Elements of Music

Elements of Music

Joseph N. Straus

Queens College and The Graduate School
The City University of New York

Upper Saddle River, NJ 07458

Library of Congress Cataloging-in-Publication Data

Straus, Joseph Nathan.
    Elements of music / Joseph N. Straus.
        p. cm.
    ISBN 0-13-034341-2
        1. Music theory. I. Title.

MT6.S788 E44 2003
781.2—dc21   2002025225

VP, Editorial Director: *Charlyce Jones Owen*
Senior acquisitions editor: *Christopher T. Johnson*
Production editor: *Laura A. Lawrie*
Manufacturing and prepress buyer: *Benjamin D. Smith*
Copy editor: *Laura A. Lawrie*
Permissions research: *Victoria Fox*
Editorial assistant: *Evette Dickerson*
Marketing manager: *Christopher Ruel*
Marketing assistant: *Scott Rich*
Director of Marketing: *Beth Mejia*
Cover image specialist: *Karen Sanatar*
Cover design: *Bruce Kenselaar*
Cover image: *Piano and music.* Source: *Patty Ridenour/Getty Images/Illustration Works*

This book was set in 10/12 New Aster by
A-R Editions, Inc. and was printed and bound by Courier Companies.
The cover was printed by Phoenix Color Corp.

Printed in the United States of America

10 9 8 7 6 5 4 3 2

ISBN 0-13-034341-2

PEARSON EDUCATION LTD., London
PEARSON EDUCATION AUSTRALIA PTY, Limited, Sydney
PEARSON EDUCATION SINGAPORE, Pte. Ltd
PEARSON EDUCATION NORTH ASIA LTD, Hong Kong
PEARSON EDUCATION CANADA, LTD., Toronto
PEARSON EDUCATIÓN DE MEXICO, S.A. de C.V.
PEARSON EDUCATION--Japan, Tokyo
PEARSON EDUCATION MALAYSIA, Pte. Ltd
PEARSON EDUCATION, Upper Saddle River, New Jersey

Contents

Preface

Who is this book for?

This book is designed for a one-semester course for two groups of students: (1) Nonmusic majors who are taking a course in music because they want to write their own music or are simply curious about how music is put together; (2) Aspiring music majors who need some extra work in fundamental topics before beginning a sequence of theory courses for music majors.

What topics does this book cover?

This book covers the traditional fundamental topics in tonal music theory: pitch notation in bass and treble clefs; rhythm and meter; major and minor scales; intervals; triads and seventh chords; simple harmonic progressions and cadences.

What makes this book different?

1. **Musical literature.** This book is immersed in musical literature. It includes an anthology of core works in diverse tonal styles (both in score and recorded on CD), and these are the source of all of the musical examples and many of the written exercises. Each musical excerpt is thus understood in its larger context; there are no isolated snippets. The theoretical concepts and musical works are integrated with each other. As students learn each basic concept, they see how it functions in music of high artistic quality. At the same time, they use their newly acquired theoretical ability to come to an intimate understanding of a small group of fine works. They learn the concepts through the musical works, and the musical works through the concepts.

2. **Flexibility.** The book is organized into six chapters: (1) pitch; (2) rhythm; (3) scales; (4) intervals; (5) triads and seventh chords; and (6) harmony. This transparent organization provides instructors with a

significant degree of flexibility. For example, teachers who prefer to teach rhythm before, or simultaneously with, early work in pitch notation will find it easy to do so. The book, with its extensive, imaginative, interactive exercises, is designed as a set of flexible resources for the teacher rather than a prescribed curricular sequence that must be followed in lockstep.

3. **Written exercises and assignments.** For each concept, there are extensive written exercises, both in traditional written and electronic formats. Many of the exercises incorporate music from the anthology and many encourage creative composition. There are far more exercises than any one class could do; the instructor will thus have a wide range of choices. Many of the exercises also work well for in-class drill and study.

4. **In-class activities.** Each lesson is accompanied by suggested in-class activities, including singing, dictation, and keyboard exercises. These activities do not comprise a course in sightsinging, dictation, or keyboard harmony; rather, they are designed to supplement and reinforce the theory lessons. The goal of these activities, and of the book as a whole, is to bring beginning students into close, intimate contact with musical materials, not only to understand them intellectually but to embody them in some way. At every stage, this book emphasizes that music is to be heard and made, not merely seen and contemplated in the abstract.

What is the goal of this book?

Learning music is like learning a foreign language. Some hard work is required to master the basic grammar and vocabulary. But once you gain a reasonable degree of fluency, a whole new world opens up to you. You can express yourself and communicate in a new language, and you can listen with far deeper understanding when others speak to you. Mastery of the basic material of music described in this book will enable you to write your own music in a more thoughtful way, enable you to talk with and learn from other musicians, and give you insight into the uses that master composers have made of these basic materials. A great adventure lies ahead of you in the following pages!

Acknowledgments

At an early stage in the writing of this book, I benefited immensely from advice offered by a large number of colleagues and friends around the country: Mark Anson-Cartwright (Hofstra University), Larry Arnold (University of North Carolina at Pembroke), Joseph Auner (State University of New York at Stony Brook), Jean Aydelotte (University of Texas at Austin), James Baker (Brown University), Amy Bauer (University of Missouri at Kansas City), Candace Brower (Northwestern University), Steven Bruns (University of Colorado at Boulder), Poundie Burstein (Hunter College, City University of New York), Eleanor Cory (Queensborough Community College, City University of New York), John Covach (University of North Carolina at Chapel Hill), Walter Everett (University of Michigan at Ann Arbor), Yayoi Everett (Emory University), Cynthia Folio (Temple University), Deborah Freedman (Missouri Western State College), Daniel Harrison (University of Rochester), Patricia Helm (Colby College), Richard Hermann (University of New Mexico), Sara Holtzschue (Queensborough Community College, City University of New York), William Horne (Loyola University), Peter Kaminsky (University of Connecticut at Storrs), Gary Karpinski (University of Massachusetts at Amherst), Stefan Kostka (University of Texas at Austin), Joseph Kraus (University of Nebraska at Lincoln), Philip Lambert (Baruch College, City University of New York), Steve Larson (University of Oregon at Portland), Stephan Lindemann (Brigham Young University), John Link (William Paterson College), Justin London (Carleton College), Elizabeth Marvin (Eastman School of Music), William Marvin (Oberlin Conservatory), John McCann (Tufts University), Jairo Moreno (Duke University), Akane Mori (Hartt School of Music), Shaugn O'Donnell (City College, CUNY), Jeffrey Perry (Louisiana State University), Mark Rimple (West Chester College), Lynne Rogers (Oberlin Conservatory), Michael Rogers (University of Oklahoma at Norman), Dean Roush (Wichita State University), Philip Rupprecht (Brooklyn College, CUNY), Matthew Santa (Texas Tech

University), Janet Schmalfeldt (Tufts University), Stephen Slottow (University of North Texas at Denton), David Smyth (Louisiana State University), James Sobaskie (University of Wisconsin at Marathon), Deborah Stein (New England Conservatory), Gary Sudano (Purdue University), Kristin Wendland (Emory University), and Norman Wick (Southern Methodist University).

As the book took shape, I received additional guidance from Ellie Hisama, Shaugn O'Donnell, and Matthew Santa, as well as from the following reviewers: Dr. Kurt Ellenberger, Grand Valley State University; Joann Feldman, Sonoma State University; Ann Usher, University of Akron; Dr. Daniel McCarthy, University of Akron; Roger Letson, De Anza College; Dr. Michael Kallstrom, Western Kentucky University; Dr Matthew Shaftel, Florida State University; Dr. Leslie Odom, University of Florida; Dr. Matthew Santa, Texas Tech University; and Gene Trantham, Bowling Green State University. When the book was in draft, four colleagues graciously offered to field-test it with their students: Robert Bowen (West Chester University), Chandler Carter (Hofstra University), Deborah Thoreson (Emory University), and Gene Trantham (Bowling Green State University). This was extremely helpful to me, as was the advice offered by several classes of my own students at Queens College (especially Michael Brooks). Hedi Siegel provided a fine translation of the text for the song by Josephine Lang. I received valuable editorial assistance from Michael Molloy and Michael Berry. At Prentice Hall, Chris Johnson guided the project from conception to completion with his customary enthusiasm and expertise. It was a pleasure to work with Laura Lawrie, the gifted and patient production editor for this book. And, as always, my deepest debt of gratitude is owed to Sally Goldfarb, peerless partner.

1 Pitch

Lesson 1: Staff

In this lesson you will learn about the five-line staff, pitches and notes, noteheads, ascending and descending motion, steps and leaps, ledger lines.

Music is written on a five-line *staff:* five parallel lines separated by four spaces.

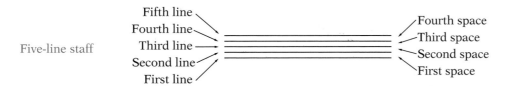

Five-line staff

A *pitch* is a musical sound at some particular point along the continuum from the lowest to the highest audible sound. A pitch is written as a *note* placed either on a line or in a space of the five-line staff. A *notehead,* which specifies where on the staff a note is to occur, is an oval shape that may be either open or filled in.

Noteheads

Use the staves below to practice writing noteheads. They should be oval (not round) in shape, and tilted to the right. Noteheads in a space should just touch the lines above and below; noteheads on a line should fill half the spaces above and below.

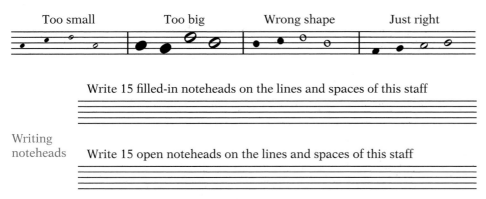

Write 15 filled-in noteheads on the lines and spaces of this staff

Writing noteheads

Write 15 open noteheads on the lines and spaces of this staff

To move from a note to a *higher sounding* note, you *ascend* on the staff. To move from a note to a *lower sounding* note, you *descend.*

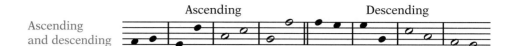

Ascending and descending

There are two kinds of melodic motion: by *step* and by *leap* (also sometimes called a skip). A step involves motion from a line up or down to an adjacent space, or from a space up or down to an adjacent line. A leap is any motion bigger than a step. Steps and leaps may be either ascending or descending.

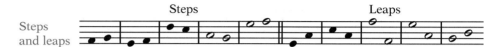

Steps and leaps

For notes that lie above or below the staff, the staff may be temporarily extended by *ledger lines*. These lines function and are spaced just like the lines of the staff, but begin just before an individual notehead and end just after it.

Ledger lines

Use the staff below to practice writing noteheads with ledger lines. Notes in the spaces above the staff need ledger lines below (not above) them; notes in the spaces below the staff need ledger lines above (not below) them.

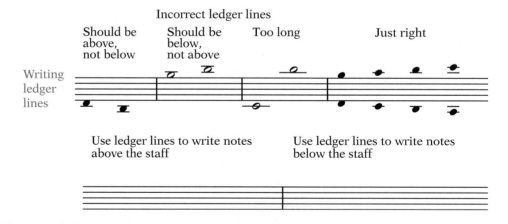

Writing ledger lines

Use ledger lines to write notes above the staff

Use ledger lines to write notes below the staff

Lesson 1: In-class activities

1. Singing. The instructor will play or sing a note. Sing the note you hear.

2. Dictation. The instructor will play two notes in succession. Identify the melodic motion as ascending or descending, step or leap. Sing the notes.

3. Dictation. The instructor will play three notes in succession. Identify the melodic motion as: (a) low-middle-high; (b) low-high-middle; (c) middle-low-high; (d) middle-high-low; (e) high-low-middle; (f) high-middle-low. Sing the notes.

Name: _____

Date: _____

Instructor's Name: _____

Lesson 1: Exercises

1-1. In these melodies, identify each motion as an ascending step (AS), descending step (DS), ascending leap (AL), or descending leap (DL). Ignore any unfamiliar notational symbols and focus only on the noteheads. Remember that a step involves motion on the staff from a line to the adjacent space, or vice versa. A leap is any motion bigger than a step.

a. Arlen, "Over the Rainbow" (the first three notes of the melody describe a melodic shape that occurs two more times).

b. Rodriguez, "La Cumparsita" (the melody involves a contrast between leaps and steps).

c. Haydn, String Quartet (the descending leaps get bigger and bigger).

d. Mozart, "Dove sono" (the melody begins mostly with steps and ends mostly with small leaps).

e. Bach, Fugue in g minor (the leap in the middle is flanked by steps before and after).

f. Lang, Song (leaps at the beginning are balanced by steps at the end).

g. Ellington, "It Don't Mean a Thing" (the melody consists mostly of small leaps).

h. Mendelssohn, Piano Trio (the leaps are usually followed by steps).

1-2. Write ascending or descending steps or leaps. Remember that a step involves motion on the staff from a line to the adjacent space, or vice versa. A leap is any motion bigger than a step.

a. Write an ascending step above each of these notes.

b. Write an ascending leap above each of these notes.

c. Write a descending step below each of these notes.

d. Write a descending leap below each of these notes.

Lesson 2: Keyboard

In this lesson you will learn about the piano keyboard, black and white keys, letter names for notes, steps and leaps, octaves, piano fingering.

In learning basic musical concepts, it is often useful to refer to the *piano keyboard*. The typical piano keyboard contains eighty-eight *keys*, some *black* and some *white*, each producing a different pitch. Moving toward the right, the pitches get higher; moving toward the left, the pitches get lower.

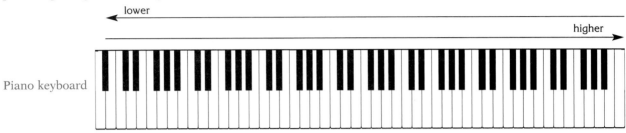

Piano keyboard

We will focus for now just on the white notes. Each white note is named with one of the first seven letters of the alphabet: A, B, C, D, E, F, G. The asymmetrical layout of the black notes (alternating groups of two and three) provides each of the seven different white notes with a distinctive location. C, for example, is always found just below the group of two black notes. The C right in the middle of the keyboard is known as *middle C*.

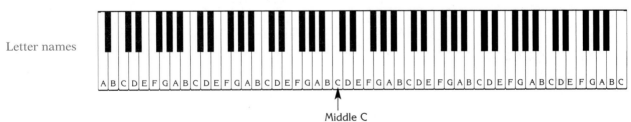

Letter names

Moving from any note to the adjacent note, up or down, is a *step*. Each step takes you from one letter of the alphabet to the next. When you get up to G, you start over again on A.

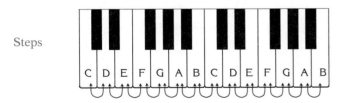

Steps

Moving from any note to a nonadjacent note is a *leap*. If you start on any note and leap up or down eight steps (counting the note you started on), you end up on another note with the same name. Eight steps comprise an *octave*. Pitches related by one or more octaves share the same name because they sound so much alike.

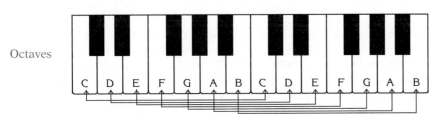

Octaves

In playing the piano, it is customary to refer to your fingers by number: the thumb is the first finger; the index finger is the second finger, and so on.

Piano fingering

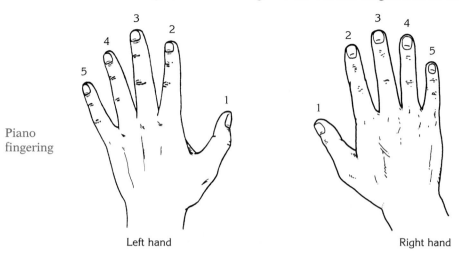

Left hand   Right hand

Lesson 2: In-class activities

1. **Singing.** The instructor will play a note. Sing the note you hear, and then the note an octave higher or lower, as requested.

2. **Singing.** The instructor will play two white notes slowly in succession. Sing the notes, then identify them as an ascending or descending step or leap.

3. **Reciting.** Recite the letter names of the notes, ascending and descending, as follows (working for speed and accuracy):
   a. ascending: A-B-C-D-E-F-G-A—B-C-D-E-F-G-A-B—C-D-E-F-G-A-B-C—D-E-F-G-A-B-C-D—E-F-G-A-B-C-D-E—F-G-A-B-C-D-E-F—G-A-B-C-D-E-F-G
   b. descending: A-G-F-E-D-C-B-A—G-F-E-D-C-B-A-G—F-E-D-C-B-A-G-F—E-D-C-B-A-G-F-E—D-C-B-A-G-F-E-D—C-B-A-G-F-E-D-C—B-A-G-F-E-D-C-B

4. **Dictation.** The instructor will play two white notes slowly in succession. Identify the interval as either an octave or not-an-octave.

5. **Playing.** The instructor will play a white note near the middle of the keyboard. Play the note you hear.

6. **Playing.** The instructor will call out a letter name (A through G). Play the requested note, then the note a step above or below, then the note an octave above or below (as instructed—white notes only).

7. **Playing.** Using the thumb of your right hand, play any white note. Then play four ascending steps (fingering: 1-2-3-4-5) and return to the starting point (fingering: 5-4-3-2-1). Using the thumb of your left hand, play any white note. Then play four descending steps (fingering: 1-2-3-4-5) and return to the starting point (fingering 5-4-3-2-1). Say the names of the notes as you play.

8. **Playing.** Using either hand, play any white note, then play as follows: octave up, step down, octave down, step down, octave up, step down, and so on. Use fingers 1 and 5 only. Name the notes as you play. Then begin again on any note, now playing as follows: octave down, step up, octave up, step up, octave down, step up, and so on. Again, use fingers 1 and 5 only and name the notes as you play.

Name: _____

Date: _____

Instructor's Name: _____

Lesson 2: Exercises

2-1. Identify the indicated notes by writing their letter names on the appropriate keys.

a.

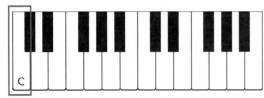

All Cs and Fs

b.

All Bs and Gs

c.

All As and Ds

d.

All Bs and Es

e.

All Cs and Gs

2-2. Provide the letter name for each indicated key.

a.

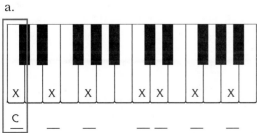

b.

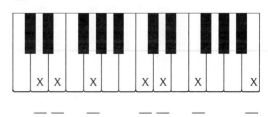

c.

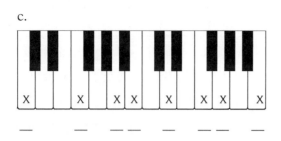

d.

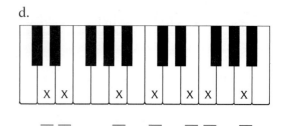

e.

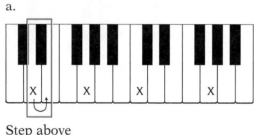

2-3. Use arrows to indicate motions (white keys only). Remember that a step involves motion from one key to an adjacent key. An octave spans eight steps.

a.

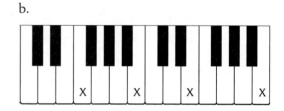

Step above

b.

Step below

c.

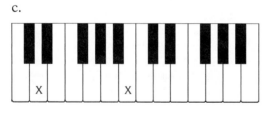

Octave above

d.

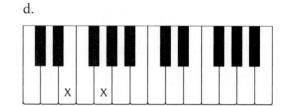

Octave above

e.

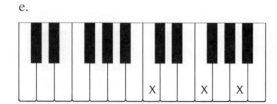

Octave below

Lesson 3: Treble clef

In this lesson you will learn about treble clef, accidentals (sharp, flat, natural), semitones, enharmonic equivalence.

A *clef* is used to identify locations on the staff with specific pitches. The most commonly used clef is the *treble clef.* This symbol, which is derived from a fancy, script G, is also called the *G clef.* It assigns the G above middle C to the second line of the staff. All of the remaining white notes of the keyboard are assigned to the other lines and spaces of the staff.

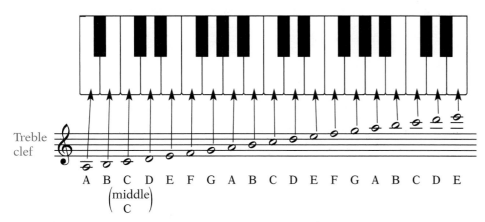

Treble clef

A B C D E F G A B C D E F G A B C D E
(middle C)

Use the staff below to practice writing the treble clef. You should write it in one continuous curve. The top of the clef extends just above the staff and the bottom extends just below it. The middle part of the clef circles around the G above middle C.

Trace these treble clefs   Write ten treble clefs

To name the black notes of the keyboard, we have to use *accidentals,*—namely, a *sharp sign* (♯) which raises a note one *semitone* and a *flat sign* (♭), which lowers a note one *semitone.* A semitone is the smallest musical distance. From any key on the keyboard to the nearest adjacent key is a semitone. The black key that lies right between the white notes C and D, for example, can be called either C♯ (because it lies a semitone above C) or D♭ (because it lies a semitone below D). Because C♯ and D♭ refer to the same pitch, they are said to be *enharmonic equivalents.* On the staff, the accidental is written before the note, but when you say the name of the note, the accidental comes after, as in "C sharp" and "D flat."

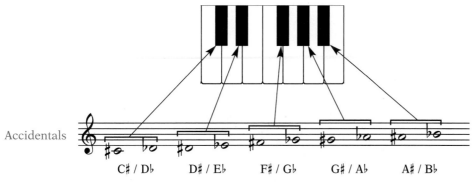

Accidentals

C♯ / D♭   D♯ / E♭   F♯ / G♭   G♯ / A♭   A♯ / B♭

A note that is neither sharp nor flat is *natural* (♮). The white notes on the keyboard are thus C♮, D♮, E♮, F♮, G♮, A♮, and B♮.

The use of sharp and flat signs is not limited to naming the black notes of the keyboard. A sharp sign raises any note by one semitone and a flat sign lowers any note by one semitone. C♭, for example, is the note a semitone below C, so C♭ is enharmonically equivalent to B. Similarly, E♯ is the note a semitone above E, so E♯ and F are enharmonic equivalents.

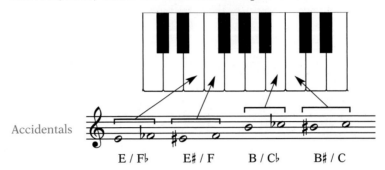

Accidentals

E / F♭   E♯ / F   B / C♭   B♯ / C

Use the staves below to practice writing accidentals. In a flat sign, the vertical line is about two spaces long. The curved portion extends to the right and is aligned horizontally with the note it modifies.

Write flat signs in front of these notes

In a sharp sign, the two vertical lines are about three spaces long and the two horizontal lines are angled slightly upward. Like the flat sign, the sharp sign is aligned with the note it modifies.

Write sharp signs in front of these notes

In the natural sign, the vertical lines are about two spaces long and the two horizontal lines are angled slightly upward. Like all accidentals, the natural sign is aligned with the note it modifies.

Write natural signs in front of these notes

Lesson 3: In-class activities

1. Note-reading. Using written exercises 3-1, 3-2, and 3-3, speak the names of the notes as accurately, steadily, and quickly as you can.

2. Singing. The instructor will play or sing each of the following melodic fragments. Sing them back, holding each note for about one second, and singing the letter name for each note.

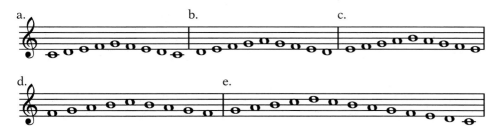

3. Singing. The instructor will play or sing each of the following melodic fragments, all highly simplified versions of melodies from the anthology. Sing them back, holding each note for about one second, and singing the letter name for each note.

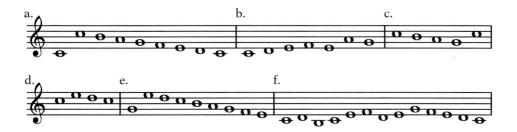

4. Dictation. Within each group, the instructor will play all three melodies in order, then play them again, one at a time, in a random order. Identify the fragment you hear and sing it back. Sing the letter name for each note.

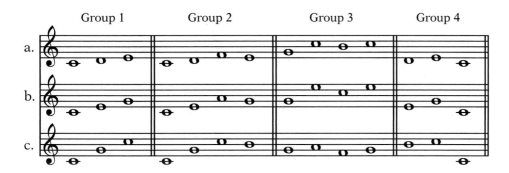

5. Playing. Play the following sequences of notes with your right hand, using the fingering provided. Play each note for approximately one second. Say the name of the note as you play.

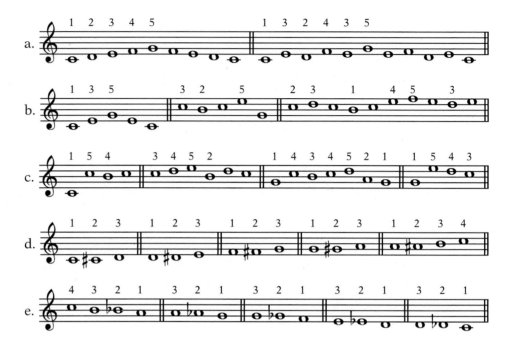

Name: _____

Date: _____

Instructor's Name: _____

Lesson 3: Exercises

3-1. Provide letter names for these notes on the treble staff (C, E, and G only). Work as quickly as you can.

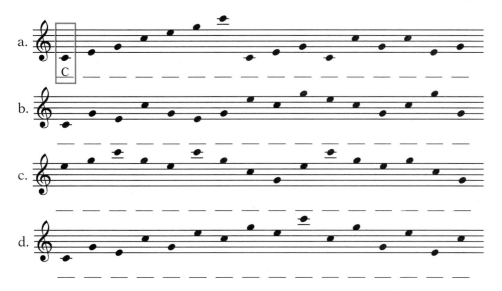

3-2. Provide letter names for these notes (C, D, E, F, G, A, and B only). Work as quickly as you can.

3-3. Provide letter names for these notes, including accidentals. (Ignore any unfamiliar symbols and just concentrate on naming the notes.)

   a. Mozart, Piano Sonata (the melodic motion is primarily stepwise).

   b. Bach, Chorale melody (the melody is in six parts, called *phrases*. The end of each phrase is identified with a symbol called a *fermata*, which indicates that a note is to be sustained for an indefinite duration.)

   c. Haydn, String Quartet (this melody is divided roughly into two halves that begin the same way but end differently).

Name: _____

Date: _____

Instructor's Name: _____

     d. Bach, Fugue in G major (the melody ascends slowly to its highpoint, then descends rapidly back to where it began).

     e. Handy, "St. Louis Blues" (the two halves of this melody begin differently but end the same).

     f. Schubert, "Heidenröslein" (the entire melody lies within one octave, from the G above middle C to the G an octave higher).

g. Mozart, "Dove sono" (the two phrases of this melody are shaped like arches, rising to a high point and then descending to their close).

3-4. Write the indicated notes on the treble staff.

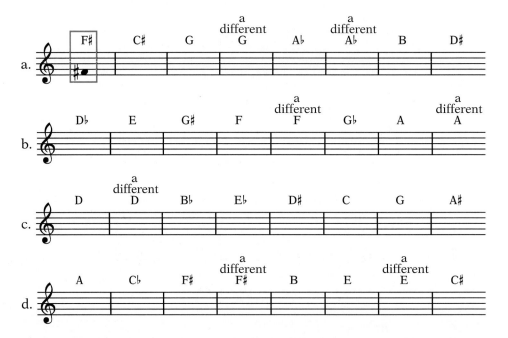

Name: _____

Date: _____

Instructor's Name: _____

3-5. Use arrows to connect these notes on the staff to the corresponding key on the keyboard.

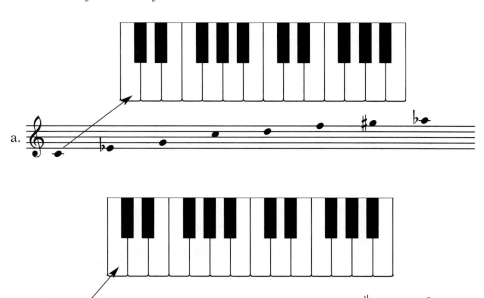

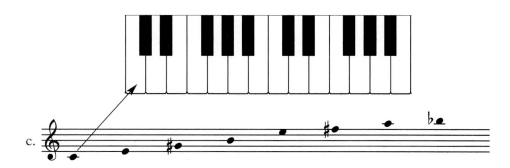

3-6. For each indicated key on the keyboard, write the corresponding note on the treble staff.

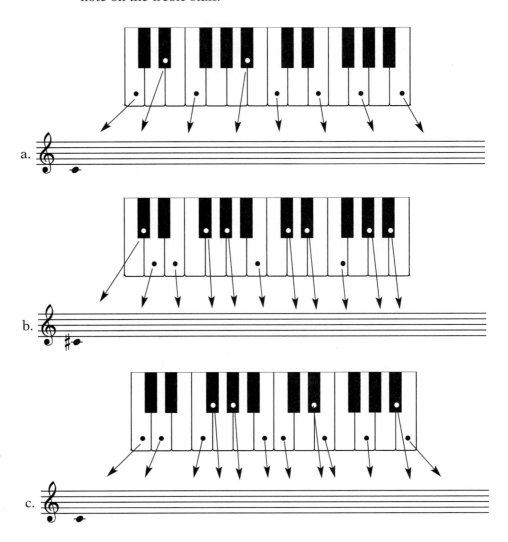

3-7. Provide enharmonic notes. Remember that enharmonic notes share the same pitch, but have different letter names.

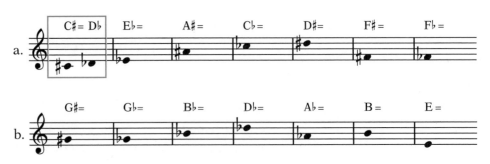

Lesson 4: Bass clef

In this lesson you will learn about bass clef, accidentals (sharp, flat, natural), semitones.

Like the treble clef, the *bass clef* is used to assign pitches to specific places on the staff. Notes written in bass clef are usually lower in pitch than notes written in treble clef. The bass clef is sometimes called an *F clef* because its design is derived from a stylized letter F. It assigns the F below middle C to the fourth line of the staff. All of the remaining notes of the keyboard are assigned to the other lines and spaces of the staff.

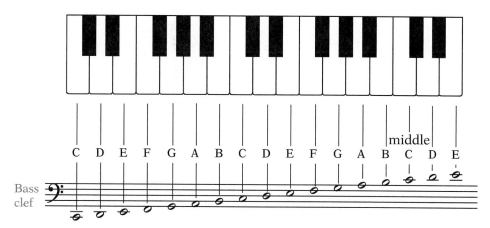

As with the treble clef, the black keys are named using *accidentals* (sharps and flats) that raise or lower any note by one *semitone*.

Use the staff below to practice writing the bass clef. The curve of the clef centers on the fourth line of the staff and the two dots surround it—one in the space above and one in the space below.

Trace these bass clefs   Write ten bass clefs

Lesson 4: In-class activities

1. Note-reading. Using written exercises 4-1, 4-2, and 4-3, speak the names of the notes as accurately, steadily, and quickly as you can.

2. Singing. The instructor will play or sing each of the following melodic fragments. Sing them back, holding each note for about one second, and singing the letter name for each note.

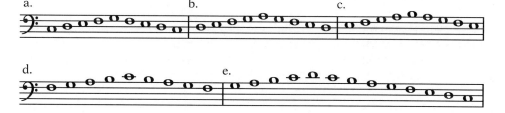

3. Singing. The instructor will play or sing each of the following melodic fragments, all highly simplified versions of melodies from the anthology. Sing them back, holding each note for about one second, and singing the letter name for each note.

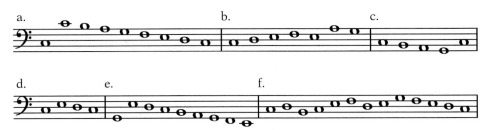

4. Dictation. Within each group, the instructor will play all three melodies in order, then play them again, one at a time, in a random order. Identify the fragment you hear and sing it back. Sing the letter name for each note.

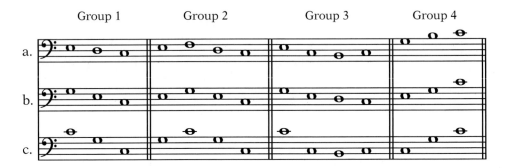

5. Playing. Play the following sequences of notes with your left hand, using the fingering provided. Play each note for approximately one second. Say the name of the note as you play.

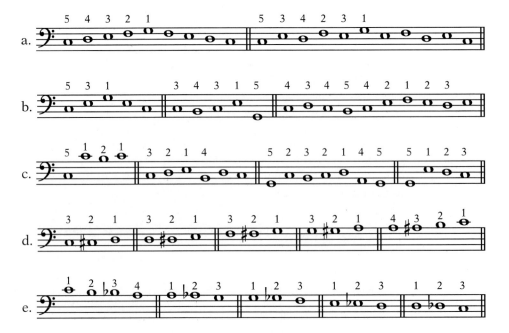

Name: _____

Date: _____

Instructor's Name: _____

Lesson 4: Exercises

4-1. Provide letter names for these notes on the bass staff (C, E, and G only). Work as quickly as you can.

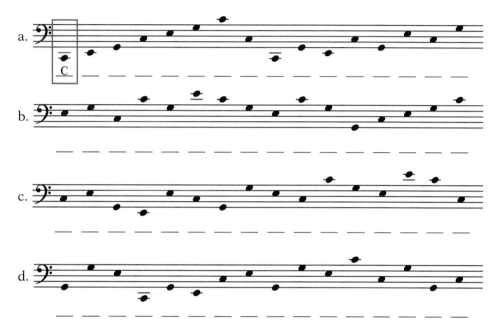

4-2. Provide letter names for these notes on the bass staff (C, D, E, F, G, A, and B). Work as quickly as you can.

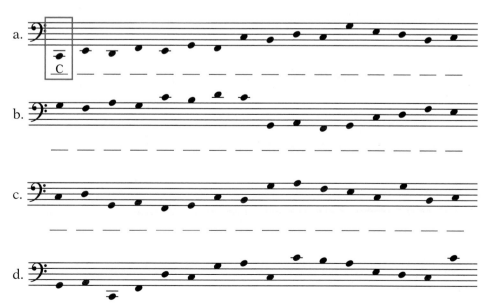

4-3. Provide letter names for these notes, including accidentals. (Ignore any unfamiliar symbols and just concentrate on naming the notes.)

a. Bach, Fugue in g minor (the melody pushes up to middle C from the C an octave below).

b. Chopin, Prelude in c minor (each note is heard simultaneously in two different octaves).

c. Mendelssohn, Piano Trio (the space outlined by the initial leap is filled in again and again).

d. Bach, Fugue in G major (this melody moves mostly by step, but contains two large ascending leaps).

Name: _____

Date: _____

Instructor's Name: _____

e. Mozart, Piano Sonata (this bass line moves around quite a bit, but always returns to A).

f. Bach, Chorale melody (the first, third, and last phrases end on C).

g. Schubert, "Death and the Maiden" (this slow, stately bass line is designed to suggest the irresistibility of death and its fixity of purpose).

h. Lang, Song (this bass line starts and ends on E♭).

4-4. Write the indicated notes on the bass staff.

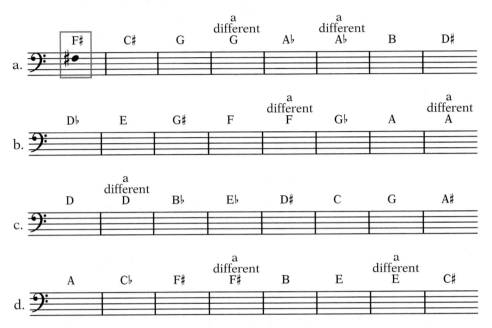

4-5. Use arrows to connect these notes on the staff to the corresponding key on the keyboard.

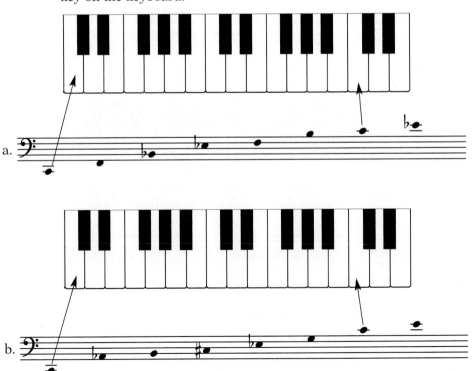

Name: _____

Date: _____

Instructor's Name: _____

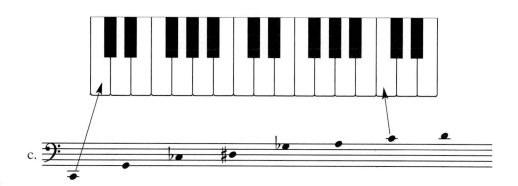

c.

4-6. For each indicated key on the keyboard, write the corresponding note on the bass staff.

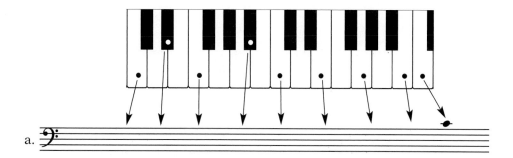

a.

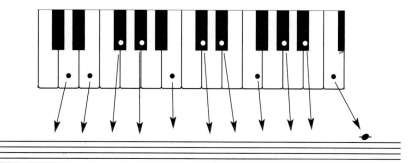

b.

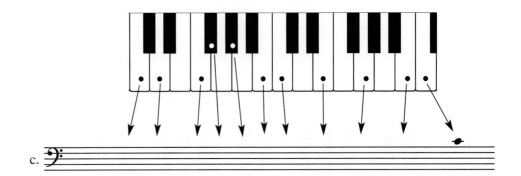

Lesson 5: Great staff

In this lesson you will learn about the great staff, octave designations.

Often music is written using two staves at the same time, with the higher notes written in treble clef and the lower notes in bass clef. That combination is called the *great staff,* and it enables us to notate any pitch.

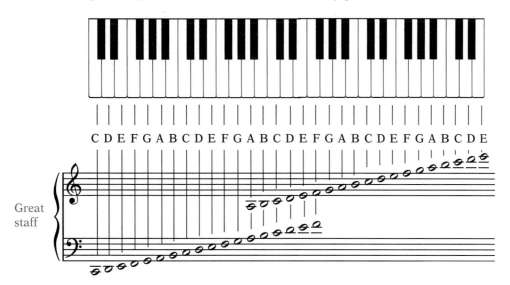

Notice that the two staves of the great staff can overlap to some extent. Middle C and the notes near it can be easily accommodated either in treble or in bass clef.

To identify a specific pitch, we will need to use not only its letter name but also its *octave designation.* Middle C, for example, is known as C4—it's the note C positioned at the beginning of the 4-octave. All of the notes above middle C, but lower then the next higher C, also lie in the 4-octave. (Octave designations actually depend on the letter name of the note, so B♯4 is in the 4-octave, although it is higher in pitch than C♭5). Every pitch can be precisely identified with a letter name and an octave designation. Our work in this book takes place between C2 and E6, as does most music.

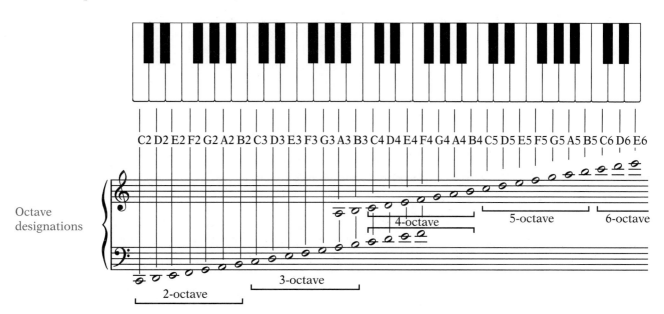

Lesson 5: In-class activities

1. Note reading. Using written worksheets 5-1, 5-2, and 5-3, speak the names of the notes as accurately, steadily, and quickly as you can.

2. Singing. The instructor will play or sing each of the following melodic fragments. Sing them back, holding each note for about one second, and singing the letter name for each note.

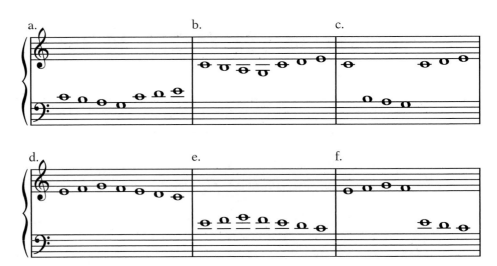

3. Singing (duets). Divide into pairs or groups to sing the following duets. Hold each note for about one second and sing the letter name for each note.

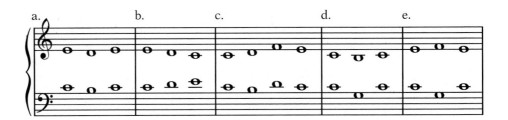

4. Dictation. Within each group, the instructor will play all three duets in order, then play them again, one at a time, in a random order. Identify the duet you hear and sing back the upper or lower part, as requested by your instructor. Sing the letter name for each note as you sing it.

Group 1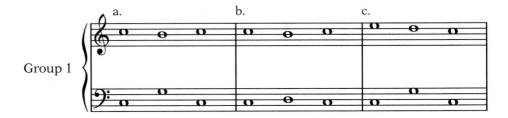

Group 2

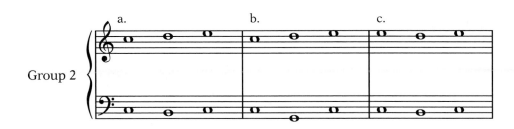

Group 3

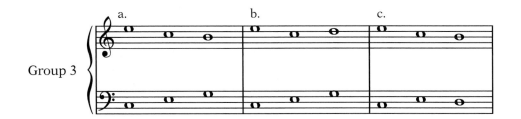

5. Playing. Play the following sequences of notes with both hands together. Use the fingering provided. Play each note for about one second.

a.

b.

Name: _____

Date: _____

Instructor's Name: _____

Lesson 5: Exercises

5-1. Provide letter names for these notes on the great staff (C, E, and G only). Work as quickly as you can.

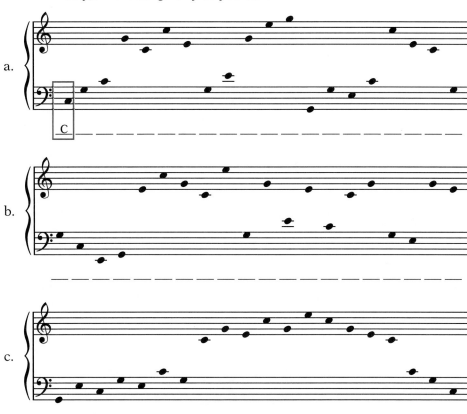

5-2. Provide letter names for these notes (C, D, E, F, G, A, and B only). Work as quickly as you can.

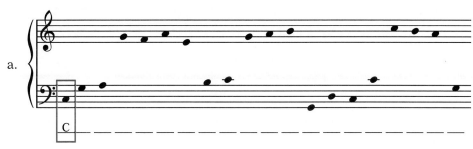

b.

c.

5-3. Provide letter names for these notes, including accidentals. For the notes in treble clef, write your answer above the staff; for the notes in bass clef, write your answer below the staff.

  a. Haydn, Quartet (these are the violin and cello melodies).

Name: _____

Date: _____

Instructor's Name: _____

    b. Chopin, Prelude in A major (the melody in the treble clef, played by the pianist's right hand, is relatively active; the melody in the bass clef, played by the pianist's left hand, hardly moves at all).

    c. Mendelssohn, Piano Trio (the right-hand melody is a memorable, beautiful tune; the left-hand melody is an accompaniment to it).

d. Bach, Chorale (the music is written for four voice parts: soprano [in treble clef with stems up]; alto [in treble clef with stems down]; tenor [in bass clef with stems up]; bass [in bass clef with stems down]. Write the correct letter names directly to the left of each note).

5-4. Write the indicated notes on the great staff. Remember that middle C is C4.

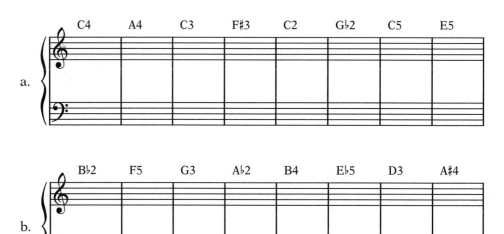

Name: _____

Date: _____

Instructor's Name: _____

5-5. Use arrows to connect these notes on the great staff to the corresponding key on the keyboard.

a.

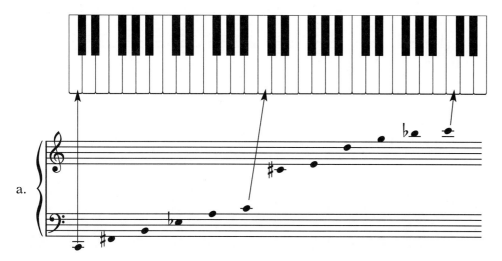

b.

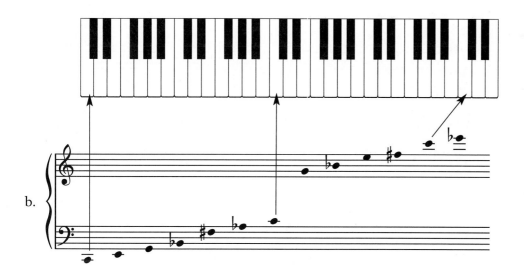

5-6. For each indicated key on the keyboard, write the corresponding note on the great staff.

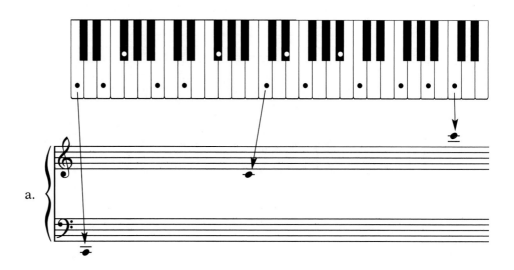

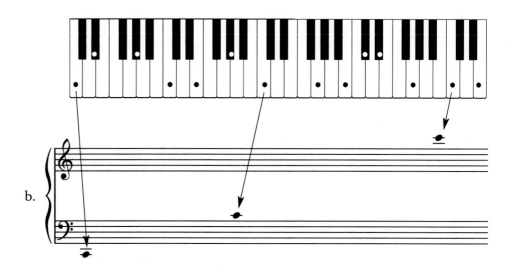

Chapter 1: Supplementary lesson

In this lesson you will learn about alto clef, tenor clef, octave sign (8va), traditional octave designations, double flats and double sharps.

Clefs are used to assign pitches to specific locations on the musical staff. In addition to treble and bass clefs studied previously, there is a group of clefs known as *C clefs* because they assign middle C to different lines of the staff. Of the C clefs, the most important are *alto clef,* which assigns middle C to the third line of the staff, and *tenor clef,* which assigns middle C to the fourth line of the staff. The alto clef is used primarily by the viola. The tenor clef is used by cello, bassoon, and trombone when their notes get too high to be written comfortably in their more usual bass clef. Which clef is used depends on custom and ease of writing notes without recourse to cumbersome ledger lines. Alto and tenor clefs are written in the same way: two vertical lines and two loops surrounding the line that represents middle C.

The highest and lowest notes require many ledger lines, and these can be confusing and hard to read. Instead, composers often use the *octave sign (8va)* to indicate that notes should be played an octave higher than written (when the sign is placed above the treble staff) or an octave lower than written (when the sign is placed below the bass staff).

Octave
sign

Pitches are identified by a combination of their letter name and their *octave designation*. In this book, we will use the system of octave designations described in Lesson 5. Another, more traditional system of octave designations is also in use.

Octave
designations

Common system	C1	C2	C3	C4	C5	C6	C7
Traditional system	CC	C	c	c1	c2	c3	c4
	Contra	Great	Small	1-line	2-line	3-line	4-line

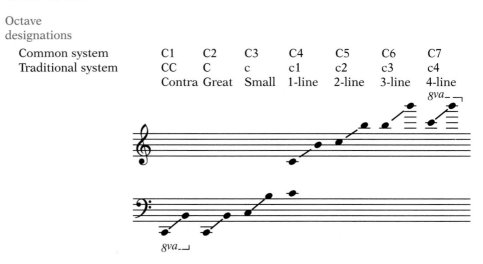

The most commonly used accidentals are the sharp sign (which raises a note by one semitone), the flat sign (which lowers a note by one semitone), and the natural sign (which cancels any previous sharp or flat). In addition, it is also possible to raise a note by two semitones using a double sharp sign or to lower a note by two semitones using a double flat sign.

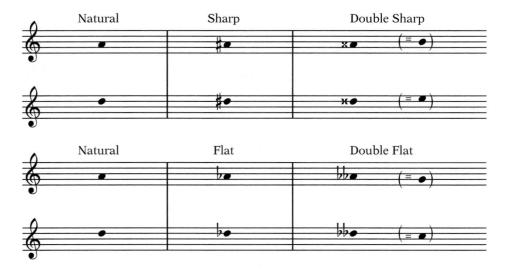

A double sharp sign is made with a simple small ✗ before the note. A double flat sign is made with two flat signs just touching each other.

2 *Rhythm and Meter*

Lesson 6: Quarter notes, half notes, and whole notes in $\frac{4}{4}$ meter

In this lesson you will learn about quarter notes, half notes, whole notes, stems, beats, measures (bars) and barlines, $\frac{4}{4}$ meter ("common time"), upbeat, downbeat, accent, conducting patterns, and tempo.

Just as *pitch* measures musical activity in *space* (high and low, up and down), *rhythm* measures musical activity in *time* (longer and shorter, before and after). The most basic unit of musical duration is called a *quarter note,* and it is written with a filled-in notehead and a *stem* (a vertical line that extends up or down from a notehead. Two quarter notes together make a *half note,* which is written as an open notehead with a stem. Similarly, two half notes combine to make a *whole note,* which is written as an open notehead with no stem.

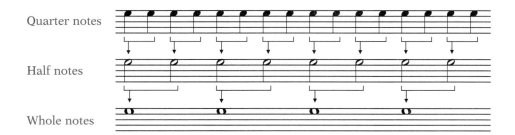

These three rhythmic values create a hierarchy of durations, from relatively short to relatively long, all in proportion to each other.

Use the staves below to practice writing quarter, half, and whole notes. The stem should be an octave in length. When the notehead is on the second space of the staff or lower, the stem goes up (from the right side of the notehead). When the notehead is on the third line of the staff or higher, the stem goes down (from the left side of the notehead).

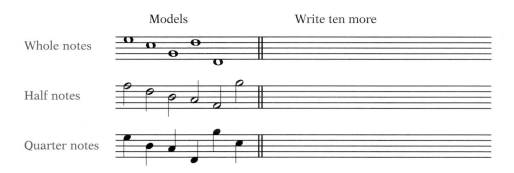

The quarter note usually serves as the *beat:* a steady, regular pulsation. The beats are grouped into *measures* (also called *bars*), which are separated by *barlines* (vertical lines through the staff). At the end of a piece or exercise, a double barline is used. A *time signature* is used to indicate which note value is acting as the beat and how many beats there are in the measure. It consists of two numbers written in a vertical stack. The number on the bottom tells which note value is acting as the beat: 4 for the quarter note, 2 for the half note, and (much less commonly) 1 for the whole note. (Other rhythmic values also can function as the beat, as we will see in later lessons.) The number on top tells how many beats there are per measure. The time signature $\frac{4}{4}$, for example, indicates that each measure contains four quarter notes. That arrangement of beats in the measure is the music's *meter.*

$\frac{4}{4}$ meter

$\frac{4}{4}$ meter is used so often that it is called "common time." Sometimes, the symbol **C** is used instead of $\frac{4}{4}$.

Common time

Within a particular meter like $\frac{4}{4}$, the actual note values need not be quarter notes so long as each measure contains the durational equivalent of four quarter notes. A measure of $\frac{4}{4}$ might contain one whole note, or two half notes, or four quarter notes, or any combination of quarter and half notes that adds up to the equivalent of four quarter notes. The rhythms may vary, but the meter stays the same.

Rhythms in $\frac{4}{4}$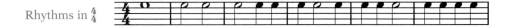

Each beat in $\frac{4}{4}$ meter has a distinctive character. The first beat of the measure is called the *downbeat,* and it receives a particular weight or *accent.* It sounds relatively strong and heavy compared to the other beats of the measure—rhythmic movement seems to depart from and return to it. The fourth beat of the measure is called the *upbeat* and, although it is relatively weak, it gives a strong sense of directed, dynamic motion toward the downbeat. The third beat receives a secondary accent—weaker than the actual downbeat, but stronger than the weak second beat that leads to it.

Accentuation in $\frac{4}{4}$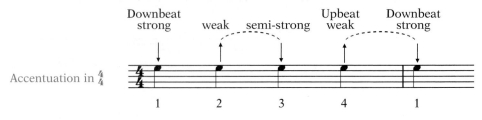

This pattern of accentuation is reflected in the gestures that a conductor uses to convey a feeling of $\frac{4}{4}$. Use your right hand and follow this pattern: down for beat 1 (the downbeat); left for beat 2; right for beat 3; then back up for beat 4 (the upbeat).

Conducting pattern for $\frac{4}{4}$

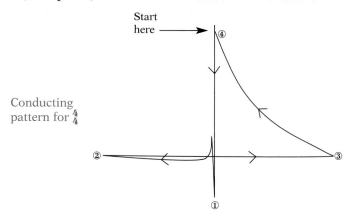

The speed of the beats—how rapidly they occur—is called the *tempo*. Tempo can be indicated in two ways: with a one-word character description (customarily in Italian) or with the number of beats per minute. Here are some common tempo names and associated numbers of beats per minute (these are approximate).

Tempo	Names	Adagio Slowly	Andante Somewhat slowly	Moderato Moderately	Allegro Fast	Presto Very fast
	Beats per minute	50	72	96	120	152

Lesson 6: In-class activities

1. Dictation. Within each group, the instructor will perform the three rhythms in a random order. Identify the rhythm you hear and tap it back.

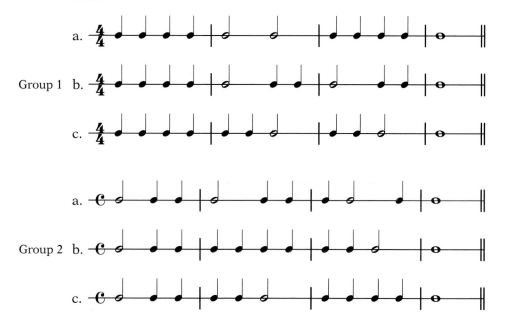

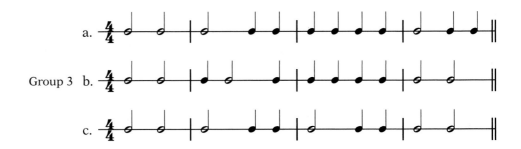

2. Solo. Suggestions for performance: (1) tap the four beats of the measure with your hand while chanting the rhythm using the syllable "ta"; (2) say the beats of the measure (1-2-3-4) while tapping the rhythm with your hand; (3) tap the beats with one hand while tapping the rhythm with the other; (4) conduct the beats with your right hand while chanting the rhythm using the syllable "ta." It is a good idea to tap four preparatory beats, or count 1-2-3-4, or conduct one preparatory measure before beginning each exercise in order to establish the tempo.

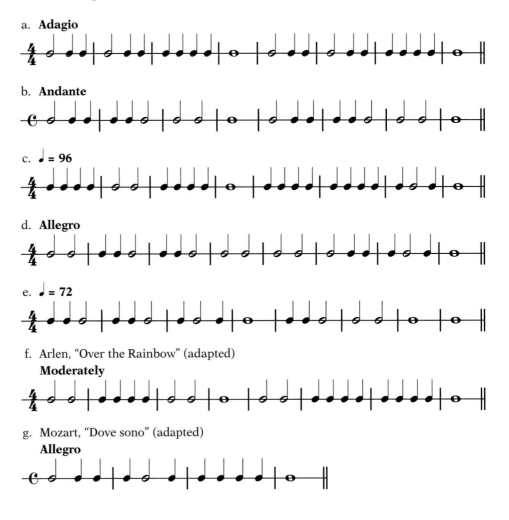

3. Duets. Suggestions for performance: (1) one student or group of students performs each part of the duet, either tapping or chanting "ta." Then switch parts; (2) a single student chants the higher rhythm while tapping the lower and then vice versa.

4. Improvisation. You are given two measures of a rhythm in $\frac{4}{4}$. Using only whole notes, half notes, and quarter notes, continue and conclude by improvising two more measures. In your improvisation, use the rhythmic values and ideas found in the two measures you are given. Three suggestions for performance: (1) improvise a two-measure continuation and conclusion; (2) perform your improvisation in continuing succession with other students, in tempo and without missing a beat. As one student concludes an improvisation, another begins immediately, either by performing all four measures (beginning with the two given measures) or just the two-measure improvisation; (3) after you complete an improvisation, another student may be asked to perform what he or she heard you do. The example below shows three possible continuations for a given opening.

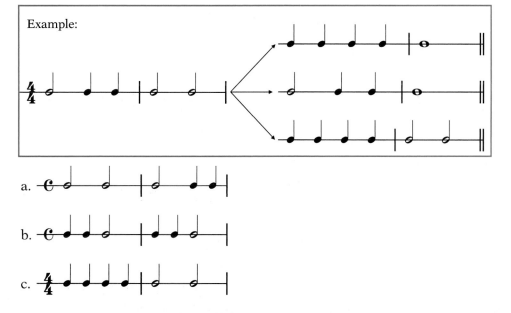

Name: _____

Date: _____

Instructor's Name: _____

Lesson 6: Exercises

6-1. Insert barlines to create complete measures in $\frac{4}{4}$ meter.

a.

b.

c.

d.

6-2. There are blank places, indicated with an arrow, in some of these measures in $\frac{4}{4}$ meter. Fill them in by adding one or more notes of the proper time-value. Remember to use quarter notes, half notes, and whole notes only.

a.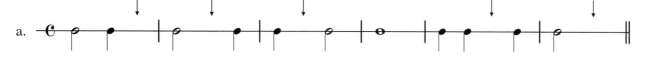

b.

c.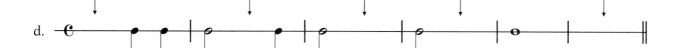

d.

6-3. Continue and complete the following short rhythmic compositions. Each will be six measures long. Be prepared to perform your compositions in class. Remember to use quarter notes, half notes, and whole notes only.

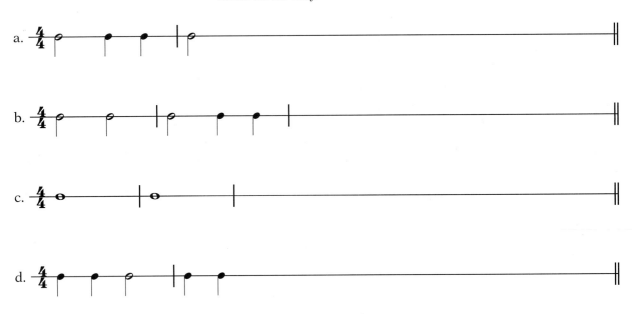

6-4. Set the following poetic texts to an appropriate rhythm. Each syllable should receive one note. Accented syllables should be placed in accented parts of the measure; unaccented syllables should be placed in unaccented parts of the measure. You should write complete, correct measures in $\frac{4}{4}$ using only quarter, half, and whole notes. Each setting is begun for you. Use as many measures as you feel you need. Be prepared to perform your settings in class.

Example:
To provide a rhythmic setting for the following text, begin by reading it aloud and determining which of its syllables is accented (marked with x) and which unaccented (marked with o):

    x   o   x   o   x   o   x   o   x   o   x   o
    What a piece of work is man! How noble in reason!

Then provide a rhythmic setting that locates the accented syllables on the strong beats of the measure (beats 1 and 3) and the unaccented syllables on the weak beats of the measure (beats 2 and 4). Be sure to provide a note for each syllable of the text and to write complete, correct measures. Here is one reasonable setting and there are certainly others (your own taste and artistic sense will guide you).

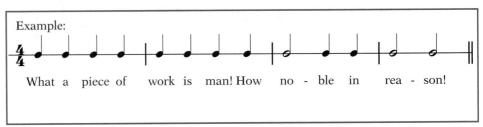

Name: _____

Date: _____

Instructor's Name: _____

a. Do not go gentle into that good night.
   Rage, rage against the dying of the light.
   (Dylan Thomas)

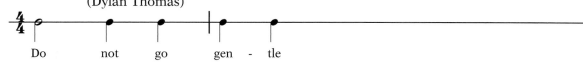

b. When in disgrace with fortune and men's eyes,
   I all alone beweep my outcast state.
   (William Shakespeare)

6-5. Set your own full name to an appropriate rhythm. Each syllable should receive a note. Accented syllables should be placed on accented beats of the measure; unaccented syllables should be placed on unaccented beats of the measure. You should write complete, correct measures in $\frac{4}{4}$ using only quarter, half, and whole notes. Be prepared to perform your settings in class.

Examples:

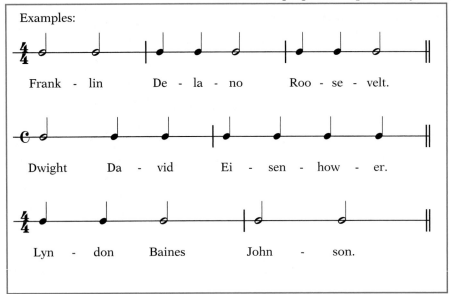

Frank - lin   De - la - no   Roo - se - velt.

Dwight   Da - vid   Ei - sen - how - er.

Lyn - don   Baines   John - son.

Your name here:

Lesson 7: Eighth notes and sixteenth notes

In this lesson you will learn about eighth notes and sixteenth notes, flags, and beams.

Just as quarter notes can be combined to create longer durations, they can be divided to create shorter ones. A quarter note can be divided into two *eighth notes*. Eighth notes are written with a filled-in notehead and a stem with a *flag*. When two eighth notes occur together in a pair, it is customary to dispense with the flags and join them with a *beam*, a horizontal line that connects the stems. Four eighth notes together also can be joined with a beam.

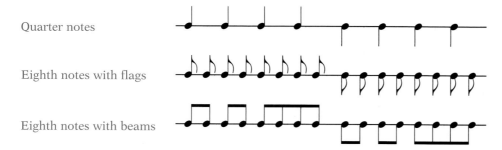

Use the staves below to practice writing eighth notes. The flag attaches at the top of an upward stem and at the bottom of a downward stem, then curves out to the right and back toward the notehead. The beam is a horizontal line that connects the ends of the stems.

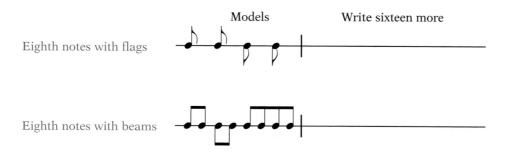

An eighth note can be divided into two *sixteenth notes*. A sixteenth note is written with a filled-in notehead and a stem with a *double flag*. Like eighth notes, sixteenth notes that occur in pairs or groups of four can be written with beams instead of flags. It is also possible for eighth notes and sixteenth notes to share a beam.

Use the staves below to practice writing sixteenth notes with double flags and double beams.

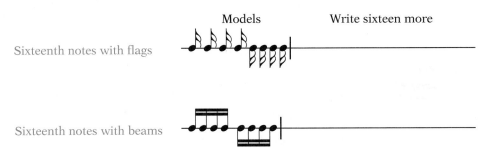

Use beams to clarify the beats, not to obscure them. Beams should not span across the boundary between the beats, particularly between beats 2 and 3.

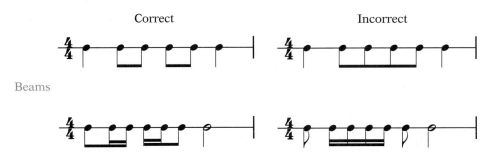

In deciding if the stems will go up to a beam above the staff or down to a beam below it, majority rules: if most of the stems would go up (because the notes lie below the middle line), then all the stems go up to the beam; if most of the stems go down (because the notes lie higher than the middle line), then all the stems go down to the beam.

If there is a tie, or if only two notes are involved, the direction of the stem is determined by the note farthest from the middle line.

Sometimes in writing for singers, composers don't use beams at all. Instead, if a syllable of text receives an eighth note or sixteenth note, it will have its own flag. In the written exercises for this book, however, we will normally use beams.

So now we have five different rhythmic values, or time-values: sixteenth, eighth, quarter, half, and whole notes. These range from the relatively short to the relatively long, all in arithmetical proportion to each other.

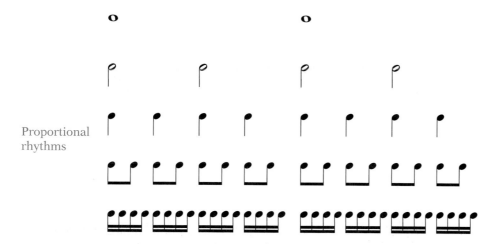

Proportional rhythms

Lesson 7: In-class activities

---

1. Dictation. Within each group, the instructor will perform the three rhythms in a random order. Identify the rhythm you hear and tap it back.

2. Solo. Suggestions for performance: (1) tap the four beats of the measure with your hand while chanting the rhythm using the syllable "ta"; (2) say the beats of the measure (1-2-3-4) while tapping the rhythm with your hand; (3) tap the beats with one hand while tapping the rhythm with the other; (4) conduct the beats with your right hand while chanting the rhythm using the syllable "ta." It is a good idea to tap four preparatory beats, or count 1-2-3-4, or conduct one

preparatory measure before beginning each exercise in order to establish the tempo.

a. **Andante**

b. **Adagio**

c. ♩ = **72**

d. Arlen, "Over the Rainbow" (adapted)
   Moderately

e. Mozart, Sonata (adapted)
   Allegro

f. Bach, Fugue in g minor

3. Duets. Suggestions for performance: (1) one student or group of students performs each part of the duet, either tapping or chanting "ta." Then switch parts; (2) a single student chants the higher rhythm while tapping the lower and then vice versa.

4. Improvisation. You are given two measures of a rhythm in ⁴⁄₄. With whole notes, half notes, quarter notes, eighth notes, and sixteenth notes available to you, continue and conclude by improvising two more measures. In your improvisation, use the rhythmic values and ideas found in the two measures you are given. Three suggestions for performance: (1) improvise a two-measure continuation and conclusion; (2) perform your improvisation in continuing succession with other students, in tempo and without missing a beat. As one student concludes an improvisation, another begins immediately, either by performing all four measures (beginning with the two given measures) or just the two-measure improvisation; (3) after you complete an improvisation, another student may be asked to perform what he or she heard you do. The example below shows three possible continuations for a given opening.

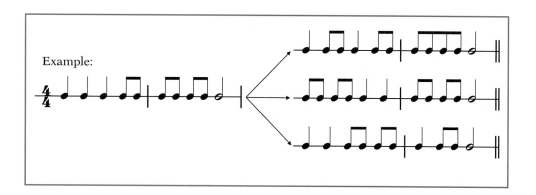

Name: _____

Date: _____

Instructor's Name: _____

Lesson 7: Exercises

7-1. Insert barlines to create complete measures in $\frac{4}{4}$ meter.

7-2. There are blank places, indicated with arrows, in some of these measures in $\frac{4}{4}$ meter. Fill them in by adding one or more notes of the proper time-value. Remember to use whole, half, quarter, eighth, and sixteenth notes only.

7-3. Rewrite the following rhythms using beams instead of flags.

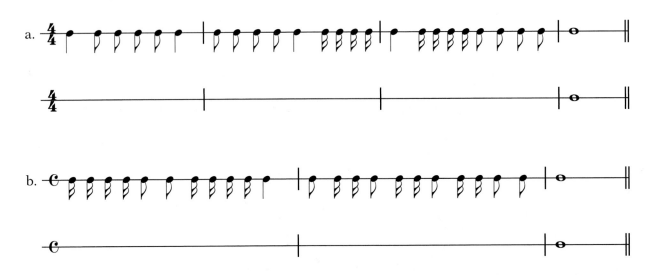

7-4. Continue and complete the following short rhythmic compositions. Each is four measures in length. Be prepared to perform your compositions in class. Remember to use whole, half, quarter, eighth, and sixteenth notes only.

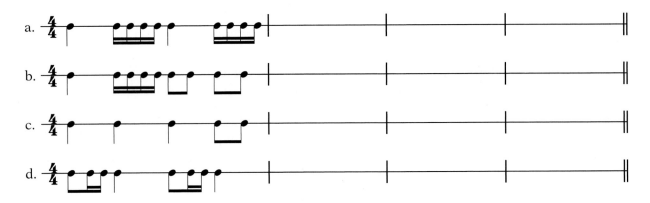

Name: _____

Date: _____

Instructor's Name: _____

7-5. Set the following poetic texts to an appropriate rhythm. Each syllable should receive a note. Accented syllables should be placed in accented parts of the measure; unaccented syllables should be placed in unaccented parts of the measure. You should write complete, correct measures in $\frac{4}{4}$ using whole notes, half notes, quarter notes, eighth notes, and sixteenth notes as appropriate. Each setting is begun for you. Use as many measures as you feel you need. Be prepared to perform your settings in class. (See Exercise 6-4 for an example of the proper procedure.)

a. Whither is fled the visionary gleam?
    Where is it now, the glory and the dream?
    (William Wordsworth)

b. Let us go then, you and I,
    When the evening is spread out against the sky
    Like a patient etherized upon a table.
    (T. S. Eliot)

Lesson 8: Dots and ties

In this lesson you will learn about the augmentation dot, dotted rhythms, ties, and anacrusis.

An *augmentation dot* placed directly after a note increases the time-value of that note by one half. In principle, any note can have its value increased in this way, but as a practical matter, we will be talking about three dotted notes: dotted half notes, dotted quarter notes, and dotted eighth notes.

Augmentation dot

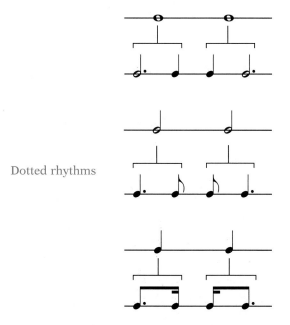

The augmentation dot gives us three new rhythmic figures called *dotted rhythms* by combining a dotted half with a quarter, a dotted quarter with an eighth, and a dotted eighth with a sixteenth. In each case, a larger value is divided into two unequal parts.

Dotted rhythms

Notice that a dotted eighth note and a sixteenth note that combine into a quarter note beat are beamed together.

Dotted eighth and sixteenth

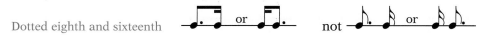

Still more rhythmic values become available through the use of the *tie*. A tie is a curved line that connects two notes of the same pitch. It combines those two notes into a single note whose duration is the sum of the two notes.

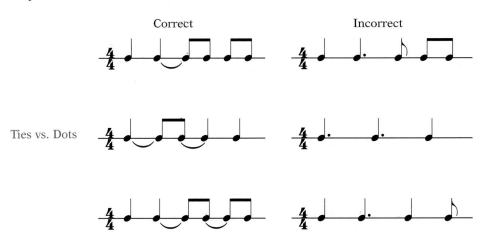

Ties

A *slur*, in contrast, is an articulation mark used to suggest a smooth connection between two or more different notes. Slurs and ties are both created with curved lines, but the slur does not affect the rhythmic values.

Do not allow a dotted note to obscure the beats of the measure, particularly beat 3. Ties should be used instead.

Correct   Incorrect

Ties vs. Dots

A piece of music may begin on the downbeat (first beat) of a measure or it may begin in the middle of an incomplete measure. An incomplete preliminary measure is called an *anacrusis,* or *pickup.* By convention, when a piece begins with an anacrusis, it will end with an incomplete measure. The durations of the anacrusis and the final measure combined will be equal to one full measure. For example, in $\frac{4}{4}$, if the anacrusis is one beat long, the final measure will be three beats long.

Anacrusis

anacrusis
(1 beat)

incomplete
final measure
(3 beats)

Lesson 8: In-class activities

1. Dictation. Within each group, the instructor will perform the three rhythms in a random order. Identify the rhythm you hear and tap it back.

2. Solo. Suggestions for performance: (1) tap the four beats of the measure with your hand while chanting the rhythm using the syllable "ta"; (2) say the beats of the measure (1-2-3-4) while tapping the rhythm with your hand; (3) tap the beats with one hand while tapping the rhythm with the other; (4) conduct the beats with your right hand while chanting the rhythm using the syllable "ta." It is a good idea to tap four preparatory beats, or count 1-2-3-4, or conduct one preparatory measure before beginning each exercise in order to establish the tempo.

   a. Bach, Chorale

   b. Mozart, "Dove sono"

    c. Mendelssohn, Piano Trio (half of the measures in this passage have the same rhythmic pattern: a dotted quarter note followed by five eighth notes).

    d. Chopin, Prelude in c minor (all four measures share the same rhythmic pattern).

  3. Duets. Suggestions for performance: (1) one student or group of students performs each part of the duet, either tapping or chanting "ta." Then switch parts; (2) a single student chants the upper rhythm while tapping the lower and then vice versa.

4. Improvisation. You are given two measures of a rhythm in $\frac{4}{4}$. With whole notes, half notes, quarter notes, eighth notes, and sixteenth notes available to you, as well as dotted rhythms, continue and conclude by improvising two more measures. In your improvisation, use the rhythmic values and ideas found in the two measures you are given. Three suggestions for performance: (1) improvise a two-measure continuation and conclusion; (2) perform your improvisation in continuing succession with other students, in tempo and without missing a beat. As one student concludes an improvisation, another begins immediately, either by performing all four measures (beginning with the two given measures) or just the two-measure improvisation; (3) after you complete an improvisation, another student may be asked to perform what he or she heard you do. The example below shows three possible continuations for a given opening.

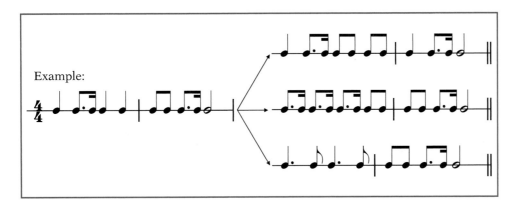

Name: _____

Date: _____

Instructor's Name: _____

Lesson 8: Exercises

8-1. Insert barlines to create complete measures in ⁴⁄₄ meter.

a.

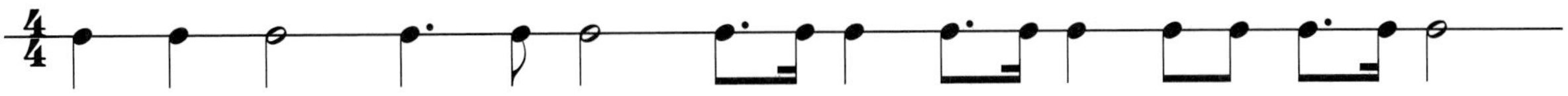

b.

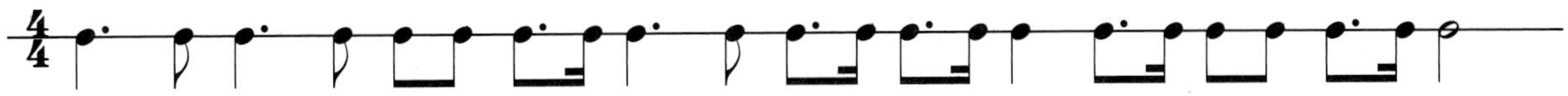

c.

d.

8-2. There are blank places, indicated with arrows, in some of these measures in ⁴⁄₄ meter. Fill them in by adding one or more notes of the proper time-value. Use dotted rhythms as appropriate.

a.

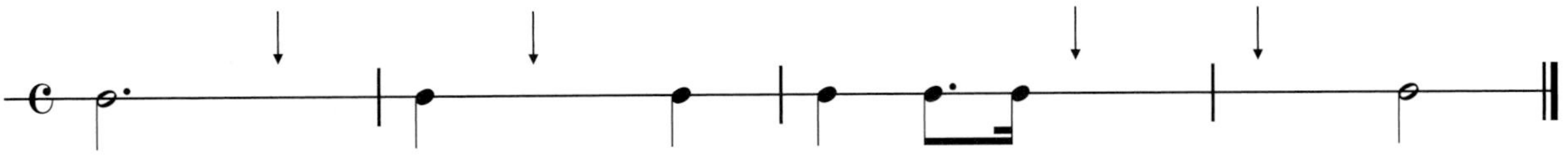

b.

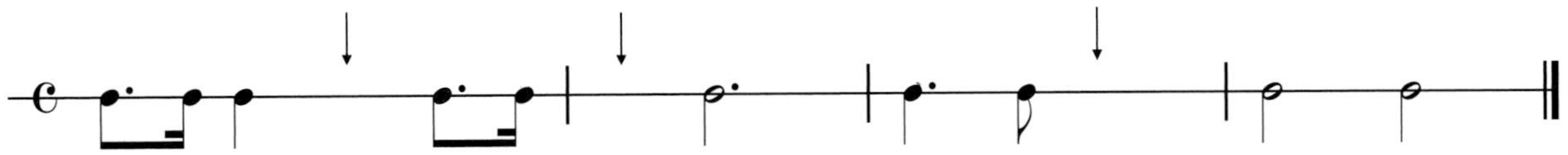

c.

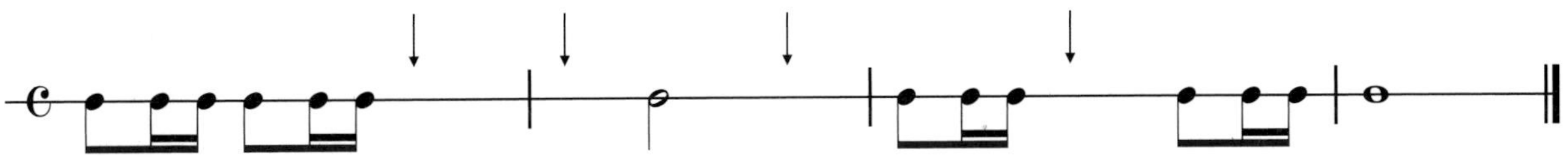

8-3. Rewrite these rhythms using dots instead of ties.

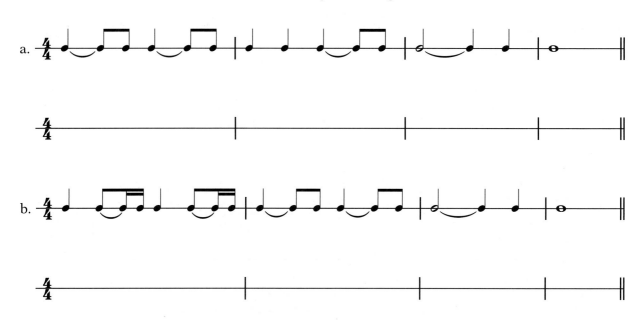

8-4. Continue and complete the following short rhythmic compositions. Each should be four measures in length. Be sure to use dotted rhythms and ties. Be prepared to perform your compositions in class.

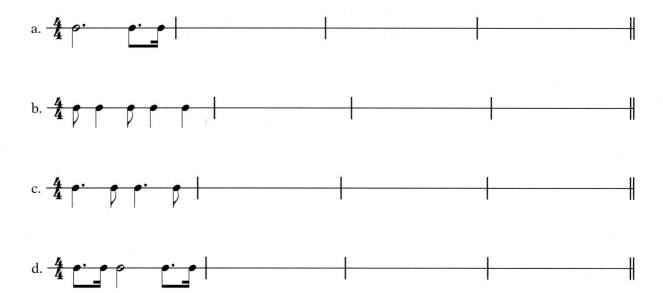

Name: _____

Date: _____

Instructor's Name: _____

8-5. Set the following poetic texts to an appropriate rhythm. Each syllable should receive a note. Accented syllables should be placed in accented parts of the measure; unaccented syllables should be placed in unaccented parts of the measure. You should write complete, correct measures in 4/4 using whole notes, half notes, quarter notes, eighth notes, sixteenth notes, and dotted rhythms as appropriate. Each setting is begun for you. Use as many measures as you feel you need. Be prepared to perform your settings in class. (See Exercise 6-4 for an example of the proper procedure.)

a. O body swayed to music, O brightening glance,
   How can we know the dancer from the dance?
   (W. B. Yeats)

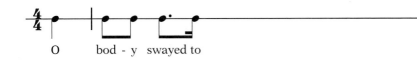

b. Because I could not stop for Death—
   He kindly stopped for me.
   (Emily Dickinson)

Lesson 9: Rests

In this lesson you will learn about rests.

Any rhythmic value can be represented by either a note or a *rest*. A rest is a silence of a certain duration. First let's consider rests that last for the duration of a whole note, half note, or quarter note.

Rests

The whole-note and half-note rests are written using the same shape, but the whole-note rest hangs below the fourth line of the staff and the half-note rest sits on the middle line. The squiggly quarter-note rest lies between the lowest and highest spaces of the staff. Use the staves below to practice writing whole- note, half-note, and quarter-note rests.

Write whole-note rests

Write half-note rests

Write quarter-note rests

Note that in ⁴⁄₄ meter, two quarter-note rests on beats 1-2 and 3-4 are normally combined into a single half-note rest. Half-note rests, however, are not used to span beats 2-3.

Using half-note and quarter-note rests

The eighth-note rest is a diagonal straight line with a short flag attached at the top. The sixteenth-note rest is formed the same way, but with a double flag.

Eighth-note rests

Sixteenth-note rests

Use the staves below to practice writing eighth-note and sixteenth-note rests.

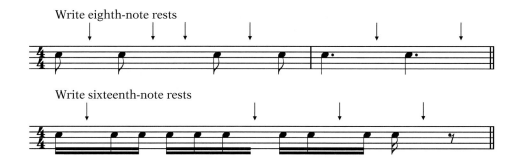

As with notes, adding a dot to a rest increases its length by half.

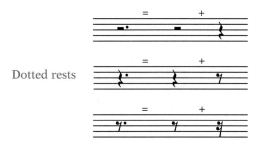

Dotted rests

In practice, the dotted half-note rest is not used in $\frac{4}{4}$ meter, because a half-note rest and a separate quarter-note rest better respect the accent on the third beat of the measure.

Dotted half-note rest in $\frac{4}{4}$

Note that while rests may be dotted, they may not be tied.

Lesson 9: In-class activities

1. Dictation. Within each group, the instructor will perform the three rhythms in a random order. Identify the rhythm you hear and tap it back.

2. Solo. Suggestions for performance: (1) tap the four beats of the measure with your hand while chanting the rhythm using the syllable "ta"; (2) say the beats of the measure (1-2-3-4) while tapping the rhythm with your hand; (3) tap the beats with one hand while tapping the rhythm with the other; (4) conduct the beats with your right hand while chanting the rhythm using the syllable "ta." It is a good idea to tap four preparatory beats, or count 1-2-3-4, or conduct one preparatory measure before beginning each exercise in order to establish the tempo.

a. **Allegro**

b. **Andante**

c. **Moderato**

d. **Lively**

e. Bach, Fugue in g minor (both measures start with a rest and end with two quarter notes).

f. Mozart, "Dove sono" (this phrase begins with an anacrusis, a pick-up to the first measure).

g. Mozart, Sonata (the rests in measure 3 occur on the beat, while the eighth notes come after the beat—that's a *syncopation,* a topic to be discussed in Lesson 13).

3. Duets. Suggestions for performance: (1) one student or group of students performs each part of the duet, either tapping or chanting "ta." Then switch parts; (2) a single student chants the higher rhythm while tapping the lower and then vice versa.

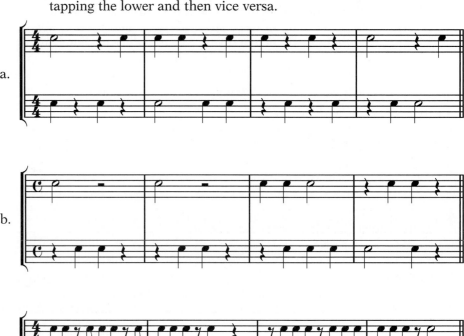

d.

4. Improvisation. You are given two measures of a rhythm in $\frac{4}{4}$. With whole notes, half notes, quarter notes, eighth notes, and sixteenth notes available to you, as well as dotted rhythms and rests, continue and conclude by improvising two more measures. In your improvisation, use the rhythmic values and ideas found in the two measures you are given. Three suggestions for performance: (1) improvise a two-measure continuation and conclusion; (2) perform your improvisation in continuing succession with other students, in tempo and without missing a beat. As one student concludes an improvisation, another begins immediately, either by performing all four measures (beginning with the two given measures) or just the two-measure improvisation; (3) after you complete an improvisation, another student may be asked to perform what he or she heard you do. The example below shows three possible continuations for a given opening.

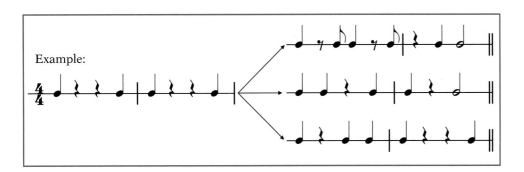

Example:

a.

b.

c.

Name: _____

Date: _____

Instructor's Name: _____

Lesson 9: Exercises

9-1. Rewrite the rhythms below, replacing each note with a rest of the same time-value.

a.

b.

9-2. Insert barlines to create complete measures in $\frac{4}{4}$ meter.

a.

b.

c.

9-3. There are blank spots, indicated with arrows, in some of these measures in $\frac{4}{4}$ meter. Fill in with a single rest to create complete measures of $\frac{4}{4}$.

9-4. Continue and complete the following short rhythmic compositions. Each should be four measures in length. Be sure to use rests. Be prepared to perform your compositions in class.

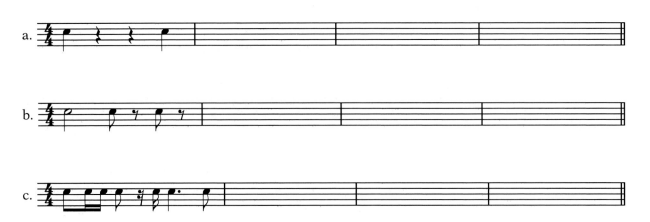

Name: _____

Date: _____

Instructor's Name: _____

9-5. Set the following poetic texts to an appropriate rhythm. Each syllable should receive a note. Accented syllables should be placed in accented parts of the measure; unaccented syllables should be placed in unaccented parts of the measure. You should write complete, correct measures in $\frac{4}{4}$ using whole notes, half notes, quarter notes, eighth notes, sixteenth notes, dotted rhythms, and rests as appropriate. Each setting is begun for you. Use as many measures as you feel you need. Be prepared to perform your settings in class. (See Exercise 6-4 for an example of the proper procedure.)

a. O Captain! my Captain! our fearful trip is done.
   (Walt Whitman)

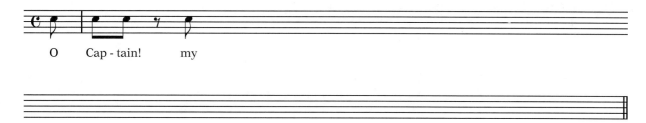

O   Cap - tain!   my

b. Heard melodies are sweet, but those unheard
   Are sweeter; therefore, ye soft pipes, play on.
   (John Keats)

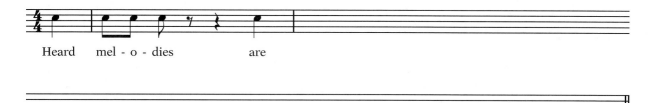

Heard   mel - o - dies   are

Lesson 10: Duple meter ($\frac{2}{4}$ and $\frac{2}{2}$)

In this lesson you will learn about $\frac{2}{4}$ and $\frac{2}{2}$ meter, *alla breve* ¢, upbeat, downbeat, and conducting patterns.

In $\frac{2}{4}$ meter, each measure consists of the time-value of two quarter notes.

As with $\frac{4}{4}$, discussed in the previous lessons, the actual note values need not be quarter notes so long as each measure contains the durational equivalent of two quarter notes. A measure of $\frac{2}{4}$ might contain one half note, two quarter notes, four eighth notes, eight sixteenth notes, or any combination of those rhythmic values that adds up to a total duration equivalent to two quarter notes.

As with $\frac{4}{4}$, the beats of $\frac{2}{4}$ meter have a different character. The first beat of the measure is the *downbeat*. It is relatively strong and receives an *accent;* it gives a sense of stability and arrival. The second beat of the measure is the *upbeat*. It is relatively weak and unaccented; it gives a sense of dynamic motion that leads to the downbeat.

$\frac{2}{4}$ is a *duple meter* because its measure contains two beats. Another important duple meter is $\frac{2}{2}$, a measure that contains two half-note beats. A measure of $\frac{2}{2}$ has the same duration as a measure of $\frac{4}{4}$, but has only two half-note beats instead of four quarter-note beats. The time signature for $\frac{2}{2}$ is often written with the symbol ¢. This meter is sometimes called *alla breve*, which is another way of saying that the measure contains two half-note beats (breves).

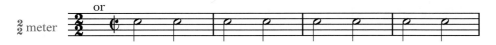

As with $\frac{4}{4}$ and $\frac{2}{4}$, a variety of rhythmic patterns can be used in $\frac{2}{2}$. The pattern of accents is the same in $\frac{2}{2}$ as in $\frac{2}{4}$: the measure consists of a weighted downbeat and a relatively weak upbeat.

The conducting pattern is the same for both meters and reflects this pattern of accents.

Conducting pattern for
$\frac{2}{4}$ and $\frac{2}{2}$

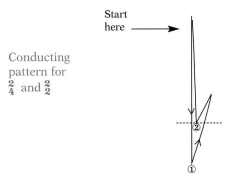

Lesson 10: In-class activities

1. Dictation. Within each group, the instructor will perform the three rhythms in a random order. Identify the rhythm you hear and tap it back.

2. Solo. Suggestions for performance: (1) tap the two beats of the measure with your hand while chanting the rhythm using the syllable "ta"; (2) say the beats of the measure (1-2) while tapping the rhythm with your hand; (3) tap the beats with one hand while tapping the rhythm with the other; (4) conduct the beats with your right hand while chanting the rhythm using the syllable "ta." It is a good idea to tap two preparatory beats, or count 1-2, or conduct one preparatory measure before beginning each exercise in order to establish the tempo.

a. Mozart, "Dove sono" (the rhythm in measures 1–4 is the same as in measures 9–12).

b. Schubert, "Heidenröslein" (this music uses flags instead of beams for eighth notes. That is common in vocal music, where each syllable of the text receives a note, and the notes have their own flags).

c. Arlen, "Over the Rainbow" (the rhythm in measures 1–2 is the same as in measures 5–6).

d. Rodriguez, "La Cumparsita" (the rhythm in measures 1–2 is the same as in measures 3–4).

3. Duets. Suggestions for performance: (1) one student or group of students performs each part of the duet, either tapping or chanting "ta." Then switch parts. (2) a single student chants the higher rhythm while tapping the lower and then vice versa.

4. Improvisation. You are given four measures of a rhythm in either $\frac{2}{4}$ or $\frac{2}{2}$. With whole notes, half notes, quarter notes, eighth notes, and sixteenth notes available to you, as well as dotted rhythms and rests, continue and conclude by improvising four more measures. In your improvisation, use the rhythmic values and ideas found in the four measures you are given. Three suggestions for performance: (1) improvise a four-measure continuation and conclusion; (2) perform your improvisation in continuing succession with other students, in tempo and without missing a beat. As one student concludes an improvisation, another begins immediately, either by performing all eight measures (beginning with the four given measures) or just the four-measure improvisation; (3) after you complete an improvisation, another student may be asked to perform what he or she heard you do. The example below shows three possible continuations for a given opening.

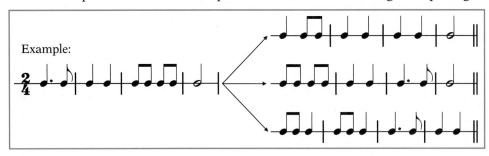

Name: _____

Date: _____

Instructor's Name: _____

Lesson 10: Exercises

10-1. Insert barlines to create complete measures in $\frac{2}{4}$ or $\frac{2}{2}$ meter.

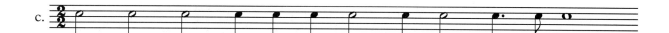

10-2. There are blank places, indicated with arrows, in some of these measures in $\frac{2}{4}$ or $\frac{2}{2}$ meter. Fill them in by adding one or more notes of the proper time-value.

10-3. Continue and complete the following short rhythmic compositions. Each should be six measures in length. Be prepared to perform your compositions in class.

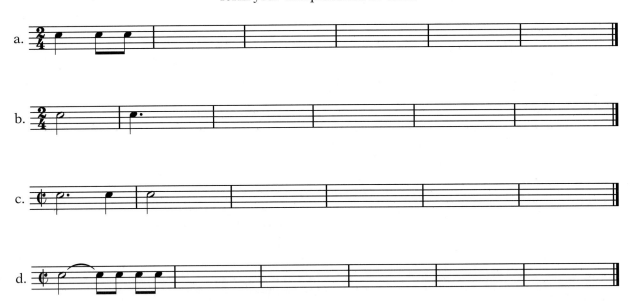

10-4. Set the following poetic texts to an appropriate rhythm. Each syllable should receive a note. Accented syllables should be placed in accented parts of the measure; unaccented syllables should be placed in unaccented parts of the measure. You should write complete, correct measures in $\frac{2}{4}$ or $\frac{2}{2}$ using whole notes, half notes, quarter notes, eighth notes, sixteenth notes, dotted rhythms, and rests as appropriate. Each setting is begun for you. Use as many measures as you feel you need. Be prepared to perform your settings in class. (See Exercise 6-4 for an example of the proper procedure.)

a. Made weak by time and fate, but strong in will
   To strive, to seek, to find, and not to yield.
   (Tennyson)

b. Since then, at an uncertain hour,
   That agony returns:
   And till my ghastly tale is told,
   This heart within me burns.
   (Coleridge)

Lesson 11: Triple meter ($\frac{3}{4}$)

In this lesson you will learn about $\frac{3}{4}$ meter and its conducting pattern.

$\frac{4}{4}$ is a *quadruple meter* because it divides the measure into four beats. $\frac{2}{4}$ and $\frac{2}{2}$ are *duple meters* because they divide the measure into two beats. The remaining principal kind of meter is *triple meter*, which divides the measure into three beats. $\frac{3}{8}$, $\frac{3}{4}$, and $\frac{3}{2}$ are all examples of triple meter and, of these, $\frac{3}{4}$ is the most commonly used.

$\frac{3}{4}$ meter indicates a measure that consists of three quarter-note beats.

$\frac{3}{4}$ meter

A variety of rhythmic figures can be used in $\frac{3}{4}$ meter. Only the whole note cannot be used—it is too long for the measure.

$\frac{3}{4}$ meter

When using rests in $\frac{3}{4}$, remember two rules: (1) a whole-note rest is used to fill the measure, not a dotted half-note rest; (2) a rest that lasts for two quarter notes should be indicated with two quarter-note rests, not one half-note rest.

Rests in $\frac{3}{4}$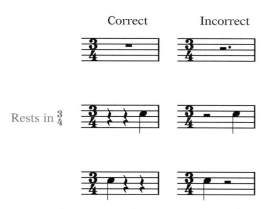

As with the other meters we have discussed, the beats of $\frac{3}{4}$ have a distinctive character. The first beat is the downbeat and is strong compared to the other two. The third beat is an upbeat that leads to the downbeat. The second beat is weaker than either of the other two—it is a kind of echo or rebound from the first beat.

Accentuation in $\frac{3}{4}$

The conducting pattern for $\frac{3}{4}$ reflects the accentual pattern.

Conducting
pattern for $\frac{3}{4}$

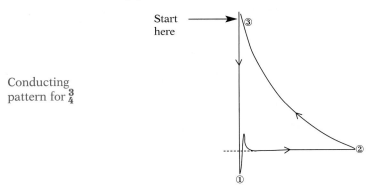

Lesson 11: In-class activities

1. Dictation. Within each group, the instructor will perform the three rhythms in a random order. Identify the rhythm you hear and tap it back.

2. Solo. Suggestions for performance: (1) tap the three beats of the measure with your hand while chanting the rhythm using the syllable "ta"; (2) say the beats of the measure (1-2-3) while tapping the rhythm with your hand; (3) tap the beats with one hand while tapping the rhythm with the other; (4) conduct the beats with your right hand while chanting the rhythm using the syllable "ta." It is a good idea to tap three preparatory beats, or count 1-2-3, or conduct one preparatory measure before beginning each exercise in order to establish the tempo.

a. Schumann, Song (this passage makes frequent use of the rhythmic figure of a dotted eighth note and a sixteenth note).

b. Lang, Song (as in the Schumann song, the combination of a dotted eighth note and a sixteenth note is common in this passage).

c. Haydn, Quartet (the rhythm in measures 1–3 is the same as in measures 5–7).

3. Duets. Suggestions for performance: (1) one student or group of students performs each part of the duet, either tapping or chanting "ta." Then switch parts; (2) a single student chants the higher rhythm while tapping the lower and then vice versa.

a.

b.

c. Chopin, Prelude (the upper part is just a bit more active rhythmically than the lower).

Andantino

d. Haydn, Quartet (these are the first violin and cello parts).

Allegro

4. Improvisation. You are given four measures of a rhythm in ¾. With half notes, quarter notes, eighth notes, and sixteenth notes available to you, as well as dotted rhythms and rests, continue and conclude by improvising four more measures. In your improvisation, use the rhythmic values and ideas found in the four measures you are given. Three suggestions for performance: (1) improvise a four-measure continuation and conclusion; (2) perform your improvisation in continuing succession with other students, in tempo and without missing a beat. As one student concludes an improvisation, another begins immediately, either by performing all eight measures (beginning with the four given measures) or just the four-measure improvisation; (3) after you complete an improvisation, another student may be asked to perform what he or she heard you do. The example below shows three possible continuations for a given opening.

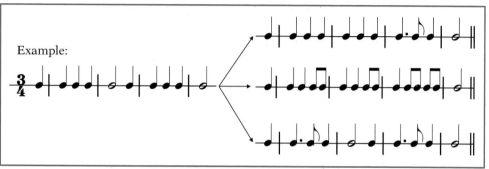

Example:

Name: _____

Date: _____

Instructor's Name: _____

Lesson 11: Exercises

11-1. Insert barlines to create complete measures in ¾ meter.

11-2. There are blank places, indicated with arrows, in some of these measures in ¾ meter. Fill them in by adding one or more notes of the proper time-value.

11-3. Continue and complete the following short rhythmic composi-tions. Each should be four measures in length. Be prepared to per-form your compositions in class.

c.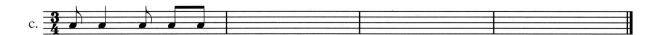

d.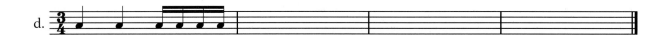

11-4. Set the following poetic texts to an appropriate rhythm. Each syllable should receive a note. Accented syllables should be placed in accented parts of the measure; unaccented syllables should be placed in unaccented parts of the measure. You should write complete, correct measures in $\frac{3}{4}$ using half notes, quarter notes, eighth notes, sixteenth notes, dotted rhythms, and rests as appropriate. Each setting is begun for you. Use as many measures as you feel you need. Be prepared to perform your settings in class. (See Exercise 6-4 for an example of the proper procedure.)

    a.   What passing-bells for these who die as cattle?
           Only the monstrous anger of the guns.
           (Wilfred Owen)

What   pas - sing - bells

    b.   And what rough beast, its hour come round at last,
           Slouches toward Bethlehem to be born?
           (W. B. Yeats)

And   what rough beast,

Lesson 12: Compound meter ($\frac{6}{8}$)

In this lesson you will learn about compound meter, $\frac{6}{8}$ meter, and its conducting pattern.

The meters we have discussed so far ($\frac{4}{4}$, $\frac{2}{4}$, $\frac{2}{2}$, and $\frac{3}{4}$) are considered *simple meters* because their beats (quarter note or half note) are divided into *two* parts (eighth notes or quarter notes) and the beat itself is a simple value. In *compound meters*, in contrast, the beat is divided into *three* parts and the beat itself is a dotted note: a dotted eighth note, dotted quarter note, or dotted half note. In $\frac{6}{8}$ meter, for example, there are two dotted quarter-note beats per measure, and each beat is divided into three eighth notes.

$\frac{6}{8}$ meter

$\frac{6}{8}$ is thus duple compound meter (two beats, each divided into three parts). $\frac{9}{8}$ (triple compound meter with three dotted quarter beats) and $\frac{12}{8}$ (quadruple compound meter with four dotted quarter beats) are also compound meters, but $\frac{6}{8}$ is the most commonly used and the one we will focus on here.

As with the other meters we have studied, many different rhythmic patterns are possible in $\frac{6}{8}$. There are two beats in the measure: the first beat is the downbeat, the second is the upbeat.

$\frac{6}{8}$ meter

A measure of $\frac{6}{8}$ has the same duration as a measure of $\frac{3}{4}$. They are both the length of six eighth notes, but they are divided differently: a measure of $\frac{6}{8}$ consists of two beats, each a dotted quarter note long, while a measure of $\frac{3}{4}$ consists of three beats, each a quarter note long.

$\frac{6}{8}$ and $\frac{3}{4}$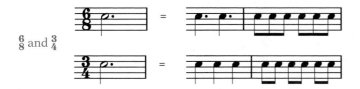

Note that beams are used to define the beat: they never span across the division between beat 1 and beat 2.

Beams in $\frac{6}{8}$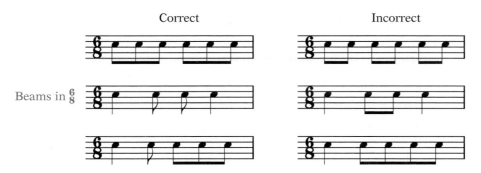

As with beams, rests should be used to clarify the beats; a rest should not span across the division between beat 1 and beat 2.

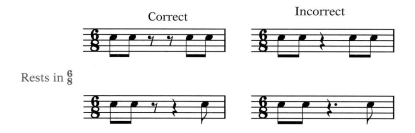

The conducting pattern for $\frac{6}{8}$ is the same as for the other duple meters, $\frac{2}{4}$ and $\frac{2}{2}$ (see Lesson 10).

Lesson 12: In-class activities

1. Dictation. Within each group, the instructor will perform the three rhythms in a random order. Identify the rhythm you hear and tap it back.

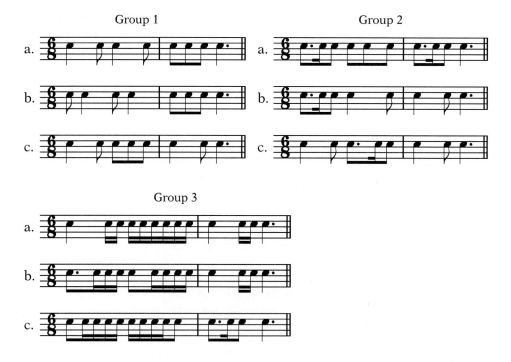

2. Solo. Suggestions for performance: (1) tap the two beats of the measure with your hand while chanting the rhythm using the syllable "ta"; (2) say the beats of the measure (1-2) while tapping the rhythm with your hand; (3) tap the beats with one hand while tapping the rhythm with the other; (4) conduct the beats with your right hand while chanting the rhythm using the syllable "ta." It is a good idea to tap two preparatory beats, or count 1-2, or conduct one preparatory measure before beginning each exercise in order to establish the tempo.

a. **Allegro**

b. ♩. = 60

c. **Presto**

d. **Andante**

e. Bach, Fugue in G Major (measures 1 and 4 have the same rhythm, as do measures 2 and 3).

f. Mozart, Sonata (the rhythms in measures 1–3 are repeated in measures 5–7).

3. Duets. Suggestions for performance: (1) one student or group of students performs each part of the duet, either tapping or chanting "ta." Then switch parts; (2) a single student chants the higher rhythm while tapping the lower and then vice versa.

d. Bach, Fugue in G Major (the two parts are rhythmically distinct—
they rarely do the same thing at the same time).

e. Mozart, Sonata (as in the Bach Fugue, the two parts are rhythmically quite independent of each other).

4. Improvisation. You are given two measures of a rhythm in $\frac{6}{8}$. Continue
and conclude by improvising two more measures. In your improvisation, use the rhythmic values and ideas found in the two measures you
are given. Three suggestions for performance: (1) improvise a two-
measure continuation and conclusion; (2) perform your improvisation
in continuing succession with other students, in tempo and without
missing a beat. As one student concludes an improvisation, another
begins immediately, either by performing all four measures (beginning
with the two given measures) or just his or her two-measure improvisation; (3) after you complete an improvisation, another student may
be asked to perform what he or she heard you do. The example below
shows three possible continuations for a given opening.

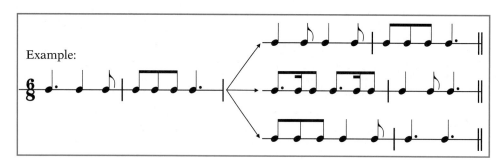

Name: _____

Date: _____

Instructor's Name: _____

Lesson 12: Exercises

12-1. Insert barlines to create complete measures in § meter.

12-2. There are blank places, indicated with arrows, in some of these measures in § meter. Fill them in by adding one or more notes of the proper time-value.

12-3. Continue and complete the following short rhythmic compositions. Each should be four measures in length. Be prepared to perform your compositions in class.

12-4. Set the following poetic texts to an appropriate rhythm. Each syllable should receive a note. Accented syllables should be placed in accented parts of the measure; unaccented syllables should be placed in unaccented parts of the measure. You should write complete, correct measures in $\frac{6}{8}$. Each setting is begun for you. Use as many measures as you feel you need. Be prepared to perform your settings in class. (See Exercise 6-4 for an example of the proper procedure.)

a. And we are here as on a darkling plain
    Swept with confused alarms of struggle and flight,
    Where ignorant armies clash by night.
    (Matthew Arnold)

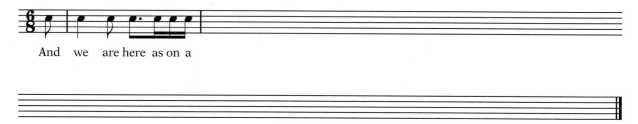

b. Had we but world enough, and time,
    This coyness, Lady, were no crime.
    (Andrew Marvell)

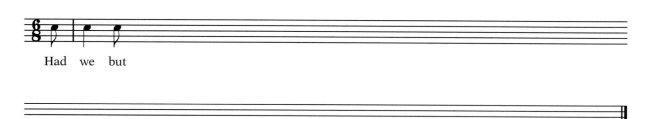

Lesson 13: Syncopation

In this lesson you will learn about syncopation, accent, ties, and subdivision.

Every meter has a fixed pattern of downbeats and upbeats, relatively accented and unaccented beats. And the beats themselves are divided into smaller units that are also either relatively accented or unaccented. *Syncopation* involves the contradiction of these underlying patterns. It makes the strong beats feel weak and the weak beats strong. In $\frac{4}{4}$ meter, for example, the first and third beats are relatively strong, while the second and fourth are relatively weak. This basic metrical framework may be contradicted in three ways:

1. A stress is placed on a weak beat by playing the note on that beat louder than normal. Often, composers use an *accent mark* to tell performers to place stress on a particular note.

Accent mark

2. A weak beat is tied to a strong beat. As a result, the weak beat receives a musical attack, but no note is attacked on a strong beat.

Ties

3. A strong beat is omitted, replaced by a rest.

Rests

Syncopations can occur in any meter. And they can occur both among the beats and among the *subdivisions* of the beats into accented and unaccented eighth notes.

Syncopations

Lesson 13: In-class activities

1. Dictation. Within each group, the instructor will perform the three rhythms in a random order. Identify the rhythm you hear and tap it back.

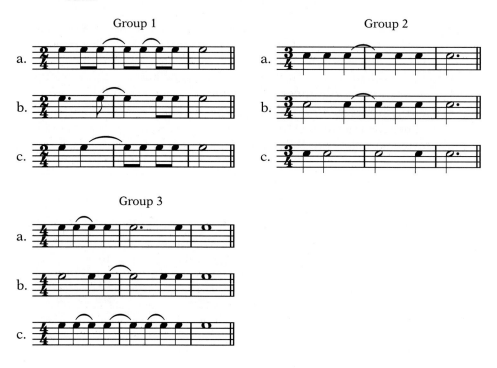

2. Solo. Suggestions for performance: (1) tap the beats with your hand while chanting the rhythm using the syllable "ta"; (2) say the beats of the measure while tapping the rhythm with your hand; (3) tap the beats with one hand while tapping the rhythm with the other; (4) conduct the beats with your right hand while chanting the rhythm using the syllable "ta." It is a good idea to tap preparatory beats, or count aloud, or conduct one preparatory measure before beginning each exercise in order to establish the tempo.

a. **Allegro**

b. **Allegro**

c. Joplin, "The Entertainer" (sixteenth notes are often joined to obscure the eighth-note beats).

d. Ellington, "It Don't Mean a Thing" (in measures 2, 4, and 6, there is a tie into the third beat of the measure).

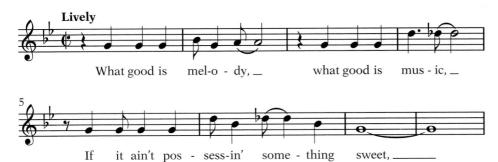

e. Handy, "St. Louis Blues" (in the first measure, a tie is used into the third beat).

3. Duets. Suggestions for performance: (1) one student or group of students performs each part of the duet, either tapping or chanting "ta." Then switch parts; (2) a single student chants the higher rhythm while tapping the lower and then vice versa.

d. Ellington, "It Don't Mean a Thing" (the lower part provides a steady background for the intensive syncopations in the upper part).

(continued)

e. Joplin, "The Entertainer" (the lower part moves in steady eighth notes against which the upper part provides nearly constant syncopations).

4. Improvisation. You are given two measures of syncopated rhythm in various meters. Continue and conclude by improvising two more measures. In your improvisation, use the rhythmic values and ideas found in the two measures you are given. Three suggestions for performance: (1) improvise a two-measure continuation and conclusion; (2) perform your improvisation in continuing succession with other students, in tempo and without missing a beat. As one student concludes an improvisation, another begins immediately, either by performing all four measures (beginning with the two given measures) or just his or her two-measure improvisation; (3) after you complete an improvisation, another student may be asked to perform what he or she heard you do. The example below shows three possible continuations for a given opening.

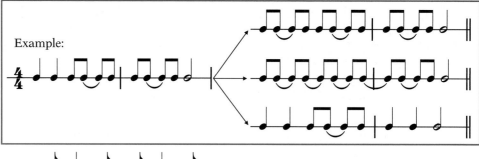

Name: ____

Date: __________________

Instructor's Name: __________________________________

Lesson 13: Exercises

13-1. Syncopate these rhythms by adding ties and accents.

a. 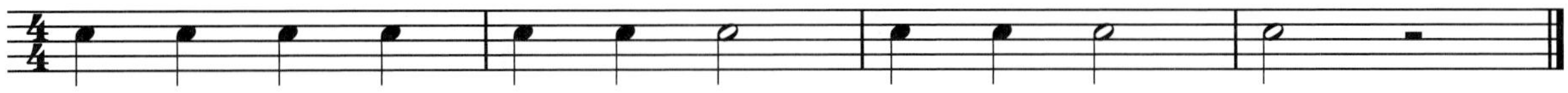

b. 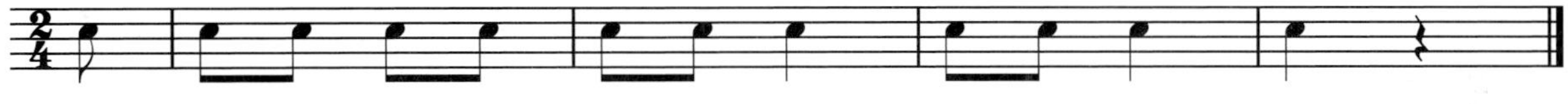

c. 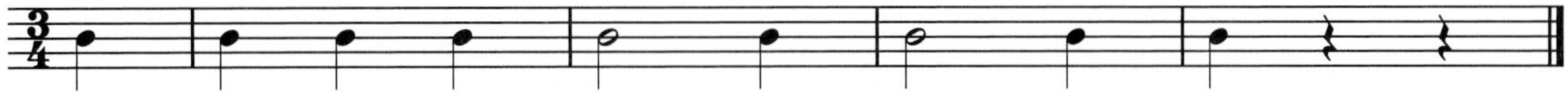

d. 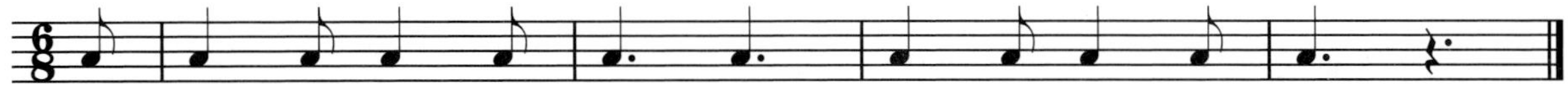

13-2. Continue and complete the following short rhythmic compositions. Each should be four measures in length. Use ties, rests, and accents to create syncopations. Be prepared to perform your compositions in class.

a. 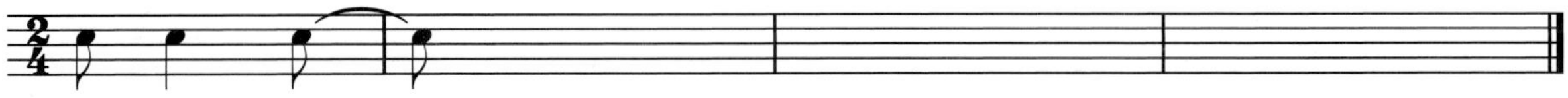

b. 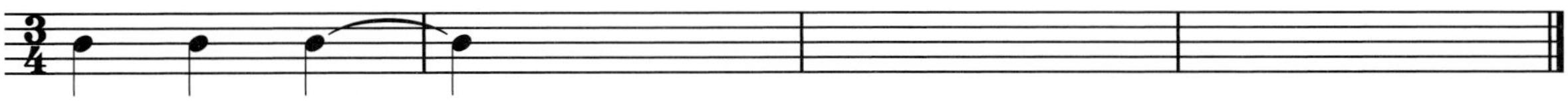

c. 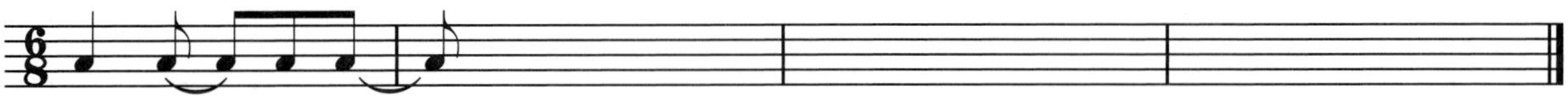

13-3. Set the following poetic texts to an appropriate rhythm. Each syllable should receive a note. Use syncopations, which will deliberately distort the natural accentuation of the words. Each setting is begun for you. Use as many measures as you feel you need. Be prepared to perform your settings in class. (See Exercise 6-4 for an example of the proper procedure.)

a. I placed a jar in Tennessee,
   And round it was, upon a hill.
   (Wallace Stevens)

b. With his ebony hands on each ivory key
   He made that poor piano moan with melody.
   (Langston Hughes)

Chapter 2: Supplementary lesson

In this lesson you will learn about rhythmic values smaller than a sixteenth note, triplets, and other duple, triple, and quadruple meters.

The hierarchy of note-values discussed in previous lessons—whole note, half note, quarter note, eighth note, sixteenth note—can be extended downward to notes of even shorter duration. A *thirty-second note* is half as long as a sixteenth note, and is written with a triple flag or beam. A *sixty-fourth note* is half as long as a thirty-second note, and is written with a quadruple flag or beam.

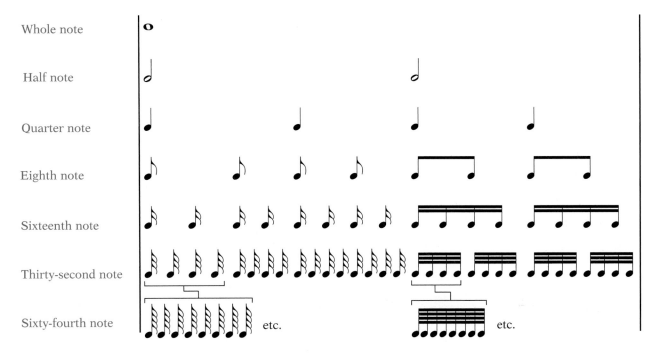

These basic note values, together with augmentation dots and ties, provide a rich variety of possible durations.

One additional kind of note-value is a *triplet,* which is used to divide into *three* parts a note that is normally divided in *two.* A quarter note, for example, is usually divided into two eighth notes, but can be divided instead into an *eighth-note triplet.*

In the same way, a whole note can be divided into a *half-note triplet;* a half note can be divided into a *quarter-note triplet;* and an eighth note can be divided into a *sixteenth-note triplet.*

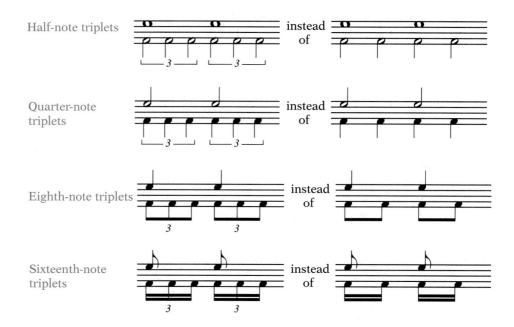

In previous lessons, we focused on the most commonly used musical meters: $\frac{4}{4}$ (or **C**), $\frac{2}{2}$ (or ¢), $\frac{2}{4}$, $\frac{3}{4}$, and $\frac{6}{8}$. Other meters are also in occasional use. Here are the main possibilities:

	Time value of the beat	Duple meter 2 beats per measure	Triple meter 3 beats per measure	Quadruple meter 4 beats per measure
Simple	Half note	$\frac{2}{2}$ or ¢	$\frac{3}{2}$	$\frac{4}{2}$
	Quarter note	$\frac{2}{4}$	$\frac{3}{4}$	$\frac{4}{4}$ or **C**
	Eighth note	$\frac{2}{8}$	$\frac{3}{8}$	$\frac{4}{8}$
Compound	Dotted half note	$\frac{6}{4}$	$\frac{9}{4}$	$\frac{12}{4}$
	Dotted quarter note	$\frac{6}{8}$	$\frac{9}{8}$	$\frac{12}{8}$
	Dotted eighth note	$\frac{6}{16}$	$\frac{9}{16}$	$\frac{12}{16}$

3 *Major and Minor Scales*

Lesson 14: Semitones and whole tones

In this lesson you will learn about diatonic semitones, chromatic semitones, and diatonic whole tones.

A *semitone* (or *half step*) is the smallest possible space between two notes. On the piano keyboard, any two adjacent keys are a semitone (or a half step) apart. Twelve semitones make up an octave.

Semitones

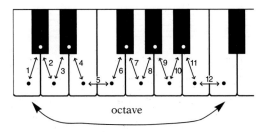

The note D, for example, lies a semitone above C♯ and a semitone below E♭. Similarly, F is a semitone above E and a semitone below F♯.

There are two kinds of semitones: *diatonic semitones* and *chromatic semitones*. A diatonic semitone consists of two notes with *different* letter names, written on a space and the adjacent line (or vice versa).

Diatonic
semitones

F♯ - G   B - C   A - B♭   E - D♯   E♭ - D   F - E

E–F and B–C are the only diatonic semitones found among the white notes (that is, they are the only white notes that have no black notes separating them). All other diatonic semitones require accidentals.

A chromatic semitone consists of two notes with the *same* letter name, written on the same line or space.

Chromatic
semitones

C - C♯   E♭ - E   A♭ - A   F - F♯   B - B♭   D♯ - D

Two semitones (or half steps) make up a *whole tone* (or *whole step*). Two notes a whole tone apart are separated by one intervening note. A *diatonic whole tone* (the only kind we will discuss here) consists of two notes with different letter names, written on a space and the adjacent line (or vice versa).

Diatonic
whole tones

Among the white notes, C–D, D–E, F–G, G–A, and A–B are diatonic whole tones (they all have a black note separating them).

Lesson 14: In-class activities

1. Singing. The instructor will play or sing the notes below. Sing the note you hear, then the note a diatonic semitone or whole tone above or below, as indicated. Sing the names of the notes (e.g., "F sharp" or "E flat").

a. diatonic semitone above

b. diatonic semitone below

c. diatonic whole tone above

d. diatonic whole tone below

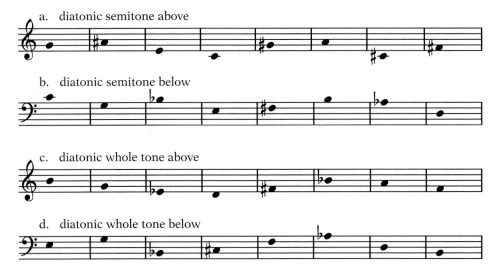

2. Dictation. The instructor will play or sing a semitone or whole tone. Identify what you hear.

3. Dictation. The instructor will play the pairs of notes within each group in a random order. Sing the notes you hear, then identify what you hear as a semitone, whole tone, or neither.

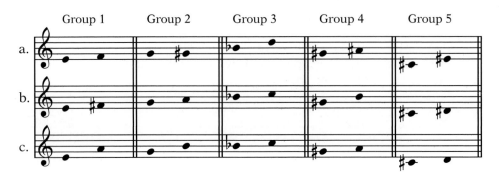

4. Playing. Play each written note, then the note a semitone or whole tone above or below, as indicated. Say the names of the notes you are playing as you play them.

  a. diatonic semitone above

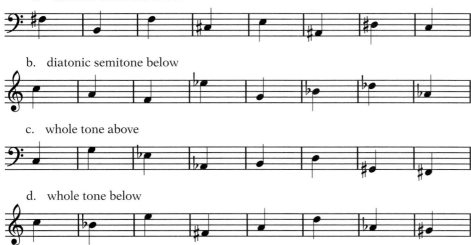

  b. diatonic semitone below

  c. whole tone above

  d. whole tone below

5. Playing. Starting on any note, play an ascending whole tone and a descending semitone in alternation until you get to an octave higher than your starting point. Then play a descending whole tone and ascending semitone in alternation until you get back to your starting point. Say the names of the notes you are playing as you play them.

Example starting on A:    etc.

etc.

Name: _____

Date: _____

Instructor's Name: _____

Lesson 14: Exercises

14-1. Write semitones and whole tones above and below these notes as directed. Use accidentals (including the natural sign) as needed. Remember to write the accidental directly before the note it modifies.

a. chromatic semitones above

b. chromatic semitones below

c. diatonic semitones above

d. diatonic semitones below

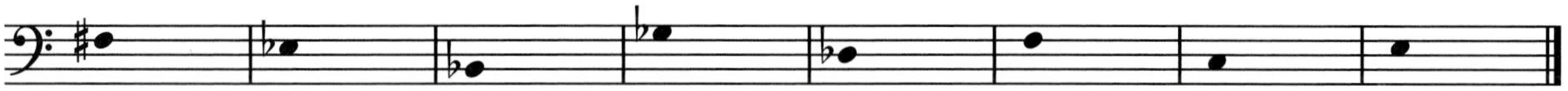

e. whole tones above

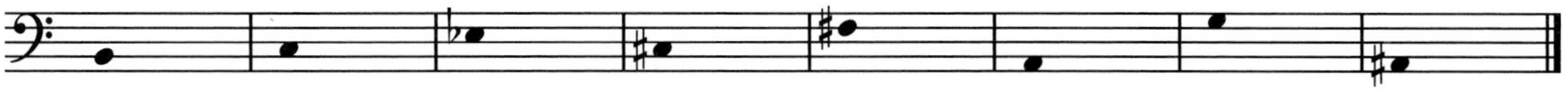

f. whole tones below

14-2. Identify these pairs of notes as chromatic semitones (CST), diatonic semitones (DST), or whole tones (WT). Remember that a chromatic semitone involves two notes with the same letter name, occupying the same line or space.

14-3. Add an accidental (sharp, flat, or natural) to the second note in each pair to create the requested interval. Remember to write the accidental directly before the note it modifies.

a. diatonic semitones

b. chromatic semitones

c. whole-tones

14-4. Identify these pairs of notes as chromatic semitones (CST), diatonic semitones (DST), or whole tones (WT). Remember that a chromatic semitone involves two notes with the same letter name, occupying the same line or space.

a. Schubert, "Heidenröslein" (in this melody, every note but one is connected by either a semitone or whole tone to the note before or after it).

Name: _____

Date: _____

Instructor's Name: _____

b. Haydn, Quartet (violin and cello only; both violin and cello make
    extensive use of diatonic semitones, particularly leading from beat
    1 to beat 2).

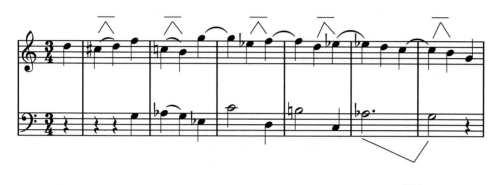

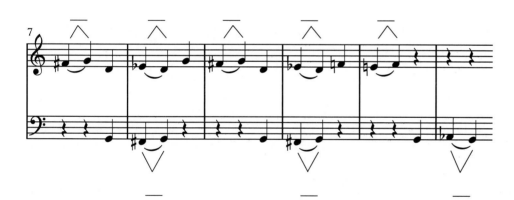

c. Bach, Fugue in g minor (Bach fills in almost every single semitone
    between C3 and C4).

d. Chopin, Prelude in c minor (at first, the bass line descends steadily, then its contour becomes more varied).

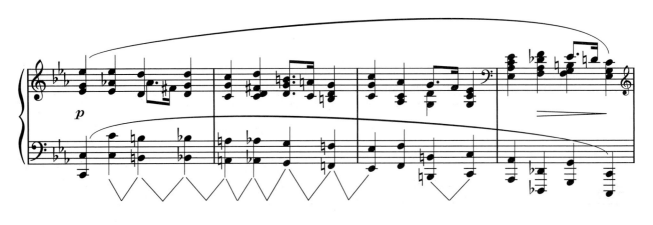

e. Mozart, "Dove sono" (the two phrases of this melody begin the same but end differently).

Name: _____

Date: _____

Instructor's Name: _____

f. Chopin, Prelude in A Major (each of the four phrases of this melody begins with the same kind of ascending step).

g. Handy, "St. Louis Blues" (the A♯ at the beginning of the melody ascends; the enharmonically equivalent B♭ toward the end of the melody descends, just as the words are "sun go down").

I hate to see __   de ev'-nin' sun   go   down _____

Lesson 15: Major scale (C major)

In this lesson you will learn about the major scale, its arrangement of semitones and whole tones, scale-degree numbers, scale-degree names, and solfège syllables.

A scale is a collection of notes used for a musical composition or part of a composition. The notes are extracted from the music and written in ascending order, within an octave. There are two scales commonly used in tonal music: *major* and *minor*. In major and minor scales, each letter name occurs once; none is omitted and none occurs more than once (except the first note, which is duplicated at the octave). Major and minor scales thus contain seven different notes.

A *major scale* consists of a particular sequence of diatonic whole tones and semitones above any given note: whole tone, whole tone, semitone, whole tone, whole tone, whole tone, semitone. A C major scale involves that sequence written starting on C—it is the only major scale that can be written without any accidentals.

C major scale

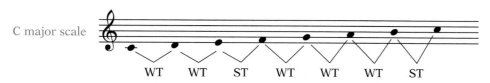

Each note of the scale is called a *scale-degree* and these are commonly numbered 1̂ through 8̂, with scale-degree 8̂ the same as scale-degree 1̂ an octave higher. Scale-degree numbers are designated by a caret (ˆ) over the number.

Scale-degree numbers

There are two semitones, between scale-degrees 3̂–4̂ and 7̂–8̂. All the other steps in the scale are whole tones.

Scale-degrees are also called by the names *tonic, supertonic, mediant, subdominant, dominant, submediant,* and *leading-tone.*

Scale-degree names

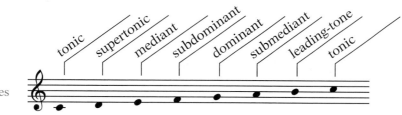

The tonic lies at the center of this naming system, with the mediant and dominant three and five steps above, and the submediant and subdominant three and five steps below.

Tonic in the middle

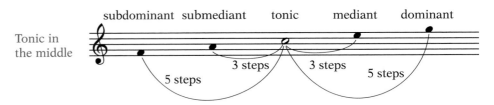

The scale-degrees are also sometimes referred to with *solfège syllables: do* (pronounced "doh"), *re* (pronounced "ray"), *mi* (pronounced "mee"), *fa* (pronounced "fah"), *sol* (pronounced "soh"), *la* (pronounced "lah"), and *ti* (pronounced "tee"). These syllables are commonly used when music is sung.

Solfège syllables

We thus have three different ways of naming each note of the C Major scale:

Note	Scale-degree number	Scale-degree name	Solfège syllable
C	$\hat{1}$ or $\hat{8}$	Tonic	*do*
D	$\hat{2}$	Supertonic	*re*
E	$\hat{3}$	Mediant	*mi*
F	$\hat{4}$	Subdominant	*fa*
G	$\hat{5}$	Dominant	*sol*
A	$\hat{6}$	Submediant	*la*
B	$\hat{7}$	Leading-tone	*ti*

Each degree of the scale has its own distinctive character, its own dynamic quality and tendencies.

Dynamic qualities

The tonic (scale-degree $\hat{1}$) embodies a sense of poised repose—it is normally both the origin and goal of melodic motion, and the other degrees of the scale tend to move toward it. It is the principal scale degree. The dominant (scale-degree $\hat{5}$) is the second most important and stable scale-degree. It lies just beyond the midpoint of the scale and can be pulled either upward or downward to the tonic. The supertonic (scale-degree $\hat{2}$), so called because it is a step above the tonic, is often pulled down one step toward the tonic, as though caught in a gravitational pull. The mediant (scale-degree $\hat{3}$), so called because it is halfway between the tonic and the dominant, is relatively stable compared to the supertonic. Melodic motion often passes downward from the mediant to the tonic via the supertonic. The subdominant (scale-degree $\hat{4}$) tends to move downward to the more stable mediant, a semitone below it. The submediant (scale-degree $\hat{6}$) is pulled downward toward the dominant, a step below it. The leading-tone (scale-degree $\hat{7}$) is so called because it has such a strong tendency to move upward to the relatively stable tonic, a semitone above it. In short, the major scale is not a neutral bunch of notes but a scene of dynamism and activity. It is a network of relations in which each scale degree has a distinctive character and role.

Lesson 15: In-class activities

1. Singing. Sing these three-note melodic fragments using scale-degree numbers, solfège syllables, or a neutral syllable like "la," as indicated by your instructor.

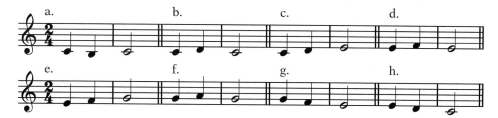

2. Singing. Sing these melodies using scale-degree numbers, solfège syllables, or a neutral syllable like "la," as indicated by your instructor.

3. Singing. Sing these melodies using scale-degree numbers, solfège syllables, or a neutral syllable like "la," as indicated by your instructor.

   a. Mozart, "Dove sono" (adapted; the melody starts in measure 9 as it did at the beginning, but diverges thereafter).

b. Haydn, Quartet (the downward leaps to each downbeat get larger and larger).

4. Singing (improvise). Continue and conclude the following short melodies (each should last four measures). Use only the notes of the C major scale, and use only whole notes, half notes, and quarter notes. Sing using scale-degree numbers, solfège syllables, or a neutral syllable like "la," as indicated by your instructor. You may perform your improvisation in continuing succession with other students, in tempo and without missing a beat. As one student concludes an improvisation, another begins immediately, beginning with the two given measures and concluding with his or her own two-measure improvisation.

5. Singing (improvise). You are given a melody in whole notes. Using only the notes of the C major scale, elaborate and decorate that melody using the suggested rhythmic values. Each improvisation is begun for you.

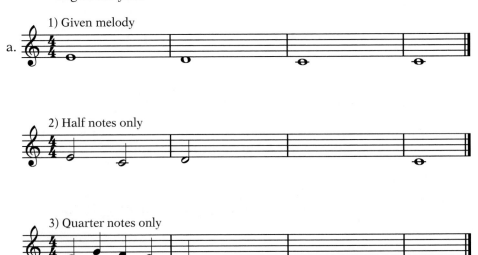

1) Given melody

b.

2) Half notes only

3) Quarter notes only

4) Half notes and quarter notes

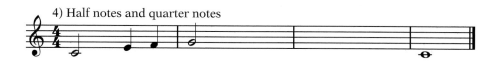

1) Given melody

c.

2) Half notes only

3) Quarter notes only

4) Half notes and quarter notes

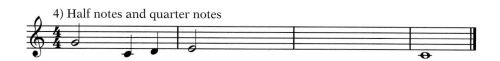

6. Singing (duets). Two students or groups of students sing the two lines of the following duets. Then switch parts. Sing using scale-degree numbers, solfège syllables, or a neutral syllable like "la," as indicated by your instructor.

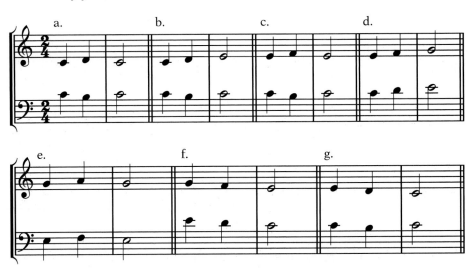

7. Dictation. The instructor will play a C major scale to establish a context and then will play a series of individual notes from the scale. Sing the note back with the correct scale-degree number or solfège syllable. The instructor will begin with C, E, and G only, then gradually add the remaining four notes.

8. Dictation. Within each group the instructor will play melodic patterns in a random order. Identify the pattern being played and then sing it back, either on a neutral syllable like "la" or using scale-degree numbers or solfège syllables.

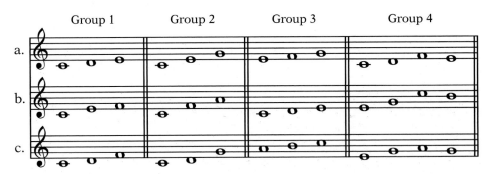

9. Playing. Learn to play a C major scale in one octave with your right hand alone and with your left hand alone (fingerings are provided).

10. Playing. Learn to play these melodies with your right hand and then, transposed an octave lower, with your left hand (fingerings provided).

a. Mozart, "Dove sono"

b. Haydn, Quartet

11. Playing (improvise). In-class activities 4 and 5 (on p. 120) involve improvisation. Instead of singing, perform your improvisations on the piano.

Name: _____

Date: _____

Instructor's Name: _____

Lesson 15: Exercises

15-1. Within the C major scale, identify these notes with scale-degree numbers, scale-degree names, and solfège syllables, as indicated.

a. scale-degree numbers

b. scale-degree names

c. solfège syllables

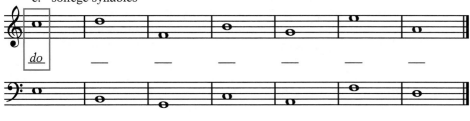

15-2. Within the C major scale, identify these notes with scale-degree numbers.

a. Haydn, Quartet (this melody features large leaps).

b. Mozart, "Dove sono" (in the first two measures, scale-degree
   $\hat{1}$ is surrounded by notes directly above and below it. The same
   thing happens to scale-degree $\hat{3}$ in measures 3–4).

c. Joplin, "The Entertainer" (the two lines here are actually a single melody played in octaves. Ignore the note in parentheses—
   it does not belong to the C major scale).

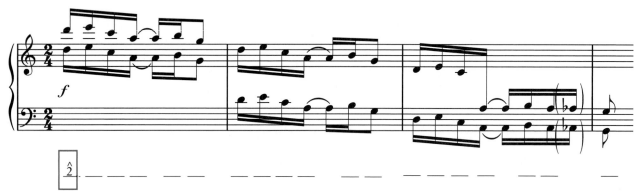

15-3. Compose a melody for each of these texts. If you wish, you may use
the rhythms you previously composed for these texts in Exercise
6-4. Use only the notes of the C major scale and remember the
dynamic tendencies of the scale-degrees. Use only whole notes,
half notes, and quarter notes. Each melody is begun for you. Play
your melodies on the piano or other instrument before handing
them in—be sure they sound the way you want them to. Be prepared to sing your melodies in class.

a. Do not go gentle into that good night.
   Rage, rage against the dying of the light.
   (Dylan Thomas)

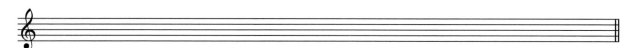

Name: _____

Date: _____

Instructor's Name: _____

b. When in disgrace with fortune and men's eyes,
   I all alone beweep my outcast state.
   (William Shakespeare)

When   in   dis - grace   with

15-4. Fill in the blanks in these melodies by adding whatever notes from
      the C major scale sound best to you (bearing in mind the dynam-
      ic tendencies of the different scale-degrees). Use only whole notes,
      half notes, and quarter notes. Play your melodies on the piano or
      other instrument before handing them in—be sure they sound the
      way you want them to. Be prepared to sing your melodies in class.

Lesson 16: Major scales other than C major

In this lesson you will learn about transposition, major scales with sharps, major scales with flats, and the circle of fifths.

Scales are named for their tonic (scale-degree $\hat{1}$). The major scale discussed in Lesson 15 has the note C as its tonic and is thus called a C major scale. But any note can be the tonic of a major scale. We simply *transpose* the scale to start on a different note, preserving its internal structure. To do so, however, requires the use of accidentals (sharps or flats). To write a G major scale, for example, requires an F♯.

G major scale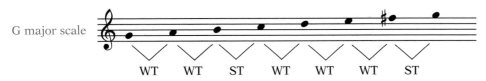

Without the F♯, there would be two steps of the wrong size: a semitone between scale-degrees $\hat{6}$ and $\hat{7}$ and a whole tone between scale-degrees $\hat{7}$ and $\hat{8}$. The F♯ makes all of the steps the correct size.

To write a major scale starting on D requires sharping both the F and the C.

D major scale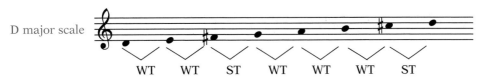

The C major scale requires no sharps or flats. The G major scale, which begins on scale-degree $\hat{5}$ of C major, requires one sharp (F♯). The D major scale, which begins on scale-degree $\hat{5}$ of G major, requires two sharps (F♯ and C♯). Every time we transpose up five steps in this way, an additional sharp is required. Notice that the sharps are added in a particular order: F♯–C♯–G♯–D♯–A♯–E♯–B♯. Like the tonics of the scales that use sharps, the sharps themselves ascend five steps each time.

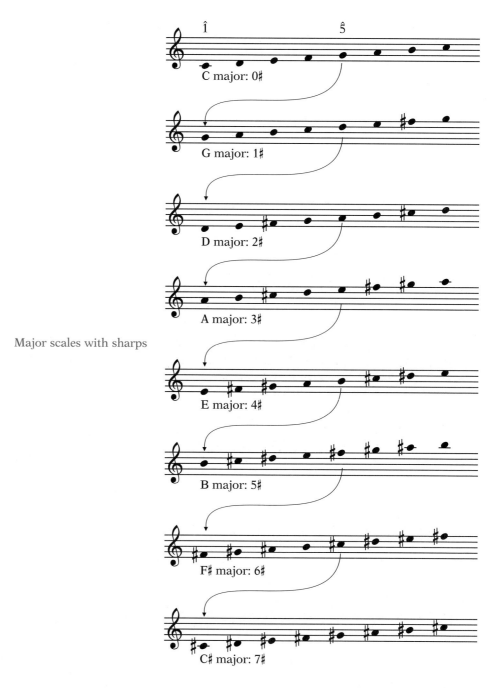

Major scales with sharps

Something similar happens moving downward by five steps. To write an F major scale, of which C is scale-degree $\hat{5}$, requires one flat (B♭).

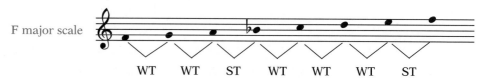

F major scale

To write a B♭ major scale, of which F is scale-degree $\hat{5}$, requires two flats (B♭ and E♭).

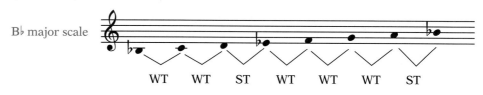

B♭ major scale

Every time we transpose down five steps, an additional flat is required. Notice that the flats are added in a certain order: B♭–E♭–A♭–D♭–G♭–C♭–F♭. Like the tonics of the scales that use flats, the flats themselves descend five steps each time.

Major scales with flats

If we start on C and move up five steps at a time in one direction and down five steps at a time in the other, we will eventually meet back in the middle, creating a *circle of fifths* on which all of the major scales and the accidentals needed to make them can be conveniently listed.

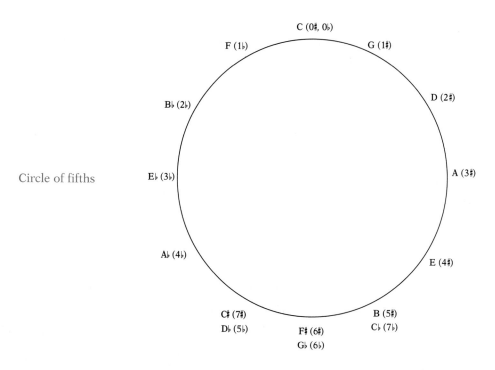

Circle of fifths

Because of enharmonic equivalence, some scales are listed twice. G♭ Major, for example, has six flats, while F♯ major has six sharps. The two scales are played with exactly the same notes on the keyboard, but are spelled differently.

The circle of fifths is the basic structure in relating major scales because the major scale is itself made up of fifths. Any major scale can be understood as a series of seven adjacent notes in the circle of fifths. Here are the notes of the C major scale identified as a contiguous segment of the circle of fifths.

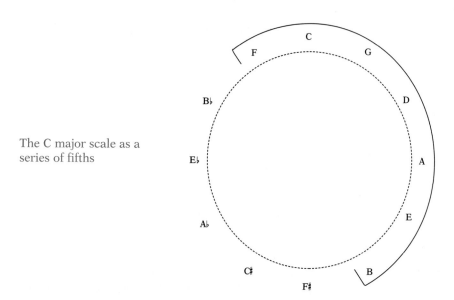

The C major scale as a series of fifths

Transposing that scale up by fifth involves shifting it one notch around clockwise. F is omitted while F♯ is added, and now we have the notes of the G major scale.

From C major
to G major

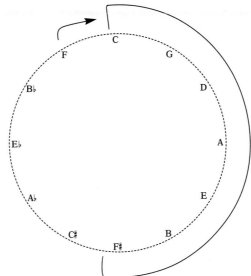

Each transposition of a major scale upward by fifth works in just this way, shifting one notch clockwise around the circle of fifths, and thus adding sharps in the prescribed order.

Transposing down by fifth involves shifting one notch counterclockwise around the circle of fifths. When C major is transposed down a fifth to F major, for example, B is omitted while B♭ is added.

From C major
to F major

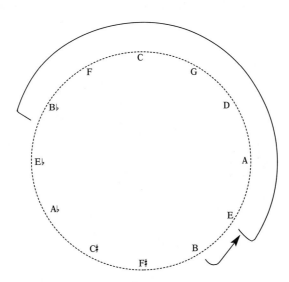

Each downward transposition by five steps shifts the collection of notes one notch counterclockwise on the circle of fifths and thus adds flats in the prescribed order.

Lesson 16: In-class activities

1. Singing. Sing the following common five-note patterns (given in D major and B♭ major). Sing using scale-degree numbers, solfège syllables, or a neutral syllable such as "la," as directed by your instructor.

2. Singing. Sing these melodies using scale-degree numbers, solfège syllables, or a neutral syllable such as "la," as directed by your instructor.

  a. Schubert, "Heidenröslein" (G major; the melody moves down toward the tonic in the first two measures, then up to the tonic in the last two measures).

  b. Mendelssohn, Piano Trio (adapted, D major; the melody creates spaces with upward leaps and fills them in with downward steps).

   c. Bach, Fugue in G major (it takes three measures for the melody to
      ascend from G4 to D5 and a single measure to get back to its start-
      ing point).

   d. Mozart, Sonata (A major; measures 5–8 begin the same as meas-
      ures 1–4 but end differently).

3. Singing (improvise). Continue and conclude the following short
melodies (each should last four measures). Use only the notes of the
G major scale (for the first melody) and the B♭ major scale (for the
second melody), and use only whole notes, half notes, quarter notes,
and eighth notes. Sing using scale-degree numbers, solfège syllables,
or a neutral syllable like "la," as indicated by your instructor. You may
perform your improvisation in continuing succession with other students, in tempo and without missing a beat. As one student concludes
an improvisation, another begins immediately, beginning with the
two given measures and concluding with his or her own two-measure
improvisation.

4. Singing (improvise). You are given a melody in whole notes. Using
only the notes of the appropriate major scale (G major for the first
melody, B♭ major for the second, and D major for the third), elaborate
and decorate that melody using the suggested rhythmic values. Each
improvisation is begun for you.

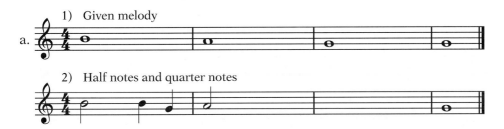

3) Quarter notes and eighth notes

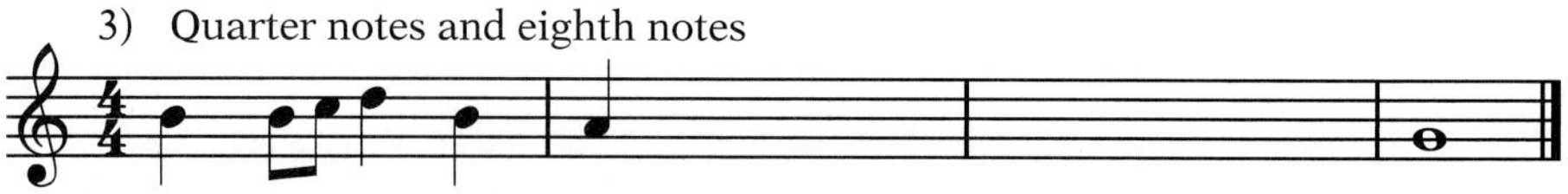

4) Eighth notes

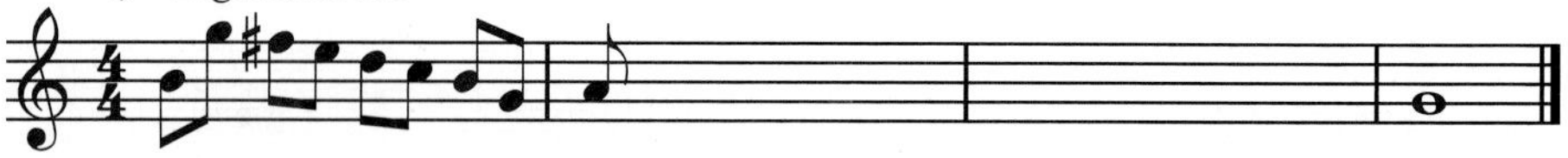

b.

1) Given melody

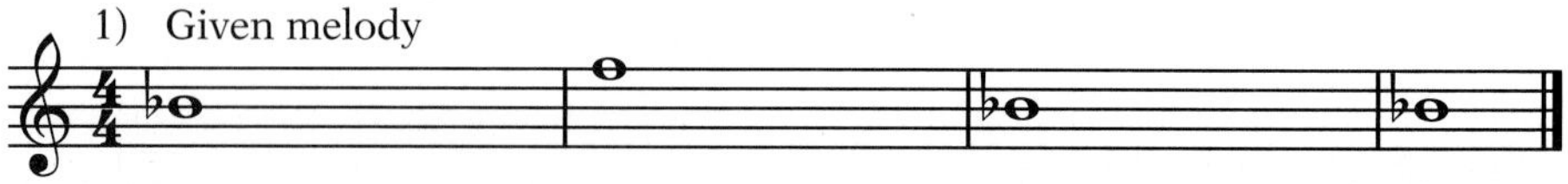

2) Half notes and quarter notes

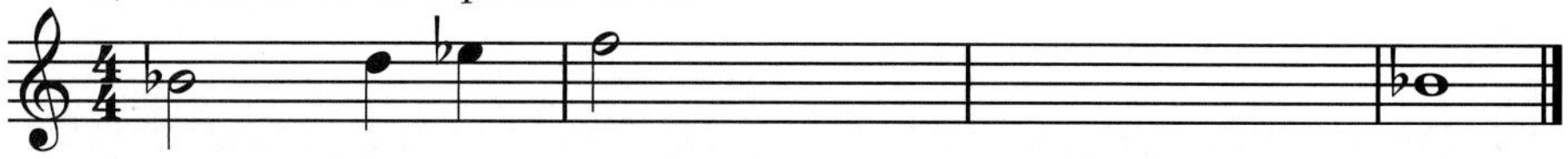

3) Quarter notes and eighth notes

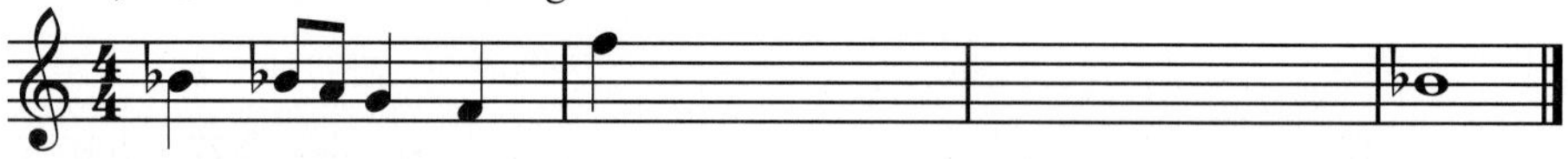

4) Eighth notes

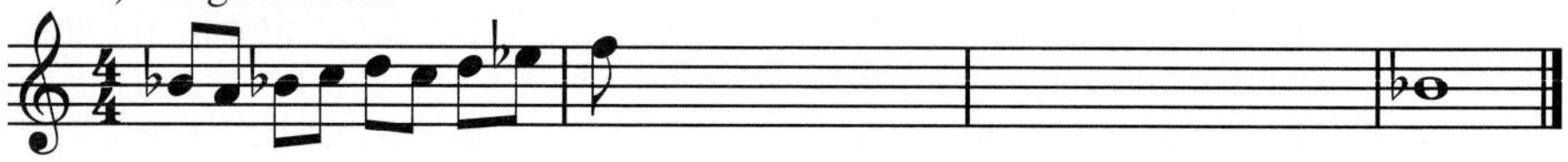

c.

1) Given melody

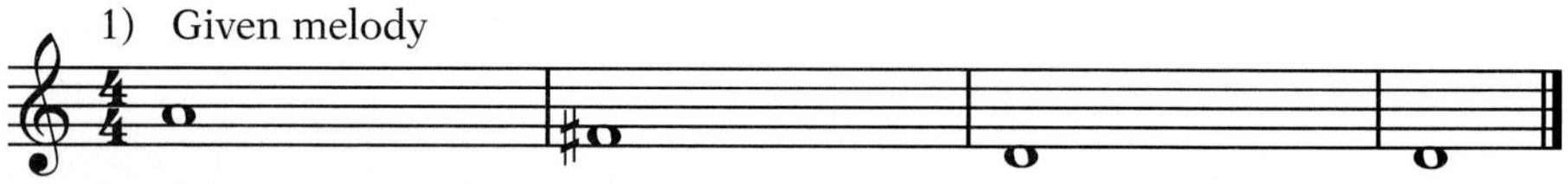

2) Half notes and quarter notes

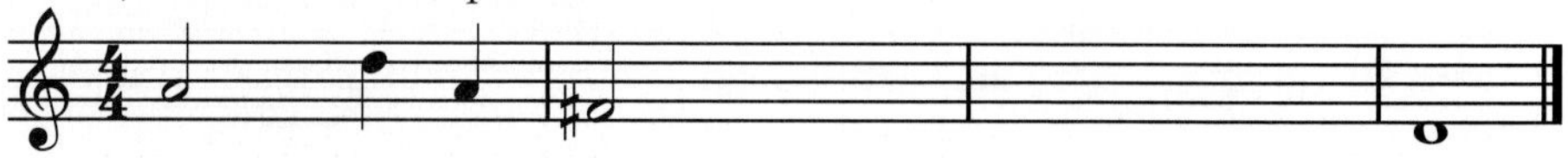

3) Quarter notes and eighth notes

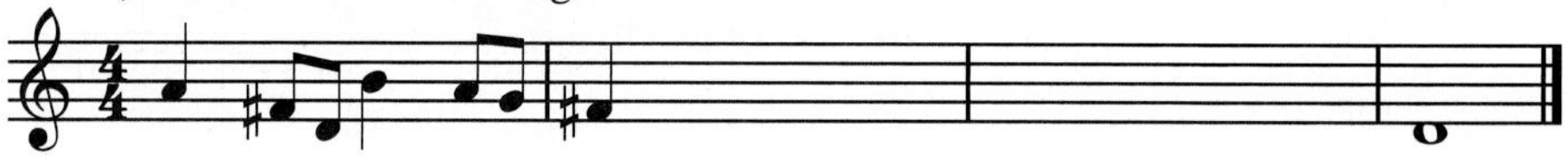

4) Eighth notes

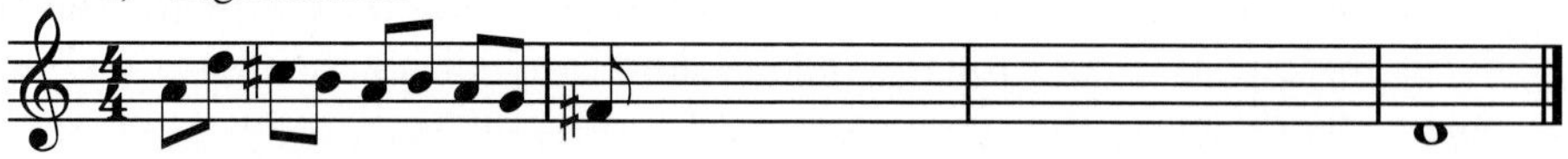

5. Singing (duets). Two students or groups of students sing the two lines of the following duets. Then switch parts. Sing using scale-degree numbers, solfège syllables, or a neutral syllable like "la," as indicated by your instructor.

6. Dictation. Within each group, the instructor will play the scales in a random order. Identify the scale played as major or not-major. Only one scale in each group is major.

7. Playing. You are given a note and told its scale-degree. Play the appropriate major scale down to its tonic, then up through an octave.

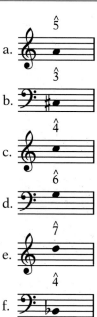

8. Playing (improvise). You are given a note and told its scale-degree. Starting with that note, improvise a short melody that ends on the tonic of the appropriate major scale. The melody should be in $\frac{4}{4}$ and use only whole notes, half notes, quarter notes, and eighth notes.

9. Playing. Learn to play major scales with hands alone and hands together. Here are the recommended fingerings for the major scales that use three or fewer accidentals.

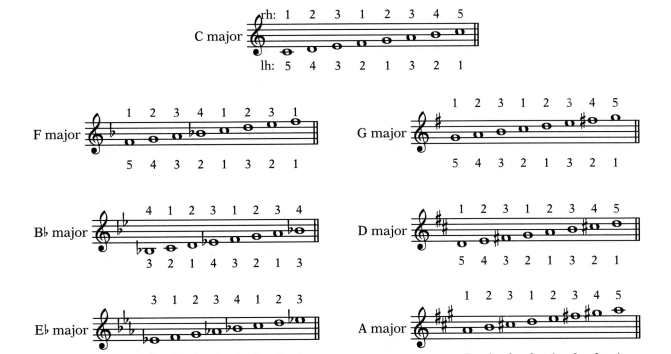

Name: _____

Date: _____

Instructor's Name: _____

Lesson 16: Exercises

16-1. Write major scales by adding the appropriate sharps or flats (major scales with three or fewer accidentals). Remember to write each accidental directly before the note it modifies.

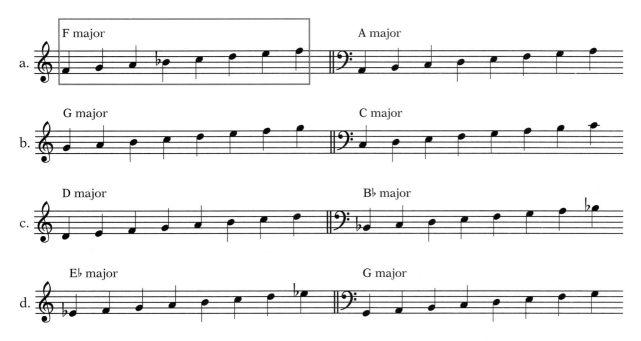

16-2. Write major scales by adding the appropriate sharps or flats (all major scales). Remember to write each accidental directly before the note it modifies.

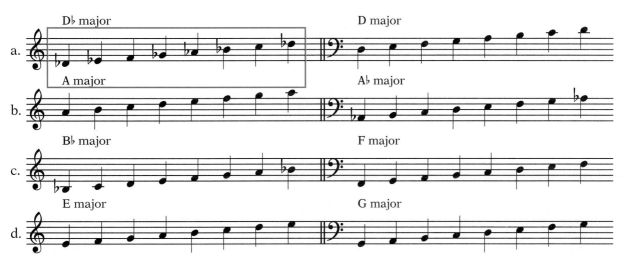

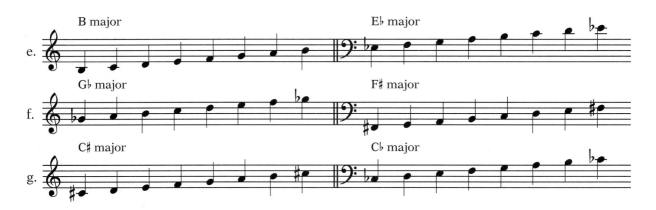

16-3. You are given a note and told what scale-degree it is. Write the appropriate major scale (scales with three or fewer accidentals).

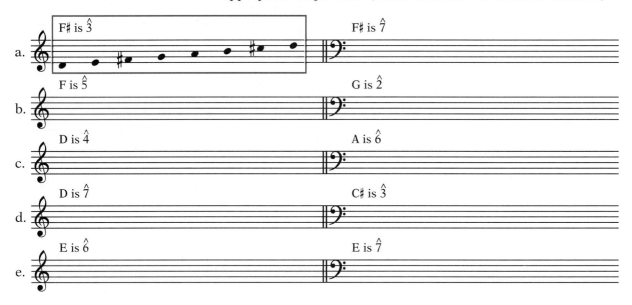

16-4. You are given a note and told what scale-degree it is. Write the appropriate major scale (all major scales).

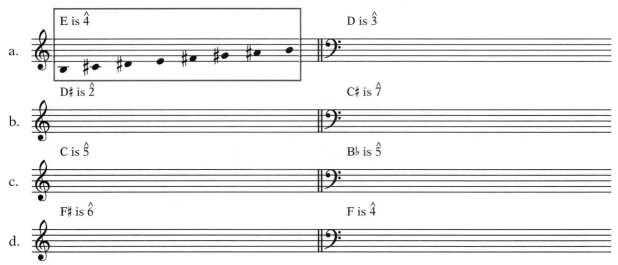

Name: _____

Date: _____

Instructor's Name: _____

16-5. You are given the name of a major scale and a scale-degree. Write the appropriate note (scales with three or fewer accidentals).

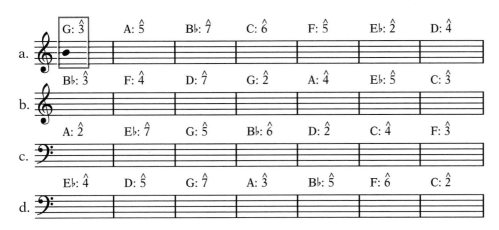

16-6. You are given the name of a major scale and a scale-degree. Write the appropriate note (all major scales).

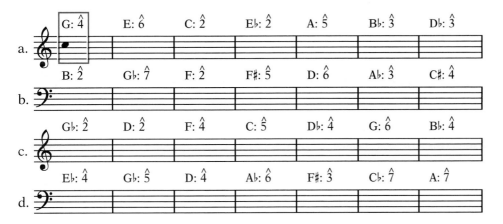

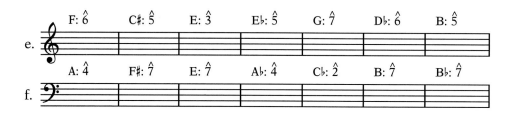

16-7. In each of these passages, identify the major scale used by writing it in the appropriate space beneath the score.

a. Chopin, Prelude (disregard the B♯ and D♯ in measure 3—they decorate the C♯ and E they precede).

b. Schubert, "Heidenröslein" (the song begins with one major scale, moves to another, then returns to its starting point. Disregard the A♯ in measure 9).

Name: _____

Date: _____

Instructor's Name: _____

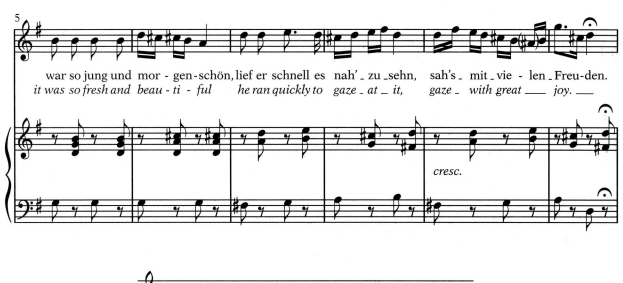

c. Schumann, Song (this song begins with one major scale then moves to another).

16-8. Transpose these melodies as requested. Play your work on a piano or other instrument before handing it in—be sure it sounds the way you want it to.

a.

Name: _____

Date: _____

Instructor's Name: _____

b.

from C major

to D major

c.

from E♭ major

to F major

16-9. Compose a melody for each of these texts. If you wish, you may use the rhythms you previously composed for these texts in Exercise 7-5. The first melody should use the notes of the D major scale; the second melody should use the notes of the F major scale. Use only whole notes, half notes, quarter notes and eighth notes. Each melody is begun for you. Play your melodies on the piano or other instrument before handing them in—be sure they sound the way you want them to. Be prepared to sing your melodies in class.

a. Whither is fled the visionary gleam?
Where is it now, the glory and the dream?
(William Wordsworth)

Whith - er   is   fled   the

b. Let us go then, you and I,
   When the evening is spread out against the sky
   Like a patient etherized upon a table.
   (T. S. Eliot)

Let   us   go   then,   you   and

16-10. Fill in the blanks in these melodies by adding whatever notes from the B♭ major scale (first melody) and G major scale (second melody) sound best to you (bearing in mind the dynamic tendencies of the different scale-degrees). Use only whole notes, half notes, quarter notes, and eighth notes. Play your melodies on the piano or other instrument before handing them in—be sure they sound the way you want them to. Be prepared to sing your melodies in class.

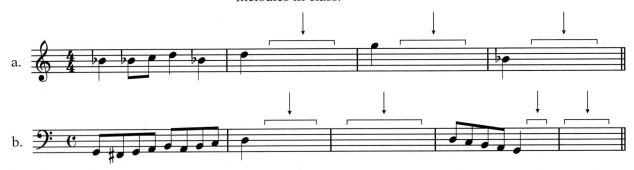

Lesson 17: Major keys and key signatures

In this lesson you will learn about major keys and key signatures.

Each major scale embodies a distinctive network of relationships. Each contains its own unique tonic, its own unique supertonic, its own unique mediant, and so on. Two major scales may have as many as six notes in common, but no two of them contain all of the same notes.

Scale-degree	$\hat{1}$	$\hat{2}$	$\hat{3}$	$\hat{4}$	$\hat{5}$	$\hat{6}$	$\hat{7}$
Name	tonic	supertonic	mediant	subdominant	dominant	submediant	leading-tone
Syllable	*do*	*re*	*mi*	*fa*	*sol*	*la*	*ti*
C major	C	D	E	F	G	A	B
G major	G	A	B	C	D	E	F♯
D major	D	E	F♯	G	A	B	C♯
A major	A	B	C♯	D	E	F♯	G♯
E major	E	F♯	G♯	A	B	C♯	D♯
B major	B	C♯	D♯	E	F♯	G♯	A♯
C♭ major	C♭	D♭	E♭	F♭	G♭	A♭	B♭
F♯ major	F♯	G♯	A♯	B	C♯	D♯	E♯
G♭ major	G♭	A♭	B♭	C♭	D♭	E♭	F
C♯ major	C♯	D♯	E♯	F♯	G♯	A♯	B♯
D♭ major	D♭	E♭	F	G♭	A♭	B♭	C
A♭ major	A♭	B♭	C	D♭	E♭	F	G
E♭ major	E♭	F	G	A♭	B♭	C	D
B♭ major	B♭	C	D	E♭	F	G	A
F major	F	G	A	B♭	C	D	E

This network of relationships within each scale is what defines a *key*. A piece is in the key of D major, for example, if it begins and ends by using the notes of the D major scale and treats D as tonic, A as dominant, C♯ as leading-tone, and so on. In pieces that are based on a particular major scale, it would be possible just to write the necessary accidentals each time they are called for, but this would be cumbersome. Instead, the necessary accidentals are simply written at the beginning of each line of the piece, right after the clef, in a *key signature*.

The A major scale, for example, uses three sharps: F♯, C♯, and G♯. Instead of writing sharp signs in front of every F, C, and G in a piece, composers just write the appropriate key signature, and all of the Fs, Cs, and Gs are automatically sharped.

This:

Key
signature

Instead of this:

The accidentals in the key signature need to be written in the proper place on the staff and in the proper order. The key of C major has a key signature of no sharps and no flats. The key of G major uses one sharp, namely F♯, and a sharp sign is placed accordingly on the top line of the treble staff and the fourth line of the bass staff.

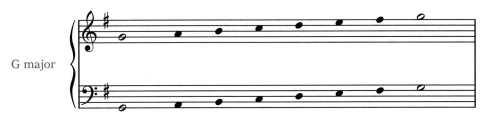

G major

That key signature indicates that every time the note F appears, in any octave, it will be played as F♯ (unless a natural sign is used temporarily to cancel it).

Shifting to a tonic five steps higher, the key of D major uses two sharps: F♯ and C♯. Sharp signs are accordingly placed on the top line of the treble and the fourth line of the bass staff (these sharp all of the Fs) and on the third space of the treble and the second space of the bass staff (these sharp all of the Cs).

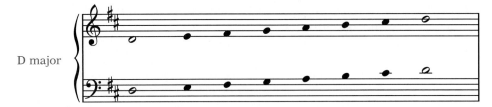

D major

Moving another five steps higher, A major uses three sharps: F♯, C♯, and G♯.

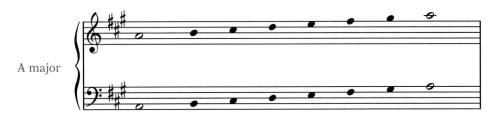

A major

Keys with flats in their signature work the same way. The key of F major, five steps below C, has a signature of one flat: B♭. Five steps below F, the key of B♭ major has a signature of two flats: B♭ and E♭. Five steps below B♭, the key of E♭ major has a signature of three flats: B♭, E♭, and A♭. As with sharps, these accidentals are written on particular lines or spaces of the treble and bass staves and apply throughout a piece in all octaves.

Major keys
with flats

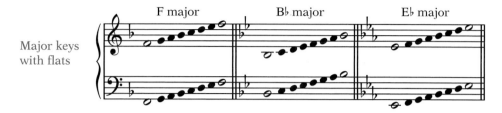

The key signatures for all of the major keys can be written conveniently around the circle of fifths.

Major key
signatures

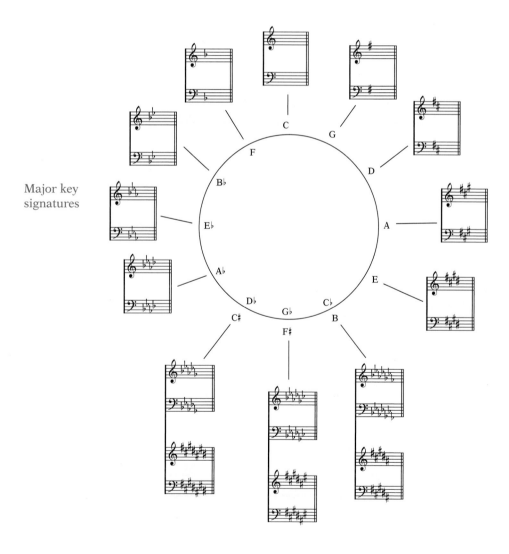

Each time you move clockwise, you add a sharp (or take away a flat). Each time you move counterclockwise, you add a flat (or take away a sharp). Notice that the sharps and flats accumulate in a particular order: F♯–C♯–G♯–D♯–A♯–E♯–B♯ for sharps and the reverse, B♭–E♭–A♭–D♭–G♭–C♭–F♭, for flats. For keys that use sharps, the tonic is a semitone above the last sharp in the signature. For keys that use flats, the tonic is the second-to-last flatted note in the signature.

Lesson 17: In-class activities

1. Singing. Sing the following common seven-note patterns (given in G major and F major). Sing using scale-degree numbers, solfège syllables, or a neutral syllable such as "la," as directed by your instructor.

2. Singing. Sing these melodies using scale-degree numbers, solfège syllables, or a neutral syllable such as "la," as directed by your instructor.

   a. Arlen, "Over the Rainbow" (the melody hovers in one place then ascends directly to the tonic).

   b. Lang, Song (the melody starts and ends on G4).

   c. Mozart, Sonata (adapted; the melody ascends to A5 before ending on A4).

   d. Schubert, "Heidenröslein" (adapted; the melody begins with a simple G Major scale).

   e. Schumann, Song (the melody descends B-A-G two times—the second one sounds like a real ending).

3. Singing (improvise). Continue and conclude the following short melodies (each should last four measures). The first melody is in D major and the second is in G major. Use dotted rhythms and/or ties as appropriate. Sing using scale-degree numbers, solfège syllables, or a neutral syllable like "la," as indicated by your instructor. You may perform your improvisation in continuing succession with other students, in tempo and without missing a beat. As one student concludes an improvisation, another begins immediately, beginning with the two given measures and concluding with his or her own two-measure improvisation.

a.

b.

4. Singing (improvise). You are given a melody in whole notes. Using only the notes of the appropriate major key, elaborate and decorate that melody using the suggested rhythmic values. Each improvisation is begun for you.

a.

1) Given melody

2) Use dotted quarter notes

3) Use ties

4) Use dotted eighth notes

b.

1) Given melody

2) Use dotted quarter notes

3) Use ties

4) Use dotted eighth notes

1) Given melody

c.

2) Use dotted quarter notes

3) Use ties

4) Use dotted eighth notes

5. Singing (duets). Two students or groups of students sing the two lines of the following duets. Then switch parts. Sing using scale-degree numbers, solfège syllables, or a neutral syllable like "la," as indicated by your instructor.

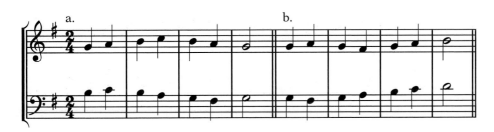

6. Playing (improvise). You are given a key signature and a note. Starting with that note, improvise a short melody that ends on the tonic of the appropriate major key.

Example

a.

b.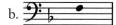

c.

d.

e.

f.

7. Playing. Learn to play the following five-finger pattern in all major keys. Play first with each hand alone and then with both hands together.

8. Playing. Learn to play the following five-finger pattern as it moves through all of the major keys. The last note of each pattern becomes the first note of the next. Alternate hands.

Name: _____

Date: _____

Instructor's Name: _____

Lesson 17: Exercises

17-1. Identify the major key represented by these key signatures (keys with three or fewer accidentals in the key signature).

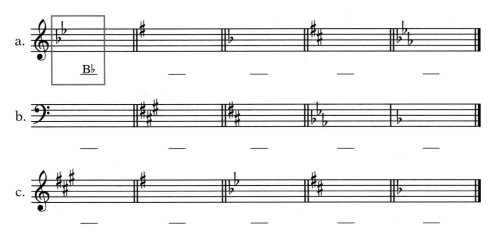

17-2. Identify the major key represented by these key signatures (all keys).

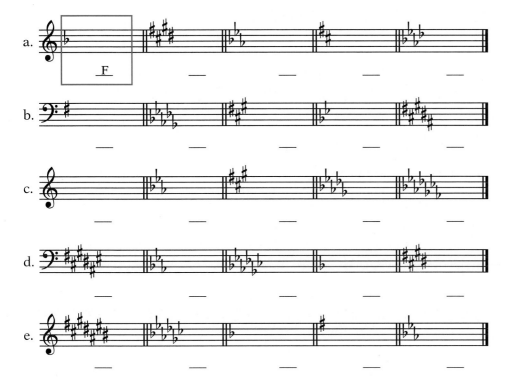

17-3. Write the key signature for these major keys (keys with three or fewer accidentals in the key signature). Remember to write accidentals in the correct order and position on the staff (see Exercise 17-1 for models).

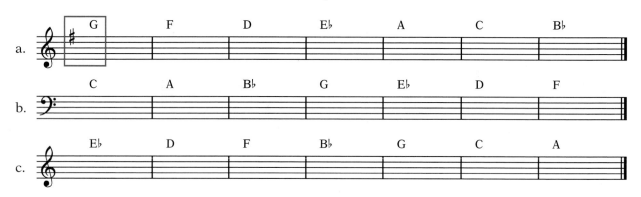

17-4. Write the key signature for these major keys (all keys). Remember to write accidentals in the correct order and position on the staff (see Exercise 17-2 for models).

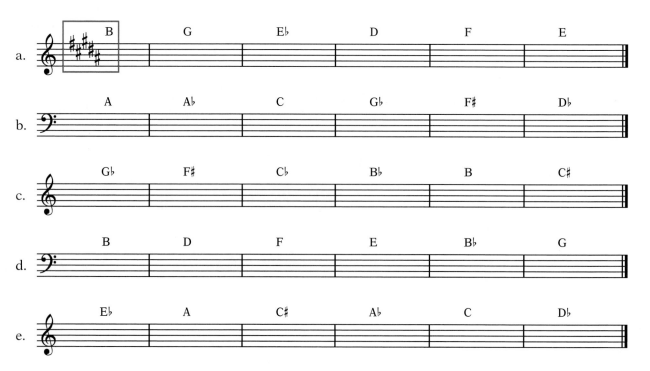

Name: _____

Date: _____

Instructor's Name: _____

17-5. Name the key of these pieces.

    a. Joplin, "The Entertainer" (disregard the notes in parentheses—
       they do not belong to the key, but serve to decorate those that do).

Key: _____

    b. Lang, Song (the bass note at the beginning and end of a phrase
       is often scale-degree Î, as it is here).

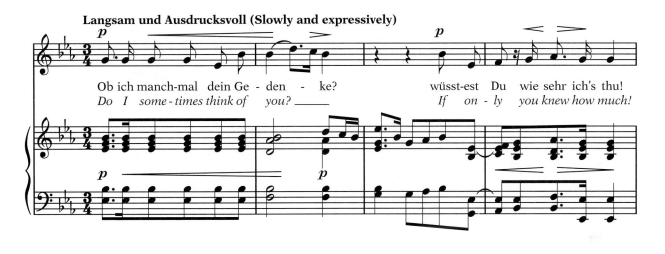

Key: _____

c. Mozart, Sonata

Key: _____

d. Schubert, "Heidenröslein" (as in the Lang song, the bass note at the beginning and end of the phrase provides scale-degree 1̂).

Key: _____

e. Chopin, Prelude (the B♯ and D♯ in measure 3 do not belong to the key).

Key: _____

f. Arlen, "Over the Rainbow"

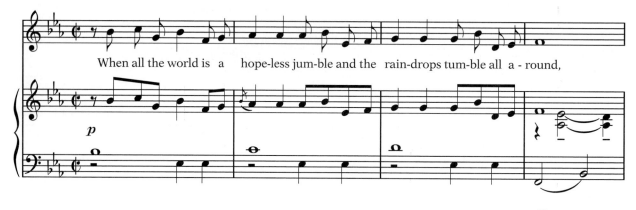

Key: _____

Name: _____

Date: _____

Instructor's Name: _____

g. Bach, Fugue

Key: _____

h. Bach, Chorale

Key: _____

i. Mozart, "Dove sono"

Do - ve so - no   i bei mo - men - ti
I   re - mem - ber days long de - part - ed,

Key: _____

j. Mendelssohn, Piano Trio

Key: _____

k. Schumann, Song

Key: _____

17-6. Compose a melody for each of these texts. If you wish, you may use the rhythms you previously composed for these texts in Exercise 8-5. Use dotted rhythms as appropriate. Each melody is begun for you. Play your melodies on the piano or other instrument before handing them in—be sure they sound the way you want them to. Be prepared to sing your melodies in class.

a. O body swayed to music, O brightening glance,
    How can we know the dancer from the dance?
    (W. B. Yeats)

b. Because I could not stop for Death—
    He kindly stopped for me.
    (Emily Dickinson)

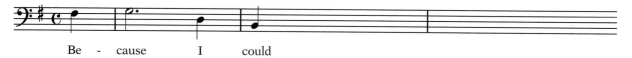

17-7. Fill in the blanks in these melodies by adding whatever notes from the appropriate major key sound best to you (bearing in mind the dynamic tendencies of the different scale-degrees). Use dotted rhythms as appropriate. Play your melodies on the piano or other instrument before handing them in—be sure they sound the way you want them to. Be prepared to sing your melodies in class.

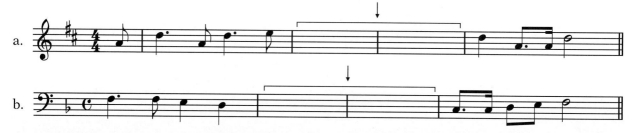

Lesson 18: Minor scale (a minor)

In this lesson you will learn about the minor scale, its arrangement of semitones and whole tones, scale-degree numbers, scale-degree names, solfège syllables, and raising scale-degrees $\hat{6}$ and $\hat{7}$.

The *minor scale* has a different arrangement of semitones and whole tones compared to the major scale. The minor scale has semitones between scale-degrees $\hat{2}$–$\hat{3}$ and $\hat{5}$–$\hat{6}$, while the major scale has semitones between scale-degrees $\hat{3}$–$\hat{4}$ and $\hat{7}$–$\hat{8}$. All other steps in the scale are whole tones. Like the C major scale, the a minor scale can be written without any accidentals.

Major and minor

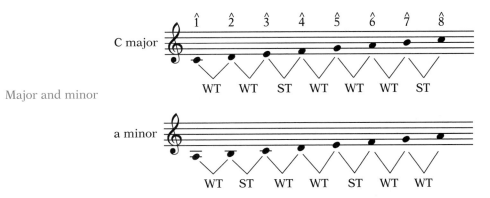

As in major, the scale degrees have names as well as numbers: tonic, supertonic, mediant, subdominant, dominant, submediant, and subtonic.

Scale-degree numbers and names

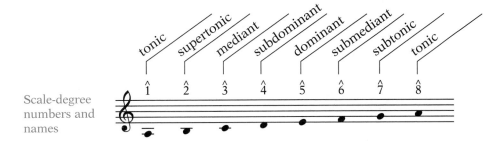

Notice that scale-degree $\hat{7}$ in minor is called the *subtonic* rather than the *leading-tone*. That is because it is a whole tone rather than a semitone below scale-degree $\hat{8}$, and thus lacks a sense of directed movement toward the tonic.

Musicians often use *solfège syllables* when singing melodies in minor. As in major, the syllable *do* is assigned to the tonic of the scale, *re* to the supertonic, and so on. Instead of *mi*, *la*, and *ti*, we use *me* (pronounced "may"), *le* (pronounced "lay"), and *te* (pronounced "tay") for scale-degrees $\hat{3}$, $\hat{6}$, and $\hat{7}$ in minor.

We thus have three ways of naming the degrees of the minor scale: with numbers, names, and solfège syllables.

Note	Scale-degree number	Scale-degree name	Solfège syllable
A	$\hat{1}$	Tonic	*do*
B	$\hat{2}$	Supertonic	*re*
C	$\hat{3}$	Mediant	*me* (*mi* in major)
D	$\hat{4}$	Subdominant	*fa*
E	$\hat{5}$	Dominant	*sol*
F	$\hat{6}$	Submediant	*le* (*la* in major)
G	$\hat{7}$	Subtonic	*te* (*ti* in major)

As with the degrees of the major scale, each degree of the minor scale has a distinctive dynamic character.

Dynamic qualities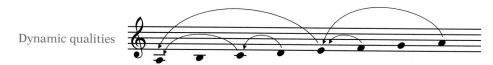

As in the major, the tonic is the principal scale-degree, with all melodic movement departing from and returning to it, and the dominant is the most important counterweight, dividing the scale nearly in half. The lack of a leading-tone means that motions often descend from the tonic toward the dominant. There is a particularly strong pull downward from the submediant to the dominant, only a semitone below. Similarly, there is a strong pull from the mediant down through the supertonic (a semitone below) to the tonic. There is thus a strong downward pull, which lends the minor scale a darker, more brooding character than the major scale.

In writing music using the minor scale, composers often create a leading-tone by raising the subtonic a semitone, making the note natural if it was flat and sharp if it was natural. Scale-degree $\hat{7}$ is now only a semitone below the tonic. When scale-degree $\hat{7}$ is raised in this way, it is called a leading-tone (rather than a subtonic) and is sung with the solfège syllable *ti* (rather than *te*).

Raising $\hat{7}$

This alteration of scale-degree $\hat{7}$ is extremely common in music that uses the minor scale.

Raising scale-degree $\hat{7}$ creates a relatively large gap of three semitones between scale-degrees $\hat{6}$ and $\hat{7}$. To smooth this out, composers sometimes raise scale-degree $\hat{6}$ as well. When scale-degree $\hat{6}$ is raised, it is still called a submediant, but is sung with the syllable *la* (rather than *le*).

Raising $\hat{6}$

Raising scale-degrees $\hat{6}$ and/or $\hat{7}$ from their natural position in the minor scale changes the dynamic qualities of the scale degrees. Now there is a flow of energy upward from scale-degree $\hat{5}$ to scale-degree $\hat{8}$, and the leading-tone truly leads upward to the tonic.

Dynamic qualities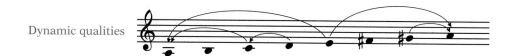

Lesson 18: In-class activities

1. Singing. Sing these three-note melodic fragments using scale-degree numbers, solfège syllables, or a neutral syllable like "la," as indicated by your instructor.

2. Singing. Sing these melodies using scale-degree numbers, solfège syllables, or a neutral syllable like "la," as indicated by your instructor.

3. Singing. Sing these melodies using scale-degree numbers, solfège syllables, or a neutral syllable like "la," as indicated by your instructor.

a. Haydn, Quartet (measures 1–4 and 5–8 begin the same but end differently).

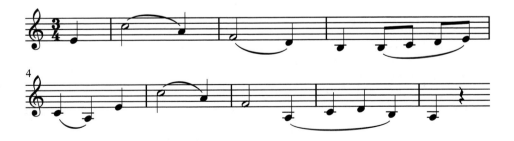

b. Mozart, Sonata (adapted; as in the passage above, measures 1–4 and 5–8 begin the same but end differently).

4. Singing (improvise). Continue and conclude the following short melodies (each should last four measures). Use only the notes of the a minor scale. Sing using scale-degree numbers, solfège syllables, or a neutral syllable like "la," as indicated by your instructor. You may perform your improvisation in continuing succession with other students, in tempo and without missing a beat. As one student concludes an improvisation, another begins immediately, beginning with the two given measures and concluding with his or her own two-measure improvisation.

5. Singing (improvise). You are given a melody in whole notes. Using only the notes of a minor (including the possibility of raising scale-degrees $\hat{6}$ and/or $\hat{7}$), elaborate and decorate that melody. (See In-class activities 15-5, 16-4, and 17-4 for models.)

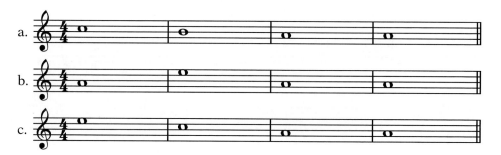

6. Singing (duets). Two students or groups of students sing the two lines of the following duets. Then switch parts. Sing using scale-degree numbers, solfège syllables, or a neutral syllable like "la," as indicated by your instructor.

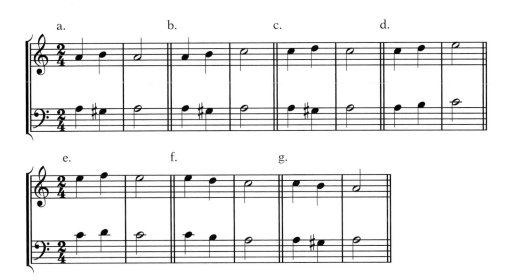

7. Dictation. The instructor will play an a minor scale to establish a context and then will play a series of individual notes from the scale. Sing the note back with the correct scale-degree number or solfège syllable. The instructor will begin with A, C, and E only, then gradually add the remaining four notes.

8. Dictation. Within each group the instructor will play melodic patterns in a random order. Identify the pattern being played and then sing it back, either on a neutral syllable like "la" or using scale-degree numbers or solfège syllables.

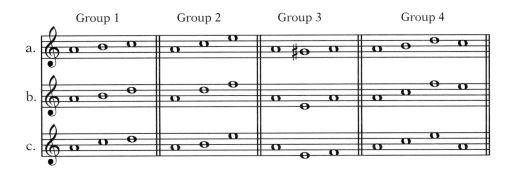

9. Playing. Learn to play an a minor scale in one octave with your right hand alone and with your left hand alone (fingerings are provided). It is conventional to raise scale-degrees $\hat{6}$ and $\hat{7}$ when ascending and restore them to their natural position when descending.

10. Playing. Learn to play these melodies sharing the playing between your left and right hands (fingerings provided).

a. Haydn, Quartet

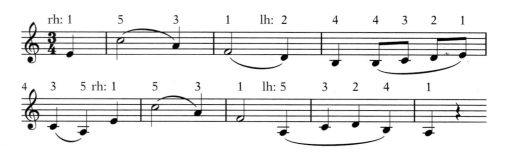

b. Mozart, Sonata (adapted)

11. Playing (improvise). In-class activities 4 and 5 (on p. 166) involve improvisation. Instead of singing, perform your improvisations on the piano.

Name: _____

Date: _____

Instructor's Name: _____

Lesson 18: Exercises

18-1. Within the a minor scale, identify these notes with scale-degree numbers, scale-degree names, and solfège syllables, as indicated. (Both G♮ and G♯ represent 7̂.)

a. scale-degree numbers

b. scale-degree names

c. solfège syllables

18-2. Within the a minor scale, identify these notes with scale-degree numbers.

a. Haydn, Quartet

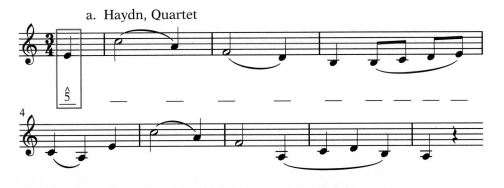

b. Mozart, Sonata (adapted)

18-3. Compose a melody in a minor for each of these texts. If you wish, you may use the rhythms you previously composed for these texts in Exercise 9-5. Each melody is begun for you. Play your melodies on the piano or other instrument before handing them in—be sure they sound the way you want them to. Be prepared to sing your melodies in class.

a. O Captain! my Captain! our fearful trip is done.
    (Walt Whitman)

b. Heard melodies are sweet, but those unheard
    Are sweeter; therefore, ye soft pipes, play on.
    (John Keats)

18-4. Fill in the blanks in these melodies by adding whatever notes from the a minor scale and whatever rhythmic values sound best to you. Bear in mind the dynamic tendencies of the different scale degrees. You may raise scale-degrees $\hat{6}$ and $\hat{7}$ when approaching the tonic from below. Play your melodies on the piano or other instrument before handing them in—be sure they sound the way you want them to. Be prepared to sing your melodies in class.

Lesson 19: Minor scales other than a minor

In this lesson you will learn about transposition, minor scales with sharps, minor scales with flats, and the circle of fifths.

Like major scales, minor scales are named for their tonic (scale-degree $\hat{1}$). The minor scale we have been considering so far has the note A as its tonic and is thus called an a minor scale. The a minor scale requires no accidentals, but *transposing* it to start on any other note will require flats or sharps to preserve its intervallic structure. To write the minor scale starting on E (the fifth degree of a minor), one sharp (F♯) is needed.

e minor scale

Without the F♯, there would be two steps of the wrong size: a semitone between scale degrees $\hat{1}$ and $\hat{2}$ and a whole-tone between scale degrees $\hat{2}$ and $\hat{3}$. The F♯ makes all of the steps the correct size.

As with the major scale, every time we transpose up five steps in this way, an additional sharp is required.

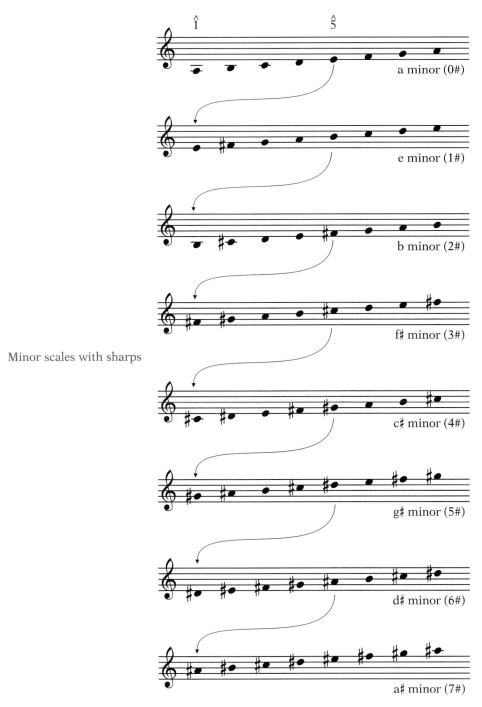

Minor scales with sharps

In contrast, to write a d minor scale, of which A is scale-degree $\hat{5}$, one flat (B♭) is needed.

d minor scale

Every time we transpose down five steps in this way, an additional flat is required.

Minor scales with flats

If we start on A and move up five steps at a time in one direction and down five steps at a time in the other, we will eventually meet back in the middle. We thus create a circle of fifths on which all of the minor scales and the accidentals needed to make them can be conveniently listed.

Circle of fifths for minor scales

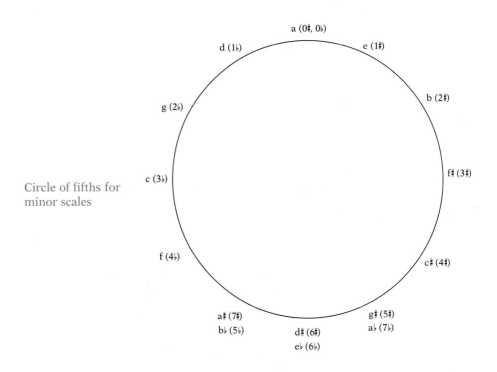

Lesson 19: In-class activities

1. Singing. Sing the following common five-note patterns (given in b minor and g minor). Sing using scale-degree numbers, solfège syllables, or a neutral syllable such as "la," as directed by your instructor. Notice that these melodies routinely use an accidental (natural or sharp) to raise scale-degree $\hat{7}$, thus creating a leading-tone.

2. Singing. Sing these melodies using scale-degree numbers, solfège syllables, or a neutral syllable such as "la," as directed by your instructor. Notice that these melodies routinely use an accidental (natural or sharp) to raise scale-degree $\hat{7}$, thus creating a leading-tone.

a. Schubert, "Death and the Maiden" (d minor; the refusal of the melody to budge from D suggests Death's inexorability).

b. Chopin, Prelude in c minor (the melody descends a long way, mostly stepwise, to its conclusion on C4).

c. Bach, Fugue in G Major (although the piece begins and ends in G major, this passage is in e minor).

d. Bach, Fugue in G Major (although the piece begins and ends in G major, this passage is in b minor).

e. Bach, Fugue in g minor

f. Bach, Fugue in g minor (although the piece begins and ends in g minor, this passage is in c minor).

g. Haydn, Quartet (this passage is in a minor).

h. Haydn, Quartet (despite the key signature this passage is in d minor).

3. Singing (improvise). Continue and conclude the following short melodies (each should last four measures). Sing using scale-degree numbers, solfège syllables, or a neutral syllable like "la," as indicated by your instructor. You may perform your improvisation in continuing succession with other students, in tempo and without missing a beat. As one student concludes an improvisation, another begins immediately, beginning with the two given measures and concluding with his or her own two-measure improvisation.

4. Singing (improvise). You are given a melody in whole notes or half notes. Using only the notes of the appropriate minor key (including the possibility of raising scale-degrees $\hat{6}$ and/or $\hat{7}$), and whatever rhythmic values you like, elaborate and decorate that melody. See In-class activities 15-5, 16-4, and 17-4 for models.

5. Singing (duets). Two students or groups of students sing the two lines of the following duets. Then switch parts. Sing using scale-degree numbers, solfège syllables, or a neutral syllable like "la," as indicated by your instructor.

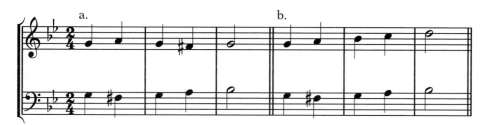

6. Dictation. Within each group, the instructor will play the scales in a random order. One is minor, one is major, and one is neither. Identify the scale played.

7. Playing. You are given a note and told its scale-degree. Play the appropriate minor scale down to its tonic, then up through an octave. When ascending, you may raise scale-degrees $\hat{6}$ and $\hat{7}$, as directed by your instructor.

8. Playing (improvise). You are given a note and told its scale-degree. Starting with that note, improvise a short melody that ends on the tonic of the appropriate minor scale. When approaching the tonic from below, you should raise scale-degrees $\hat{6}$ and $\hat{7}$.

9. Playing. Learn to play minor scales with hands alone and hands to-gether. Here are five minor scales that have the same piano fingering.

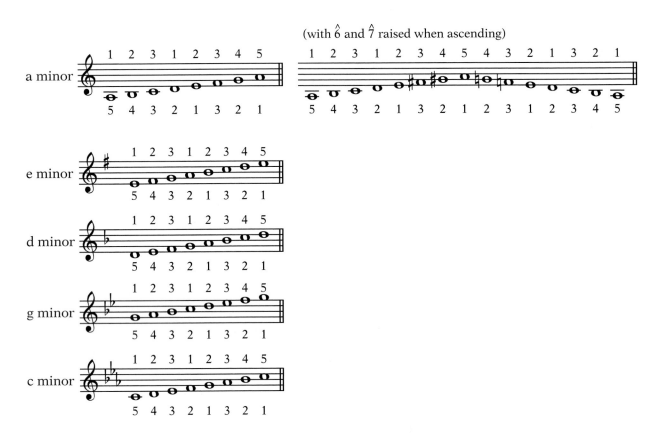

Name: _____

Date: _____

Instructor's Name: _____

Lesson 19: Exercises

19-1. Write minor scales by adding the appropriate sharps or flats (minor scales with three or fewer accidentals).

19-2. Write minor scales by adding the appropriate sharps or flats (all minor scales).

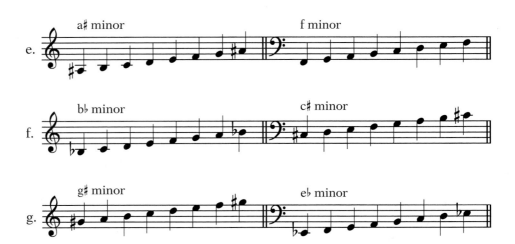

19-3. You are given a note and told what scale-degree it is. Write the appropriate minor scale (scales with three or fewer accidentals).

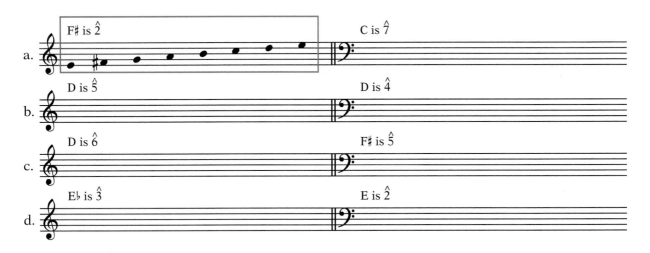

19-4. You are given a note and told what scale-degree it is. Write the appropriate minor scale (all minor scales).

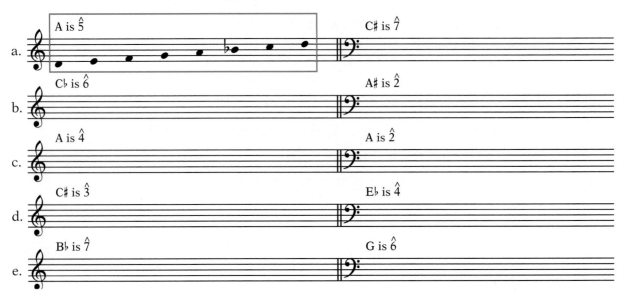

Name: _____

Date: _____

Instructor's Name: _____

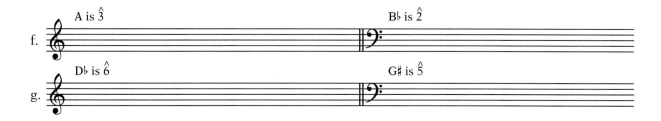

19-5. You are given the name of a minor scale and a scale-degree. Write the appropriate note (scales with three or fewer accidentals).

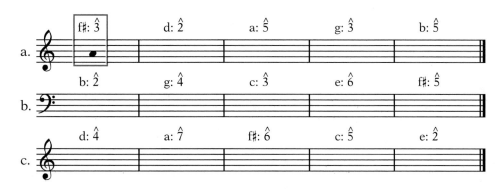

19-6. You are given the name of a minor scale and a scale-degree. Write the appropriate note (all minor scales).

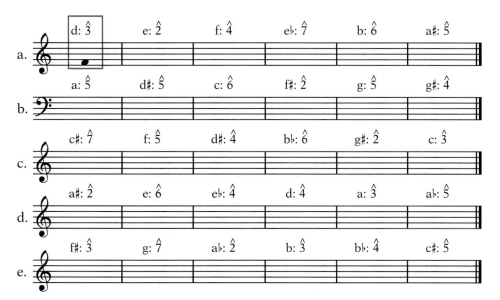

19-7. In these passages, identify the *major* or *minor* scales being used by writing them in the appropriate space beneath the score.

a. Bach, Fugue in G Major (the third scale is the same as the first).

Name: _____

Date: _____

Instructor's Name: _____

   b. Bach, Fugue in g minor (remember that scale-degree $\hat{7}$ is rou-
       tinely raised in minor scales. Disregard the C♯ in parentheses in
       measure 5.)

c. Schumann, Song (disregard the B♭ in parentheses in measure 5—it does not belong to the prevailing scale, but merely decorates the A, which does).

Name: _____

Date: _____

Instructor's Name: _____

    d. Mendelssohn, Piano Trio (here are three similar passages taken from three different places in the work. Disregard the notes in parentheses—they merely decorate notes that belong to the prevailing scales).

19-8. Transpose these melodies as requested. Play your work on a piano or other instrument before handing it in—be sure it sounds the way you want it to.

a.
from a minor

to b minor

b.
from a minor

to g minor

Name: _____

Date: _____

Instructor's Name: _____

19-9. Compose a melody for each of these texts. The first is in e minor and the second is in g minor. If you wish, you may use the rhythms you previously composed for these texts in Exercise 10-4. Each melody is begun for you. Play your melodies on the piano or other instrument before handing them in—be sure they sound the way you want them to. Be prepared to sing your melodies in class.

a. Made weak by time and fate, but strong in will
   To strive, to seek, to find, and not to yield.
   (Alfred, Lord Tennyson)

b. Since then, at an uncertain hour,
   That agony returns:
   And till my ghastly tale is told,
   This heart within me burns.
   (Samuel Taylor Coleridge)

19-10. Fill in the blanks in these melodies by adding whatever notes from the appropriate minor scale and whatever rhythmic values sound best to you. Bear in mind the dynamic tendencies of the different scale-degrees. You may raise scale-degrees $\hat{6}$ and $\hat{7}$ when approaching the tonic from below. Play your melodies on the piano or other instrument before handing them in—be sure they sound the way you want them to. Be prepared to sing your melodies in class.

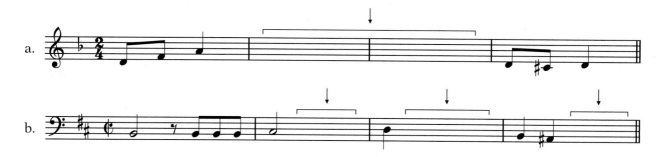

Lesson 20: Minor keys and key signatures

In this lesson you will learn about minor keys, minor key signatures, relative keys, and parallel keys.

As with the major scale, each minor scale embodies a network of relationships, with its own unique tonic, supertonic, mediant, and so on. This network of relationships is what defines a *key*. A piece is in the key of d minor, for example, if it begins and ends by using the notes of the d minor scale and treats D as tonic, F as mediant, A as dominant, and so on.

Scale-degree Name Syllable	$\hat{1}$ tonic *do*	$\hat{2}$ supertonic *re*	$\hat{3}$ mediant *me*	$\hat{4}$ subdominant *fa*	$\hat{5}$ dominant *sol*	$\hat{6}$ submediant *le*	$\hat{7}$ subtonic *te*
a minor	A	B	C	D	E	F	G
e minor	E	F♯	G	A	B	C	D
b minor	B	C♯	D	E	F♯	G	A
f♯ minor	F♯	G♯	A	B	C♯	D	E
c♯ minor	C♯	D♯	E	F♯	G♯	A	B
⎰g♯ minor	G♯	A♯	B	C♯	D♯	E	F♯
⎱a♭ minor	A♭	B♭	C♭	D♭	E♭	F♭	G♭
⎰d♯ minor	D♯	E♯	F♯	G♯	A♯	B	C♯
⎱e♭ minor	E♭	F	G♭	A♭	B♭	C♭	D♭
⎰a♯ minor	A♯	B♯	C♯	D♯	E♯	F♯	G♯
⎱b♭ minor	B♭	C	D♭	E♭	F	G♭	A♭
f minor	F	G	A♭	B♭	C	D♭	E♭
c minor	C	D	E♭	F	G	A♭	B♭
g minor	G	A	B♭	C	D	E♭	F
d minor	D	E	F	G	A	B♭	C

As with the major scale, the accidentals needed for each minor scale can be gathered into a *key signature*, and the key signatures for all of the minor scales can be summarized in a *circle of fifths*. The sharps and flats are added (and written) in just the same order as in major.

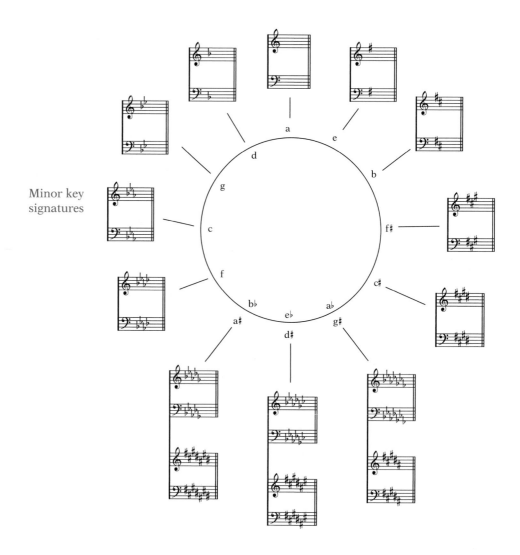

Minor key signatures

Major and minor scales that share the same key signature are called *relative keys*. Relative keys use the same notes, but ordered differently. For example, F major and d minor both use the same seven notes, but F major arranges those notes to begin on F and d minor arranges them to begin on D. Similarly, D major and b minor are relative scales.

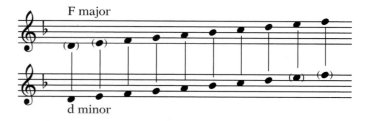

Relative minor scales

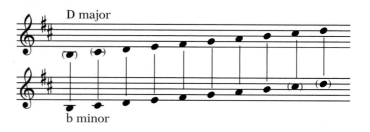

Major scales begin on scale-degree $\hat{3}$ of their relative minors; minor scales begin on scale-degree $\hat{6}$ of their relative majors.

The relative major and minor key signatures can be gathered into a double circle of fifths, with the major keys listed around the outside, the minor keys around the inside, and their shared key signatures between.

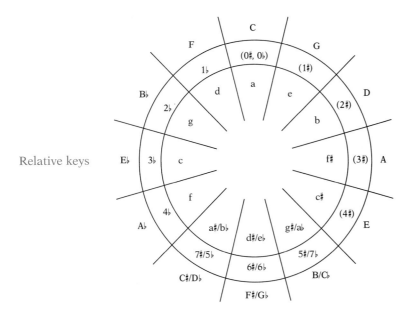

Relative keys

Major and minor scales that share the same tonic are called *parallel keys*. Parallel keys share not only the same tonic but also the same supertonic, subdominant, and dominant as well. C major and c minor, B♭ major and b♭ minor, D major and d minor, are all parallel keys. They differ only in scale-degrees $\hat{3}$, $\hat{6}$, and $\hat{7}$. But those differences can have a powerful expressive effect. Lots of music creates a change of mood by shifting from minor to major, or vice versa, while retaining the same tonic.

Lesson 20: In-class activities

1. Singing. Sing the following common seven-note patterns (given in e minor and d minor). Sing using scale-degree numbers, solfège syllables, or a neutral syllable such as "la," as directed by your instructor.

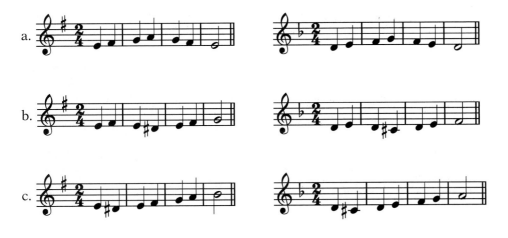

2. Singing. **Sing these melodies using scale-degree numbers, solfège syllables, or a neutral syllable such as "la," as directed by your instructor.**

a. Rodriguez, "La Cumparsita" (adapted; the melody leaps from G4 to G5, then fills in by step the space thus opened).

b. Chopin, Prelude in c minor (adapted; the generally descending shape of the melody contributes to its gloomy character).

c. Schubert, "Death and the Maiden" (the upward push of the melody reflects a young woman's desire to evade death).

d. Ellington, "It Don't Mean a Thing" (adapted; the melody stays between G4 and D4).

3. Singing (improvise). Continue and conclude the following short melodies (each should last four measures). Use only the notes of the appropriate minor scale. Sing using scale-degree numbers, solfège syllables, or a neutral syllable like "la," as indicated by your instructor. You may perform your improvisation in continuing succession with other students, in tempo and without missing a beat. As one student concludes an improvisation, another begins immediately, beginning with the two given measures and concluding with his or her own two-measure improvisation.

4. Singing (improvise). You are given a melody in dotted half notes. Using only the notes of the appropriate minor key (including the possibility of raising scale-degrees $\hat{6}$ and/or $\hat{7}$), and whatever rhythmic values you like, elaborate and decorate that melody. See In-class activities 15-5, 16-4, and 17-4 for models.

5. Singing (duets). Two students or groups of students sing the two lines of the following duets. Then switch parts. Sing using scale-degree numbers, solfège syllables, or a neutral syllable like "la," as indicated by your instructor.

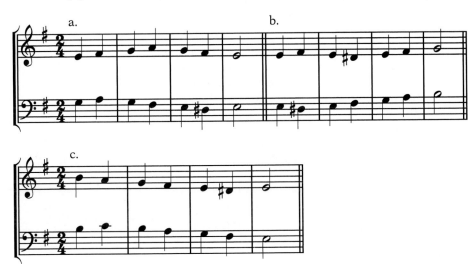

6. Playing (improvise). You are given a key signature and a note. Starting with that note, improvise a short melody that ends on the tonic of the appropriate minor key.

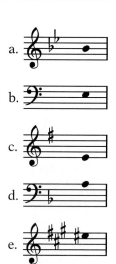

7. Playing. Learn to play the following five-finger pattern in all minor keys. Play first with each hand alone and then with both hands together.

8. Playing. Learn to play the following five-finger pattern as it moves through all of the minor keys. The last note of each pattern becomes the first note of the next. Alternate hands.

Name: _____

Date: _____

Instructor's Name: _____

Lesson 20: Exercises

20-1. Identify the minor key represented by these key signatures (keys with three or fewer flats or sharps in the key signature).

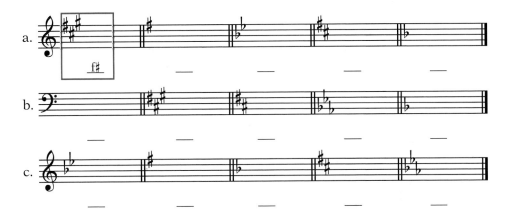

20-2. Identify the minor key represented by these key signatures (all keys).

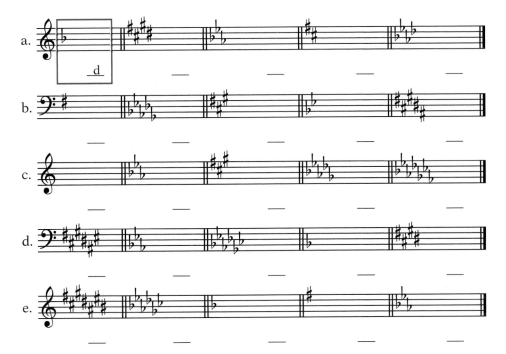

f.

g.

20-3. Write the key signature for these minor keys (keys with three or fewer accidentals in the key signature). Be sure to write sharps or flats in the correct order and position on the staff (see Exercise 20-1 for models).

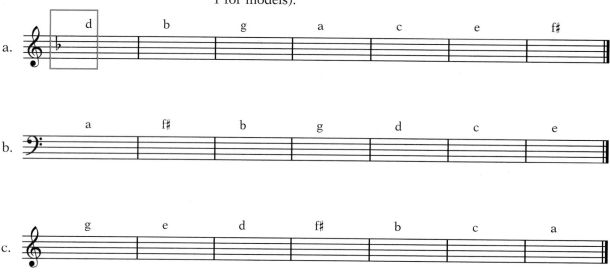

a.

    d   b   g   a   c   e   f♯

b.

    a   f♯   b   g   d   c   e

c.

    g   e   d   f♯   b   c   a

20-4. Write the key signature for these minor keys (all keys). Be sure to write sharps or flats in the correct order and position on the staff (see Exercise 20-2 for models).

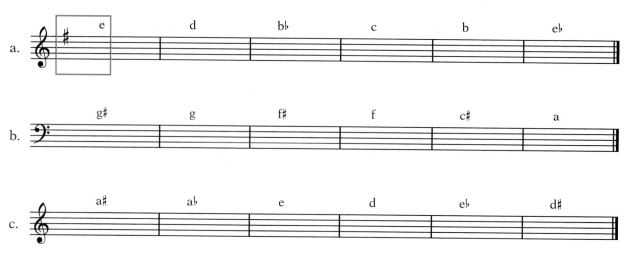

a.

    e   d   b♭   c   b   e♭

b.

    g♯   g   f♯   f   c♯   a

c.

    a♯   a♭   e   d   e♭   d♯

Name: _____

Date: _____

Instructor's Name: _____

20-5. Name the key of these pieces. Remember that scale-degree $\hat{7}$ is routinely raised in minor keys.

a. Chopin, Prelude (notice that both staves are written in bass clef).

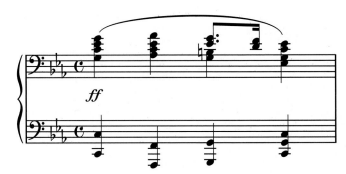

Key _____

b. Schubert, "Death and the Maiden" (notice that both staves are written in bass clef).

Key _____

c. Rodriguez, "La Cumparsita" (disregard the C♯ in measures 2 and 4—it does not belong to the scale, but embellishes the D, which does).

Key _____

d. Mozart, Sonata (disregard the embellishing notes in parentheses).

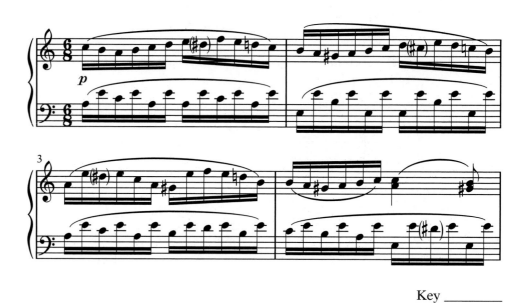

Key _____

e. Ellington, "It Don't Mean a Thing" (the D♭ in measure 3 is a wonderfully expressive note, but it does not belong to the key—that's part of the reason it sounds so expressive).

Key _____

Name: _____

Date: _____

Instructor's Name: _____

f. Haydn, Quartet

Key _____

g. Bach, Fugue

Key _____

20-6. Name the two keys (one major and one minor) represented by these key signatures (keys with three or fewer sharps or flats in the key signature). Write the major key first with an upper case letter, then the minor key with a lower case letter.

20-7. Name the two keys (one major and one minor) represented by these key signatures (all keys). Write the major key first with an upper case letter, then the minor key with a lower case letter.

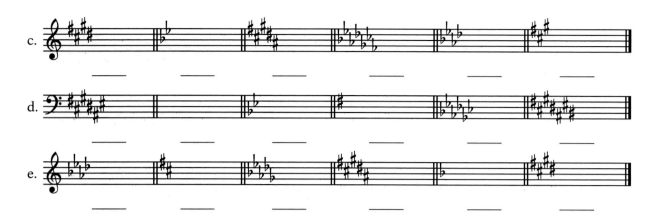

20-8. For each minor key, name the relative major and provide their shared key signature (keys with three or fewer accidentals in the key signature). Remember to write the sharps and flats in the prescribed order and position.

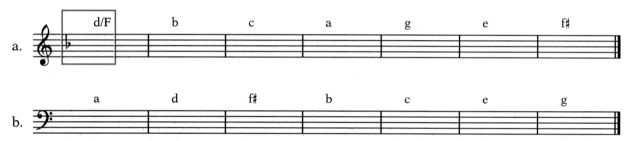

20-9. For each minor key, name the relative major and provide their shared key signature (all keys). Remember to write the sharps and flats in the prescribed order and position.

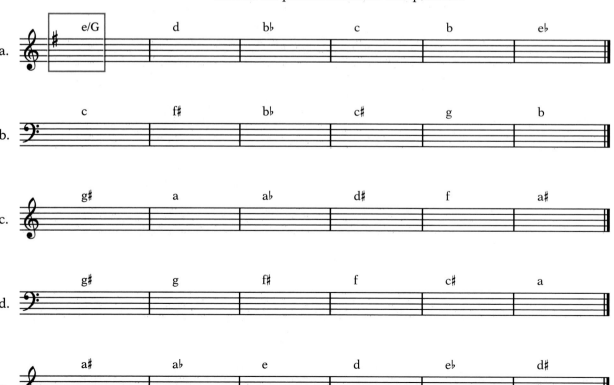

Name: _____

Date: _____

Instructor's Name: _____

20-10. Compose a melody for each of these texts. If you wish, you may use the rhythms you previously composed for these texts in Exercise 11-4. Each melody is begun for you. Play your melodies on the piano or other instrument before handing them in—be sure they sound the way you want them to. Be prepared to sing your melodies in class.

a. What passing-bells for these who die as cattle?
Only the monstrous anger of the guns.
(Wilfred Owen)

b. And what rough beast, its hour come round at last,
Slouches toward Bethlehem to be born?
(W. B. Yeats)

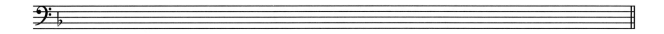

20-11. Fill in the blanks in these melodies by adding whatever notes from the appropriate minor scale and whatever rhythmic values sound best to you. Bear in mind the dynamic tendencies of the different scale-degrees. You may raise scale-degrees $\hat{6}$ and $\hat{7}$ when approaching the tonic from below. Play your melodies on the piano or other instrument before handing them in—be sure they sound the way you want them to. Be prepared to sing your melodies in class.

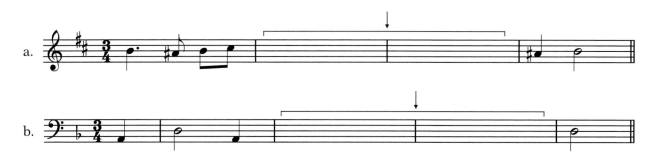

Chapter 3: Supplementary lesson

In this lesson you will learn about the harmonic minor, the melodic minor, modes, and the pentatonic scale.

The minor scale we have been discussing so far is called the *natural minor*. The natural minor is the basic form of the minor scale, and key signatures are always based on it. But as we observed in Lesson 18, scale-degrees $\hat{6}$ and $\hat{7}$ are frequently raised one semitone above their position in the natural minor. These alterations create new, varied forms of the minor scale.

The first common variant is the *harmonic minor*. It creates a leading tone by raising scale-degree $\hat{7}$ a semitone from its position in the natural minor.

Harmonic minor

In the natural minor, scale-degree $\hat{7}$ is called the subtonic and is a whole step below the tonic. In the harmonic minor, scale-degree $\hat{7}$ is called the leading-tone and is only a semitone below the tonic. It is as though the leading tone has been borrowed from the parallel major.

In the harmonic minor, there are three semitones: between scale-degrees $\hat{2}$–$\hat{3}$ and $\hat{5}$–$\hat{6}$ (as in the natural minor) and $\hat{7}$–$\hat{8}$ (borrowed from the parallel major). There is also a gap between scale-degrees $\hat{6}$–$\hat{7}$. This interval, a semitone larger than a whole tone, is called an *augmented second* (for reasons to be explained in Chapter 4).

Harmonic minor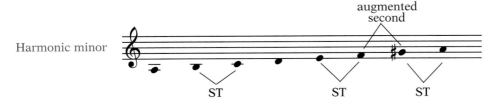

To create the harmonic minor by raising scale-degree $\hat{7}$ from its position in the natural minor, an accidental will always be required. If scale-degree $\hat{7}$ in the natural minor is flat, it must be made natural, and if scale-degree $\hat{7}$ in the natural minor is natural, it must be made sharp.

A second common variant is the *melodic ascending minor*. Like the harmonic minor, it creates a leading-tone by raising scale-degree $\hat{7}$ a semitone from its position in the natural minor. It then smooths out the gap between scale-degrees $\hat{6}$–$\hat{7}$ by also raising scale-degree $\hat{6}$ by a semitone. This variant is thus particularly suitable for singing or playing a melody that ascends to the tonic.

Melodic ascending minor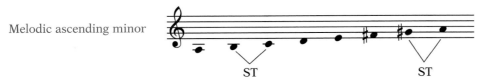

Now there are two semitones, between scale-degrees $\hat{2}$–$\hat{3}$ and $\hat{7}$–$\hat{8}$. All the other steps in the scale are whole tones. The melodic ascending is thus very similar to the major, differing only in the placement of one of its semitones—between $\hat{2}$ and $\hat{3}$ in minor and between $\hat{3}$ and $\hat{4}$ in major.

The natural minor still remains the basic form of the minor on which the key signature is based. To write a melodic ascending minor scale, scale-degrees $\hat{6}$ and $\hat{7}$ will always require an accidental.

One final variant of the minor scale is called the *melodic descending minor*. When descending melodically from the tonic, the raised seventh degree (leading tone) and sixth degrees are no longer necessary and revert to their position in the natural minor. As a result, the melodic descending minor is identical to the natural minor and thus requires no further discussion.

Six additional scales were in common use in Medieval and Renaissance music (before around 1600). These are called the *modes*, or *Church modes*, and they persist in more recent folk and popular music. They can be written using only the white notes.

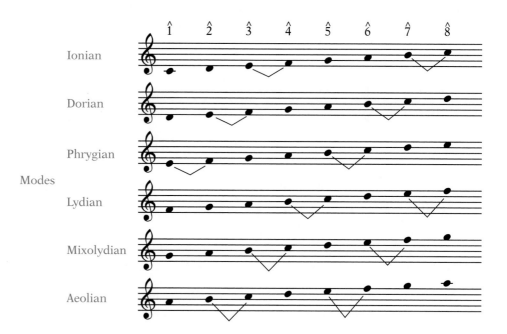

The six modes, like all other scales, may be transposed to start on any note. Notice the distinctive position of the two semitones in each mode and the way in which modal scales and key signatures relate to major and minor scales and key signatures.

Mode name	In relation to major and minor scales	Position of semitones	Key signature
Ionian	Same as major	$\hat{3}$–$\hat{4}$, $\hat{7}$–$\hat{8}$	Normal for major
Dorian	Natural minor with raised sixth degree	$\hat{2}$–$\hat{3}$, $\hat{6}$–$\hat{7}$	One sharp more (or one flat less) than signature for minor
Phrygian	Natural minor with lowered second degree	$\hat{1}$–$\hat{2}$, $\hat{5}$–$\hat{6}$	One flat more (or one sharp less) than signature for minor
Lydian	Major with raised fourth degree	$\hat{4}$–$\hat{5}$, $\hat{7}$–$\hat{8}$	One sharp more (or one flat less) than signature for major
Mixolydian	Major with lowered seventh degree	$\hat{3}$–$\hat{4}$, $\hat{6}$–$\hat{7}$	One flat more (or one sharp less) than signature for major
Aeolian	Same as minor	$\hat{2}$–$\hat{3}$, $\hat{5}$–$\hat{6}$	Normal for minor

One final scale in reasonably common use, particularly in folk and popular music, is the *pentatonic scale,* so called because it contains five notes.

Pentatonic scale

It can be thought of as a major scale with scale-degrees $\hat{4}$ and $\hat{7}$ omitted (it thus contains no semitones). Like all other scales, it can be transposed to start on any note.

4 Intervals

Lesson 21: Interval size

In this lesson you will learn about intervals, melodic and harmonic intervals, interval size, and compound intervals.

An *interval* is the distance between two notes. When the two notes occur at the same time, the interval is *harmonic*. When one note occurs before the other, the interval between them is *melodic,* and may be either ascending or descending.

Harmonic intervals

Melodic intervals

Intervals are identified by both their *size* (to be discussed in this lesson) and their *quality* (to be discussed in the next lesson). The size of an interval is the number of steps it contains, *disregarding any accidentals.* A *unison* spans a single step—the notes are on the same line or space of the staff.

Unisons

A *second* spans two steps. The actual number of semitones between the notes may vary, but if one note is on a space and the other is on the adjacent line (or vice versa), the interval is a second. We have previously referred to this interval as a *step.*

Seconds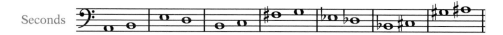

A *third* spans three steps. As with seconds, the actual number of semitones may vary, but if the two notes are on adjacent lines or adjacent spaces, the interval is a third.

Thirds

The remaining intervals—fourths, fifths, sixths, sevenths, and octaves—are calculated in the same way.

Fourths

Fifths

Sixths

Sevenths

Octaves

Intervals smaller than an octave are called *simple*. Intervals larger than an octave are *compound*, because they consist of a simple interval plus one or more octaves. A compound second is usually called a ninth (octave plus a second) and a compound third is usually called a tenth (octave plus a third). Other compound intervals are just called by their simple names.

Simple   Compound

Second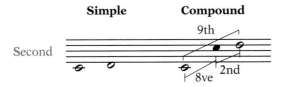

Third

Fourth

Fifth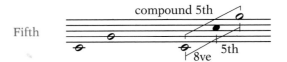

Sixth

Seventh

Lesson 21: In-class activities

Reciting. There are only seven letter-pairs for each interval size. Drill and memorize those pairs as follows.

a. Seconds. The letter-pairs for seconds are C–D, D–E, E–F, F–G, G–A, A–B, and B–C. Your instructor will name a note. Provide the note a second above or below, as requested.

b. Thirds. The letter-pairs for thirds are C–E, D–F, E–G, F–A, G–B, A–C, and B–D. Your instructor will name a note. Provide the note a third above or below, as requested.

c. Fourths. The letter-pairs for fourths are C–F, D–G, E–A, F–B, G–C, A–D, and B–E. Your instructor will name a note. Provide the note a fourth above or below, as requested.

d. Fifths. The letter-pairs for fifths are C–G, D–A, E–B, F–C, G–D, A–E, and B–F. Your instructor will name a note. Provide the note a fifth above or below, as requested.

e. Sixths. The letter-pairs for sixths are C–A, D–B, E–C, F–D, G–E, A–F, and B–G. Your instructor will name a note. Provide the note a sixth above or below, as requested.

f. Sevenths. The letter-pairs for sevenths are C–B, D–C, E–D, F–E, G–F, A–G, and B–A. Your instructor will name a note. Provide the note a seventh above or below, as requested.

Name: _____

Date: _____

Instructor's Name: _____

Lesson 21: Exercises

21-1. Identify the numerical size of these simple intervals. Remember to disregard any accidentals—they do not affect the numerical size of an interval (1 = unison, 2 = second, 3 = third, 4 = fourth, 5 = fifth, 6 = sixth, 7 = seventh, 8 = octave).

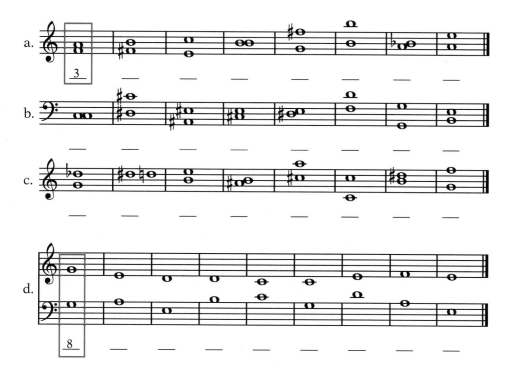

21-2. Identify the numerical size of these compound intervals. Remember to disregard any accidentals—they do not affect the numerical size of an interval. Compound seconds and thirds should be identified as ninths and tenths. Larger intervals should be identified as their simple equivalents (1 = unison, 2 = second, 3 = third, 4 = fourth, 5 = fifth, 6 = sixth, 7 = seventh, 8 = octave, 9 = ninth, 10 = tenth).

21-3. Write intervals of the proper size as indicated. Remember to disregard any accidentals—they do not affect the numerical size of an interval.

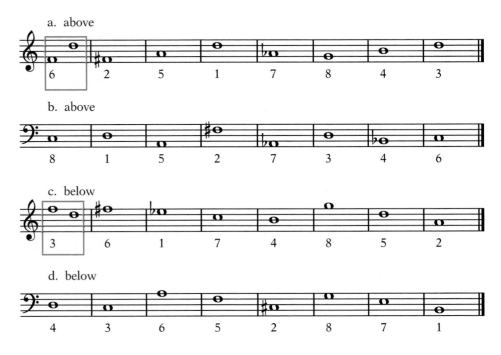

Name: _____

Date: _____

Instructor's Name: _____

21-4. Identify the numerical size of these intervals. Remember to disregard any accidentals—they do not affect the numerical size of an interval.

   a. Arlen, "Over the Rainbow" (each measure contains a leap down from B♭, and the leaps get bigger each time).

When all the world is a   hope-less jum-ble and the   rain-drops tum-ble all a - round,

   b. Chopin, Prelude in c minor (this bass line features wide leaps, mostly fourths and fifths).

   c. Schubert, "Heidenröslein" (all of these intervals, between bass and melody, are compound).

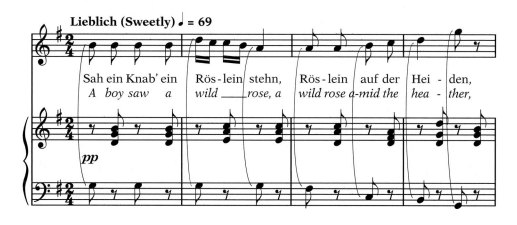

Lieblich (Sweetly) ♩ = 69

Sah ein Knab' ein | Rös-lein | stehn, | Rös-lein | auf der | Hei - | den,
A boy saw   a | wild ___ rose, a | wild rose a-mid the | hea - | ther,

pp

Lesson 22: Seconds and thirds

In this lesson you will learn about interval quality, natural intervals, major and minor intervals, diminished and augmented intervals, and enharmonic intervals.

Intervals of the same numerical *size* may vary in *quality* depending on the number of semitones they contain. If a second contains only one semitone, it is a *minor second* (familiar already as a semitone or a half step). If a second contains two semitones, it is a *major second* (familiar already as a whole tone or whole step). A *natural interval* is formed without any accidentals. There are seven *natural seconds,* all either major or minor.

Natural seconds

If both notes of a natural second are raised or lowered by the same amount, the size and quality of the interval remain the same.

Natural seconds transposed
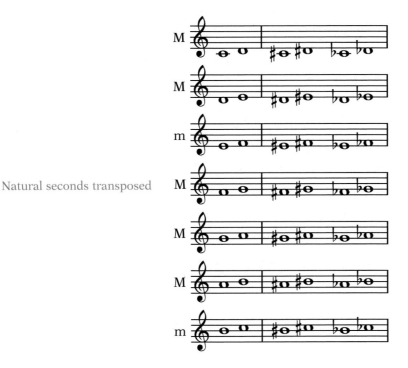

If a minor second, or any minor interval, is compressed by lowering the upper note or raising the bottom note by a semitone, it becomes *diminished.* But diminished seconds—intervals made up of adjacent letter-names that are enharmonically the same pitch—are rare and we will not consider them further here. If a major second, or any major interval, is expanded by lowering the bottom note or raising the upper note by a semitone, it becomes *augmented.*

Major, minor, and augmented seconds

Like seconds, thirds can be *diminished, minor, major,* or *augmented.* The seven *natural thirds,* formed without any accidental, are all either major (contains four semitones or two whole tones) or minor (contains three semitones or one whole tone and one semitone).

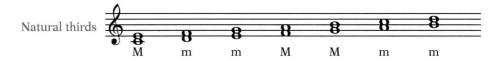

Natural thirds

Raising or lowering both notes by the same amount preserves the size and quality of the interval.

Natural thirds transposed

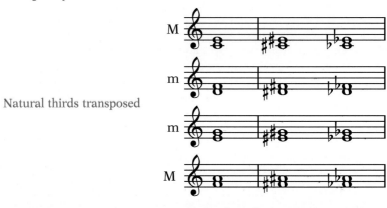

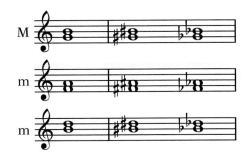

Natural thirds transposed (cont.)

When a minor third is compressed by a semitone, it becomes *diminished;* when a major third is expanded by semitone, it becomes *augmented.* But these are rare in music and will not concern us further here; instead, we will concentrate on major and minor thirds.

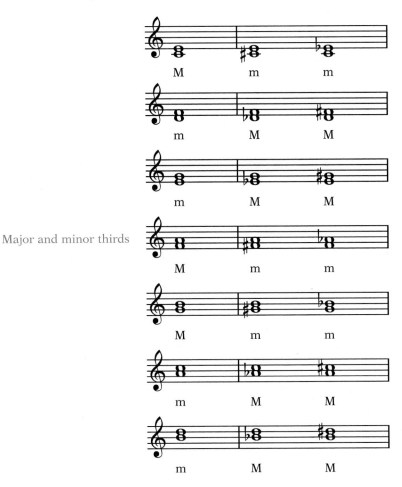

Major and minor thirds

In sum, there are four kinds of seconds and thirds (diminished, minor, major, and augmented), but only minor, major, and augmented seconds and minor and major thirds are in common use.

	Diminished	Minor	Major	Augmented
Seconds (number of semitones)	~~C♯–D♭~~ ~~0~~	C–D♭ 1	C–D 2	C–D♯ 3
Thirds (number of semitones)	~~C♯–E♭~~ ~~2~~	C–E♭ 3	C–E 4	~~C–E♯~~ ~~5~~

Intervals that span the same number of semitones but are spelled with different note names are *enharmonic intervals*. C–D♯ and C–E♭, for example, both span three semitones. But one is a second and the other is a third and they have correspondingly different musical roles to play.

Lesson 22: In-class activities

1. Singing. Sing the following melodies. The lyrics identify the qualities of the natural seconds and thirds.

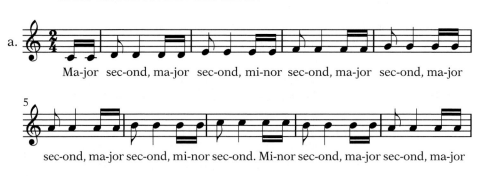

Ma-jor sec-ond, ma-jor sec-ond, mi-nor sec-ond, ma-jor sec-ond, ma-jor

sec-ond, ma-jor sec-ond, mi-nor sec-ond. Mi-nor sec-ond, ma-jor sec-ond, ma-jor

sec-ond, ma-jor sec-ond, mi-nor sec-ond, ma-jor sec-ond, ma-jor sec-ond.

Ma-jor third, mi-nor third, mi-nor third, ma-jor third, ma-jor third, mi-nor third,

mi-nor third, yes!   Mi-nor third, ma-jor third,   ma-jor third, mi-nor third,

mi-nor third, ma-jor third,   mi-nor third, yes!

2. Dictation. The instructor will play the pairs of notes within each group in a random order. Sing the notes you hear, then identify the interval as a minor second, major second, minor third, major third, or none of the above. In Groups 1–6, the three intervals are m2, M2, or neither of these; in Groups 7–12, the three intervals are m3, M3, or neither of these.

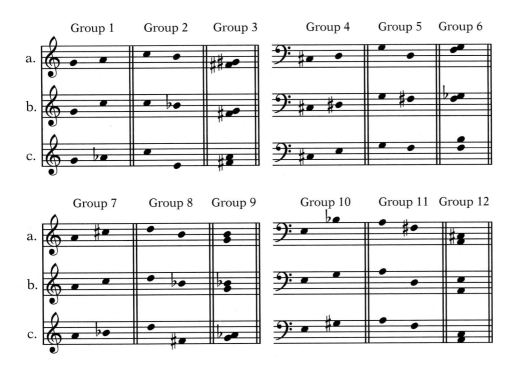

3. Playing. Play the following melody two times. The first time, identify the qualities of the thirds as you play them. The second time, identify the qualities of the seconds as you play them. Transpose to other major keys.

Name: _____

Date: _____

Instructor's Name: _____

Lesson 22: Exercises

22-1. Identify the quality of these natural seconds (m = minor, M = major).

22-2. Identify the quality of these seconds (m = minor, M = major, A = augmented).

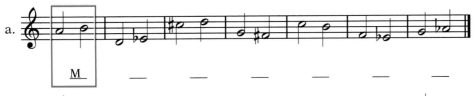

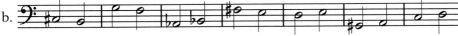

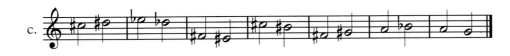

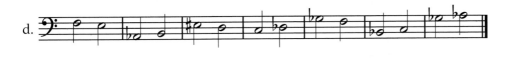

22-3. Add an accidental (sharp, flat, or natural) to the top note to create seconds of the desired quality (m = minor, M = major, A = augmented). Do not alter the bottom note.

22-4. Write seconds as indicated (m = minor, M = major, A = augmented).

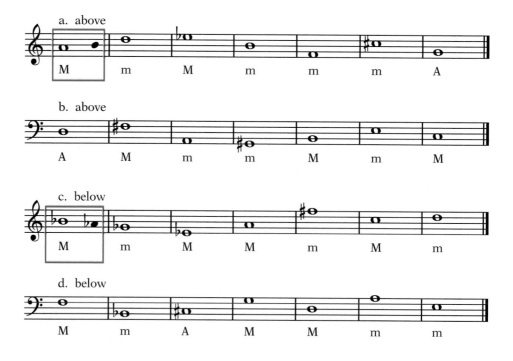

Name: _____

Date: _____

Instructor's Name: _____

22-5. Identify the quality of these natural thirds (m = minor, M = major).

a.

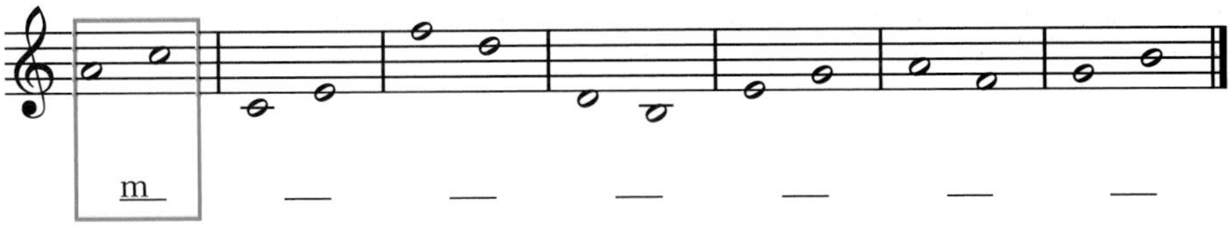

    m   __   __   __   __   __   __

b.

    __   __   __   __   __   __

22-6. Identify the quality of these thirds (m = minor, M = major).

a.

    m   __   __   __   __   __   __

b.

    __   __   __   __   __   __   __

c.

    __   __   __   __   __   __   __

d.

    __   __   __   __   __   __

22-7. Add an accidental (sharp, flat, or natural) to the top note to create thirds of the desired quality (m = minor, M = major). Do not alter the bottom note.

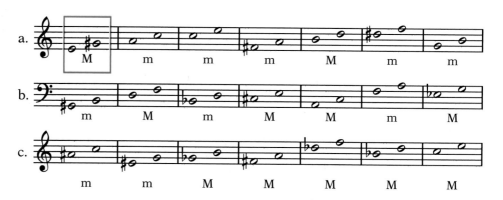

22-8. Write thirds as indicated (m = minor, M = major).

a. above

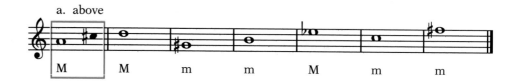

b. above

c. below

d. below

Name: _____

Date: _____

Instructor's Name: _____

22-9. Identify these intervals as seconds (minor, major, augmented) or thirds (major, minor).

a. Haydn, Quartet (thirds, ascending and descending, are a persistent feature of this melody).

b. Schubert, "Death and the Maiden" (the first two seconds go down, the next two go up).

c. Bach, Chorale (the voice pairs—soprano-alto, alto-tenor, and tenor-bass—are often very close to each other, either a third or a second apart).

Lesson 23: Sixths and sevenths

In this lesson you will learn about sixths and sevenths, enharmonic intervals, and interval inversion.

Sixths and sevenths behave like seconds and thirds. Natural sixths and sevenths are either major or minor (a minor sixth contains eight semitones, a major sixth contains nine semitones, a minor seventh contains ten semitones, and a major seventh contains eleven semitones).

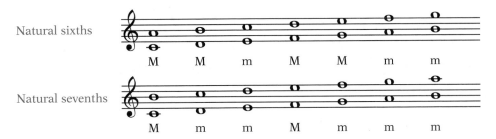

  When a natural sixth or seventh is transposed up or down, it retains the same quality.

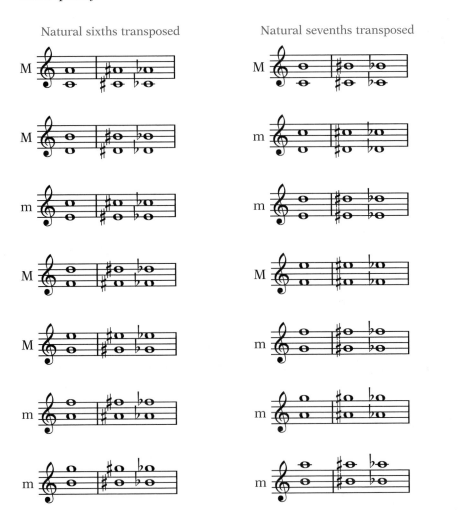

When minor sixths and sevenths are compressed by a semitone, they become diminished; when major sixths and sevenths are expanded, they become augmented. Of these, augmented sevenths, diminished sixths, and augmented sixths will not concern us further. We will focus on major and minor sixths and major, minor, and diminished sevenths.

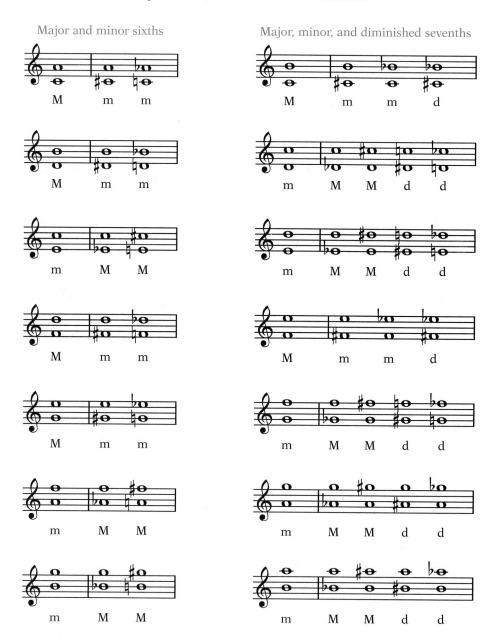

In sum, there are four kinds of sixths and sevenths (diminished, minor, major, and augmented), but only major and minor sixths and major, minor, and diminished sevenths will be discussed here.

	Diminished	Minor	Major	Augmented
Sixths (number of semitones)	C♯–A♭ 〈✕〉 7	C–A♭ 8	C–A 9	C–A♯ 〈✕〉 10
Sevenths (number of semitones)	C♯–B♭ 9	C–B♭ 10	C–B 11	C–B♯ 〈✕〉 12

As noted earlier, intervals that span the same number of semitones but are spelled with different note names, are *enharmonic intervals*. C♯–A♯ and C♯–B♭, for example, both span nine semitones, but one is a sixth and the other is a seventh.

When an octave is divided into two parts, each part is said to be the *inversion* of the other. Conversely, an interval can be combined with its inversion to make up an octave.

Dividing an octave

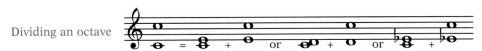

An interval is *inverted* by reversing its upper and lower notes (bottom becomes top and top becomes bottom). To invert an interval, either move the upper note down an octave or move the lower note up an octave.

Inverting intervals

When an interval is inverted, certain predictable things happen to the size and quality. In size, seconds become sevenths (and vice versa) and thirds become sixths (and vice versa).

Inverting intervals (size)

Second ← inverts to → **Seventh**

Third ← inverts to → **Sixth**

In quality, major intervals become minor (and vice versa), diminished intervals become augmented (and vice versa).

Inverting intervals (quality)

Minor ← inverts to → **Major**

Diminished ← inverts to → **Augmented**

For the seconds, thirds, sixths, and sevenths, the inversions work like this:

Inverting intervals

d2	m2	M2	A2	d3	m3	M3	A3
↕	↕	↕	↕	↕	↕	↕	↕
A7	M7	m7	d7	A6	M6	m6	d6

Lesson 23: In-class activities

1. Singing. Sing the following melody. The lyrics identify the qualities of the natural sixths.

Ma-jor sixth, ma-jor sixth,   mi-nor sixth, ma-jor sixth,   ma-jor sixth, mi-nor sixth,   mi-nor sixth, yes!

2. Singing. Sing the following melodies. Identify the qualities of the sixths and sevenths.

a. Arlen, "Over the Rainbow" (this melody features large upward leaps).

b. Haydn, Quartet (the downward leaps that lead from beat 3 to beat 1 get larger and larger).

c. Bach, Fugue in g minor (from the highest note to the lowest note of the melody is a diminished seventh).

d. Bach, Fugue in G Major (this melody features two large upward leaps).

e. Joplin, "The Entertainer" (this melody begins by repeating the sixth from E4 to C5, then explores the inversion of that interval: the third from C5 to E5).

f. Mendelssohn, Trio (the two halves of this melody begin with an upward leap and then fill in that space with descending steps).

3. Dictation. The instructor will play the pairs of notes within each group in a random order. Sing the notes you hear, then identify the interval as a minor sixth, major sixth, minor seventh, major seventh, or none of the above. In Groups 1–6, the three intervals are m6, M6, or neither of these; in Groups 7–12, the three intervals are m7, M7, or neither of these.

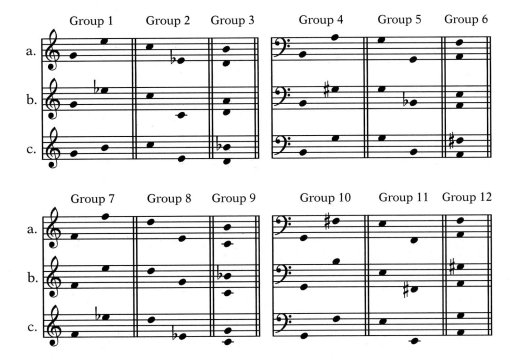

4. Playing. Play the following melody two times. The first time, identify the qualities of the sevenths as you play them. The second time, identify the qualities of the sixths as you play them. Transpose to other major keys.

Name: _____

Date: _____

Instructor's Name: _____

Lesson 23: Exercises

23-1. Identify the quality of these natural sixths (m = minor, M = major).

23-2. Identify the quality of these sixths (m = minor, M = major).

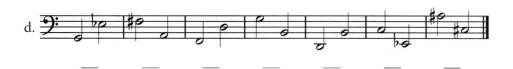

23-3. Add an accidental (sharp, flat, or natural) to the top note to create sixths of the desired quality (m = minor, M = major). Do not alter the bottom note.

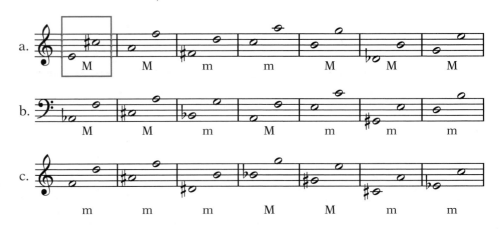

23-4. Identify the quality of these sixths (m = minor, M = major). Then write the inversion and identify its quality.

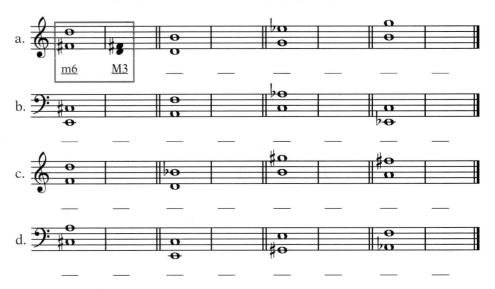

23-5. Write sixths as indicated (m = minor, M = major).

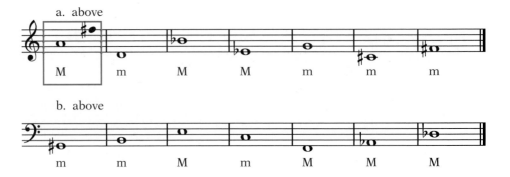

Name: _____

Date: _____

Instructor's Name: _____

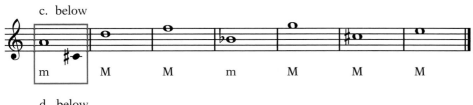

c. below

m   M   M   m   M   M   M

d. below

m   M   m   M   m   m   m

23-6. Identify the quality of these natural sevenths (m = minor, M = major).

a.

m   ___   ___   ___   ___   ___   ___

b.

___   ___   ___   ___   ___   ___   ___

23-7. Identify the quality of these sevenths (d = diminished, m = minor, M = major).

a.

m   ___   ___   ___   ___   ___   ___

b.

___   ___   ___   ___   ___   ___   ___

c.

___   ___   ___   ___   ___   ___   ___

d.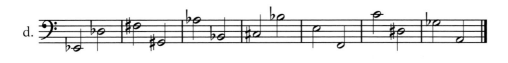

___   ___   ___   ___   ___   ___   ___

23-8. Add an accidental (sharp, flat, or natural) to the top note to create sevenths of the desired quality (d = diminished, m = minor, M = major). Do not alter the bottom note.

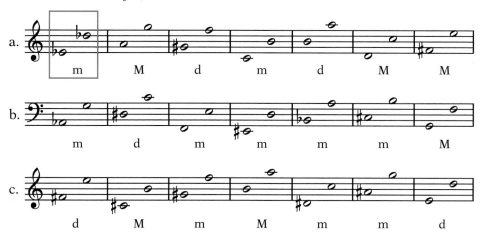

23-9. Identify the quality of these sevenths (d = diminished, m = minor, M = major). Then write the inversion and identify its quality.

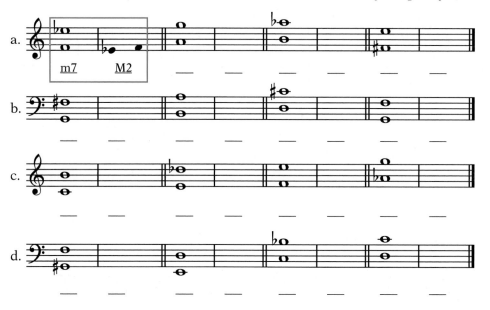

23-10. Write sevenths as indicated (d = diminished, m = minor, M = major).

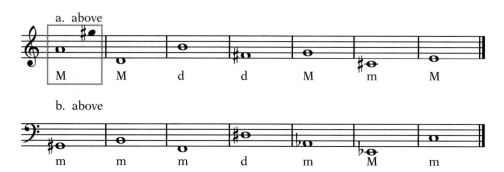

Name: _____

Date: _____

Instructor's Name: _____

c. below

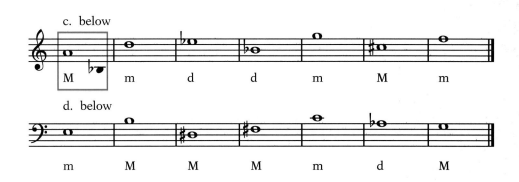

M   m   d   d   m   M   m

d. below

m   M   M   M   m   d   M

23-11. Identify these intervals as sixths (major or minor) or sevenths (diminished, minor or major).

a. Arlen, "Over the Rainbow"

b. Bach, Fugue in g minor (the large leap at the beginning opens up a space that is gradually filled in).

c. Bach, Fugue in G Major (apart from the two big upward leaps, the melody moves almost entirely stepwise).

d. Mendelssohn, Trio (the large leap at the beginning of measure 1 is answered by one even larger at the beginning of measure 3).

e. Haydn, Quartet (this melody is unusual in having more leaps than steps).

Lesson 24: Fourths and fifths, unisons and octaves

In this lesson you will learn about perfect intervals, fourths and fifths, unisons and octaves, interval inversion, and enharmonic intervals.

Because of the relative purity of their sound, unisons, fourths, fifths, and octaves are *perfect* intervals. Perfect intervals cannot be major or minor. They can only be *diminished* (if compressed by semitone), *perfect*, or *augmented* (if expanded by semitone).

The seven natural fourths are all perfect, except for F–B, which is augmented.

Natural fourths

The augmented fourth is sometimes called the *tritone* because it spans three whole tones (it contains six semitones, or exactly one half of the twelve-semitone octave). Perfect fourths, in contrast, span two whole tones and a semitone (or five semitones).

Augmented fourth (tritone)   Perfect fourth

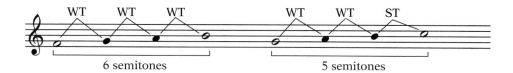

Transposing a natural fourth preserves its size and quality.

Natural fourths transposed

If a perfect fourth is expanded by semitone, it becomes augmented; if a perfect fourth is compressed by semitone, it becomes diminished. Diminished fourths are rare, however, and we will concentrate only on perfect and augmented fourths here.

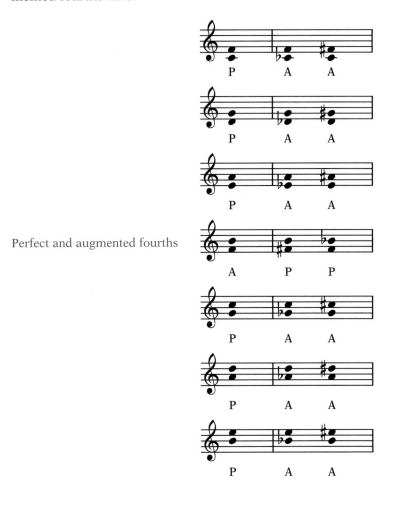

Perfect and augmented fourths

Fourths invert to fifths. Perfect intervals invert to perfect intervals and (as with seconds, thirds, sixths, and sevenths) diminished intervals invert to augmented intervals, and vice versa.

Inverting fourths and fifths

Perfect 4th ⟷ Perfect 5th

Augmented 4th ⟷ Diminished 5th

All the natural fifths are perfect except for B–F, which is diminished.

Natural fifths

A perfect fifth contains seven semitones (or three whole tones and a semitone); a diminished fifth contains six semitones (or two whole tones and two semitones).

Perfect fifth   Diminished fifth

Transposing a natural fifth preserves its size and quality.

Natural fifths transposed

If a perfect fifth is expanded by a semitone, it becomes augmented; if it is compressed by a semitone, it becomes diminished. Augmented fifths are rare, however, and we will be concerned here only with perfect and diminished fifths.

Perfect and diminished fifths

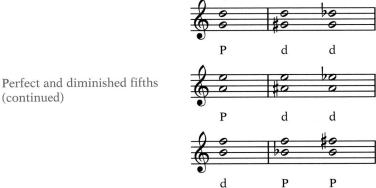

Perfect and diminished fifths (continued)

A diminished fifth and an augmented fourth both contain six semitones. They are thus *enharmonic* intervals: they are the same absolute size but span a different number of steps.

Diminished fifth   Augmented fourth

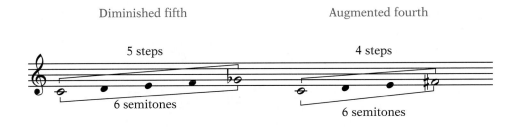

Two notes on the same pitch create a perfect unison.

Perfect unisons
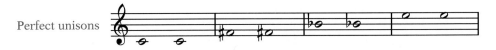

If one of the notes is a semitone higher than the other, but still maintains the same letter name, then the interval is an *augmented unison* (there is no such thing as a diminished unison). Normally, we will just refer to such intervals as *chromatic semitones*.

Augmented unisons (chromatic semitones)

The octave is like the unison. A perfect octave is a single note repeated an octave higher or lower.

Perfect octaves

As with the other perfect intervals, compressing a perfect octave by a semitone produces a diminished octave; expanding a perfect octave by a semitone produces an augmented octave. But diminished and augmented octaves will not be discussed further here.

Lesson 24: In-class activities

1. Singing. Sing the following melodies. The lyrics identify the qualities of the natural fourths and fifths.

a.

Per - fect fourth, per - fect fourth,   per - fect fourth, aug-men-ted fourth,

per - fect fourth,   per - fect fourth,   per - fect fourth,   yes!

b.

Per - fect fifth,   per - fect fifth,   per - fect fifth,   per - fect fifth,

per - fect fifth,   per - fect fifth,   di - min-ished fifth,   yes!

2. Singing. Sing the following melodies. Identify the qualities of the fourths and fifths.

   a. Arlen, "Over the Rainbow" (the downward leaps arrive on successively lower notes: G–F–Eb–D).

   b. Chopin, Prelude in c minor (this bass line moves mainly in fourths and fifths).

   c. Lang, Song (the interval in measure 4 is given an expressive, yearning quality by the fermatas over both notes—they should be sustained as long as the singer thinks appropriate).

d. Schubert, "Death and the Maiden"

3. Dictation. The instructor will play the pairs of notes within each group in a random order. Sing the notes you hear, then identify the interval as a perfect fourth, perfect fifth, augmented fourth/diminished fifth (without distinction), or none of the above.

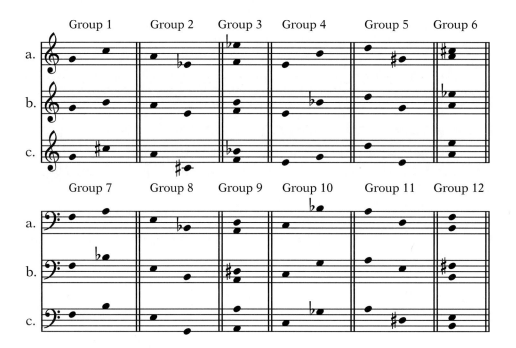

4. Playing. Play the following melody two times. The first time, identify the qualities of the fourths as you play them. The second time, identify the qualities of the fifths as you play them. Transpose to other major keys.

Name: _____

Date: _____

Instructor's Name: _____

Lesson 24: Exercises

24-1. Identify the quality of these natural fourths (P = perfect, A = augmented).

a.

b.
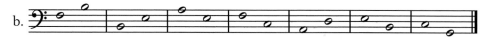

24-2. Identify the quality of these fourths (P = perfect, A = augmented).

a.

b.

c.

d.

24-3. Add an accidental (sharp, flat, or natural) to the top note to create fourths of the desired quality (P = perfect, A = augmented). Do not alter the bottom note.

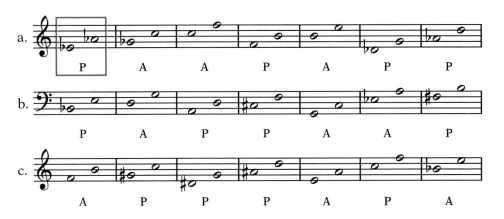

24-4. Write fourths as indicated (P = perfect, A = augmented).

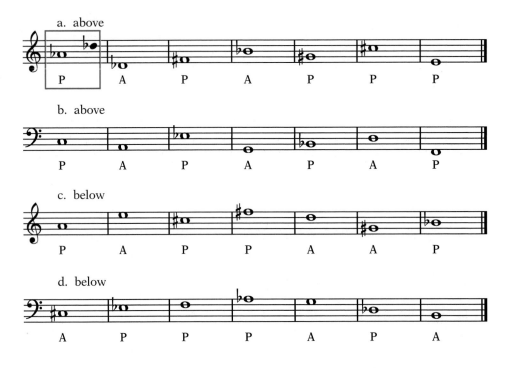

24-5. Identify the quality of these natural fifths (d = diminished, P = perfect).

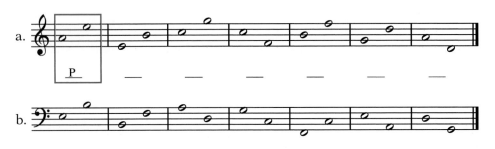

Name: _____

Date: _____

Instructor's Name: _____

24-6. Identify the quality of these fifths (d = diminished, P = perfect).

24-7. Add an accidental (sharp, flat, or natural) to the top note to create fifths of the desired quality (d = diminished, P = perfect). Do not alter the bottom note.

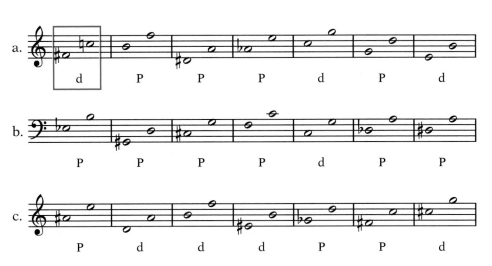

24-8. Write fifths as indicated (d = diminished, P = perfect).

24-9. You are given a fourth or a fifth. Identify its quality (d = diminished, P = perfect, A = augmented). Then write its inversion and identify its quality.

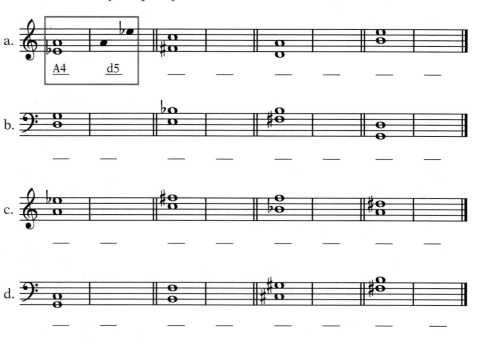

Name: _____

Date: _____

Instructor's Name: _____

24-10. Identify these intervals as fourths (perfect or augmented) or fifths (diminished or perfect).

a. Arlen, "Over the Rainbow"

b. Chopin, Prelude in c minor

c. Lang, Song

d. Schubert, "Death and the Maiden" (the melody consists mainly of two large downward leaps, and then two large intervals filled in by step, also descending).

Lesson 25: Intervals in a major key

In this lesson you will learn about intervals in a major key, intervals in relation to scale-degrees, and consonance and dissonance.

Within a *major* scale, the intervals formed between the tonic and the other scale-degrees are all *major* or *perfect:* major second, major third, perfect fourth, perfect fifth, major sixth, and major seventh.

Intervals in relation
to the tonic

It is also interesting to think about the intervals that can be formed with all of the degrees of a major scale, not just the tonic. The most common interval in the major scale is the perfect fourth (or, if the interval is inverted, the perfect fifth)—there are six of them.

Six perfect fourths

Indeed, the entire major scale can be described as a chain of perfect fourths or perfect fifths. (You read the fifths going clockwise and the fourths going counterclockwise.)

Circle of fourths/fifths

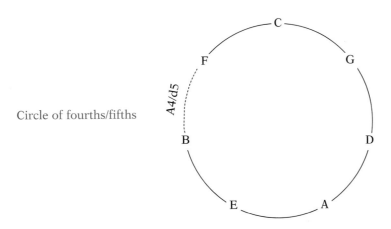

In addition to its six perfect fourths (or fifths), the major scale contains five whole tones (or minor sevenths), four minor thirds (or major sixths), three major thirds (or minor sixths), two semitones (or major sevenths), and a single, unique augmented fourth (or diminished fifth).

Other intervals

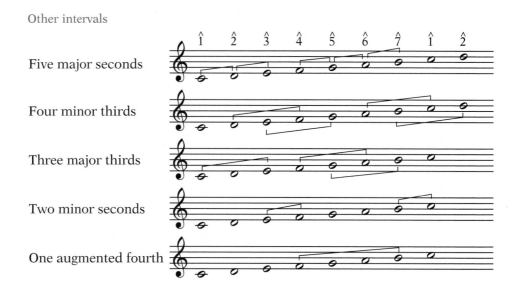

Five major seconds

Four minor thirds

Three major thirds

Two minor seconds

One augmented fourth

Every kind of interval occurs a different number of times, ranging from a maximum of six (perfect fourths/fifths) to a minimum of one (augmented fourth/diminished fifth). Because there is only one of them, the augmented fourth/diminished fifth plays an important key-defining role: it uniquely identifies the major scale to which it belongs.

Harmonic intervals are classified as either *consonant* or *dissonant*. Consonant intervals are those that sound relatively harmonious, whose notes blend well together, and are relatively stable. Composers use consonant intervals at points of arrival or conclusion. Dissonant intervals are those that sound relatively tense and unstable, with the notes rubbing against each other rather then blending together. Composers use dissonant intervals to propel music forward, because dissonances require some kind of continuation—they cannot be used at points of arrival or conclusion.

Major and minor thirds and sixths are consonant. So are all perfect intervals, with one partial exception: the perfect fourth, which is only consonant when a major or minor third or perfect fifth is sounding below it. When the lower note of the perfect fourth is also the lowest sounding note, the perfect fourth is usually treated as a dissonance. Major and minor seconds and sevenths are dissonant, as are all augmented and diminished intervals.

Consonance	**Major and minor thirds and sixths** **Perfect fifths, octaves, and unisons** **Perfect fourths (sometimes)**
Dissonance	**Seconds and sevenths** **Augmented or diminished intervals** **Perfect fourths (sometimes)**

Lesson 25: In-class activities

1. Singing. (duets). Sing one or more to a part, and then switch parts. Identify the melodic intervals (within each part) and the harmonic intervals (between the parts).

   a. In this duet, the intervals between the parts are all consonances.

   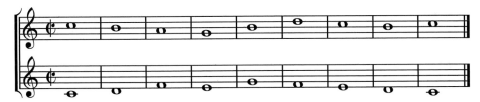

   b. In this duet, the intervals between the parts are all consonances.

   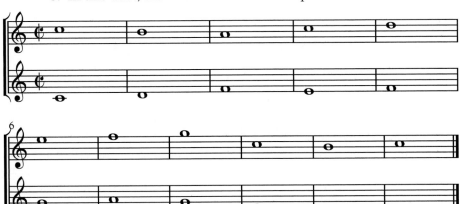

   c. Bach, Chorale (these are the soprano and bass voices in the first phrase of the chorale).

   d. Bach, Chorale (these are the soprano and bass voices in the last phrase of the chorale).

e. Haydn, Quartet (after singing this duet, listen to the first four measures of the piece from which it was adapted. Many pieces can be understood as elaborations of a simple, consonant duet like this one).

f. Mozart, "Dove sono" (after singing this duet, listen to the first eight measures of the piece from which it was adapted).

g. Mozart, Sonata (after singing this duet, listen to the first eight measures of the piece from which it was adapted).

2. Dictation. The instructor will play the three brief duets in a random order within each group. Identify the duet and sing it back.

Group 2

Group 3

3. Playing. Practice major scales in thirds and fifths. These can be played with either hand alone or with both hands together. The example is given in D major and also should be transposed to other major keys.

4. Playing. You are given an interval that occurs in more than one major key. Improvise a short progression of intervals that leads to the tonic note of one of the possible keys played in unison or an octave apart. Use only thirds, fifths, and sixths (in addition to the concluding unison or octave).

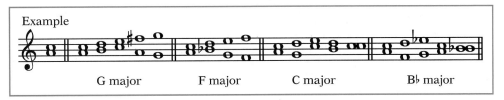

Example

G major   F major   C major   B♭ major

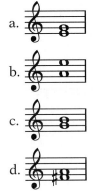

a.

b.

c.

d.

5. Playing. You are given an augmented fourth (which represents scale-degrees $\hat{4}$ and $\hat{7}$ in one key) and its enharmonic interval, a diminished fifth (which represents scale-degrees $\hat{7}$ and $\hat{4}$ in a different key). Play the resolution of each interval to scale-degrees $\hat{1}$ and $\hat{3}$ in the appropriate key.

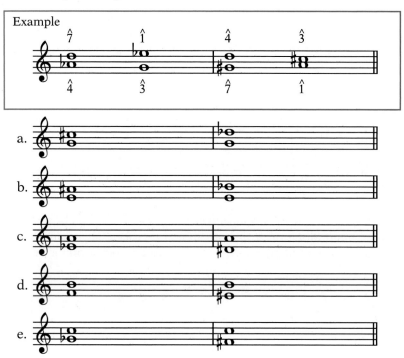

Name: _____

Date: _____

Instructor's Name: _____

Lesson 25: Exercises

25-1. For the given keys, identify the requested intervals.

> a. G major: its four minor thirds <u>A–C, B–D, E–G, F♯–A</u>

b. G major: its three major thirds _____

c. F major: its five major seconds _____

d. D major: its two minor seconds _____

e. B♭ major: its one augmented fourth _____

f. A major: its six perfect fourths _____

g. E♭ major: its four minor thirds _____

25-2. For any major key, identify the interval between these scale-degrees, always calculating upward from the first note to the second.

> a. $\hat{1}$–$\hat{5}$ <u>P5</u>

b. $\hat{1}$–$\hat{3}$ ____

c. $\hat{1}$–$\hat{6}$ ____

d. $\hat{1}$–$\hat{7}$ ____

e. $\hat{4}$–$\hat{6}$ ____

f. $\hat{5}$–$\hat{7}$ ____

g. $\hat{3}$–$\hat{4}$ ____

h. $\hat{4}$–$\hat{7}$ ____

i. $\hat{7}$–$\hat{4}$ ____

j. $\hat{5}$–$\hat{6}$ ____

k. $\hat{5}$–$\hat{1}$ ____

l. $\hat{5}$–$\hat{2}$ ____

m. $\hat{7}$–$\hat{5}$ ____

n. $\hat{2}$–$\hat{6}$ ____

o. $\hat{2}$–$\hat{7}$ ____

p. $\hat{6}$–$\hat{1}$ ____

25-3. Name the major scales that contain these intervals.

a. F–A = $\hat{1}$–$\hat{3}$ in F, $\hat{4}$–$\hat{6}$ in C, $\hat{5}$–$\hat{7}$ in B♭

b. G–B = $\hat{1}$–$\hat{3}$ in _____ , $\hat{4}$–$\hat{6}$ in _____ , $\hat{5}$–$\hat{7}$ in _____

c. E–F = $\hat{3}$–$\hat{4}$ in _____ , $\hat{7}$–$\hat{8}$ in _____

d. D–A = $\hat{1}$–$\hat{5}$ in _____ , $\hat{2}$–$\hat{6}$ in _____ , $\hat{3}$–$\hat{7}$ in _____ , $\hat{4}$–$\hat{1}$ in _____ , $\hat{5}$–$\hat{2}$, in _____ , $\hat{6}$–$\hat{3}$ in _____

e. F♯–A = $\hat{2}$–$\hat{4}$ in _____ , $\hat{3}$–$\hat{5}$ in _____ , $\hat{6}$–$\hat{1}$ in _____ , $\hat{7}$–$\hat{2}$ in _____

f. B♭–C = $\hat{1}$–$\hat{2}$ in _____ , $\hat{2}$–$\hat{3}$ in _____ , $\hat{4}$–$\hat{5}$ in _____ , $\hat{5}$–$\hat{6}$ in _____ , $\hat{6}$–$\hat{7}$, in _____

g. B♭–E = $\hat{4}$–$\hat{7}$ in _____

h. G♯–D = $\hat{7}$–$\hat{4}$ in _____

i. A♭–D = $\hat{4}$–$\hat{7}$ in _____

j. C♯–G = $\hat{7}$–$\hat{4}$ in _____

k. A–E♭ = $\hat{7}$–$\hat{4}$ in _____

25-4. Identify these intervals.

Name: _____

Date: _____

Instructor's Name: _____

25-5. Identify these intervals.

a. Bach, Chorale

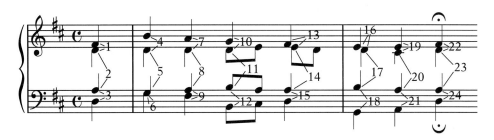

1. M3	4. ____	7. ____	10. ____	13. ____	16. ____	19. ____	22. ____
2. ____	5. ____	8. ____	11. ____	14. ____	17. ____	20. ____	23. ____
3. ____	6. ____	9. ____	12. ____	15. ____	18. ____	21. ____	24. ____

b. Mendelssohn, Piano Trio

1. m3	4. ____	7. ____	10. ____	13. ____	16. ____
2. ____	5. ____	8. ____	11. ____	14. ____	17. ____
3. ____	6. ____	9. ____	12. ____	15. ____	18. ____

25-6. Compose duets by adding a melody above the given melody (some notes are already provided). Play your duet on the piano or other instrument before handing it in—be sure it sounds the way you want it to. Be prepared to sing in class both the melody you are given and the melody you have composed. Your melody should follow these guidelines:

1. Use only whole notes.

2. Create only the following intervals between the two melodies: thirds, fifths, sixths, octaves. Identify each interval by writing the appropriate number beneath the staff.

3. Don't write two consecutive fifths or octaves between the melodies.

4. Write a melody that moves mainly by step. Your melody should be as smooth, connected, and directed as the melodies you are given.

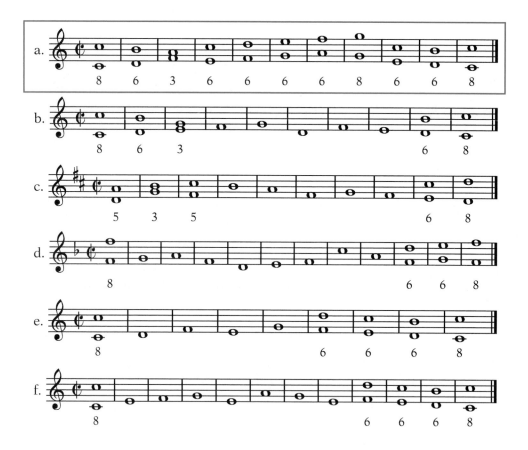

Lesson 26: Intervals in a minor key

In this lesson you will learn about intervals in a minor key, and intervals in relation to scale-degrees.

In a *minor* scale, all of the intervals formed with the tonic, with one exception, are *minor* or *perfect:* major second (that's the exception), minor third, perfect fourth, perfect fifth, minor sixth, and minor seventh.

Intervals in relation to the tonic

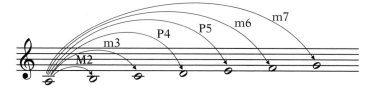

In a major scale, the intervals formed with the third, sixth, and seventh scale-degrees are all major; in a minor scale these intervals are all minor. And that is precisely what gives the two scales their different, contrasting characters.

Considering all of the intervals (not just those formed in relation to the tonic), the minor scale (like the major) has six perfect fourths/perfect fifths, five major seconds/minor sevenths, four minor thirds/major sixths, three major thirds/minor sixths, two minor seconds/major sevenths, and one augmented fourth/diminished fifth. But those intervals are formed by different scale-degrees.

Six perfect fourths

Five major seconds

Four minor thirds

Three major thirds

Two minor seconds

One augmented fourth

Also like the major scale, the minor scale can be described as a chain of perfect fourths/perfect fifths.

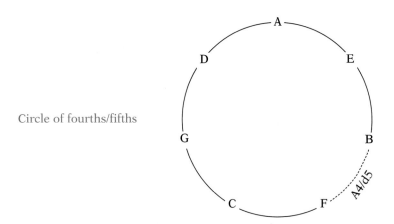

Circle of fourths/fifths

The alteration of scale-degrees $\hat{6}$ and $\hat{7}$, so common in minor, creates new intervals. The most important and distinctive of these is the augmented second (and its inversion, the diminished seventh) when $\hat{7}$ is raised to create a leading-tone.

Augmented second/
diminished seventh

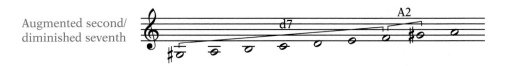

Like the augmented fourth/perfect fifth in major, this unique, distinctive interval involves the leading tone and thus serves to identify the tonic of the minor scale to which it belongs.

Lesson 26: In-class activities

1. Singing (duets). Sing one or more to a part, and then switch parts. Identify the melodic intervals (within each part) and the harmonic intervals (between the parts).

   a. In this duet, the intervals between the parts are all consonances.

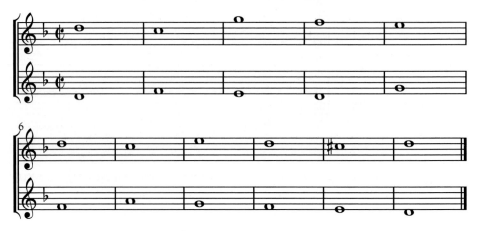

b. In this duet, the intervals between the parts are all consonances.

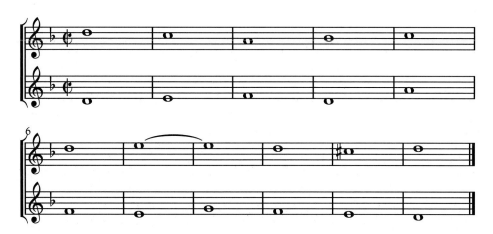

c. Bach, Chorale (these are the soprano and bass voices).

d. Ellington, "It Don't Mean a Thing" (after singing this duet, listen to the passage from which it was adapted—see if you can figure out which one. Many pieces can be understood as elaborations of a simple, consonant duet like this one).

e. Chopin, Prelude in c minor, adapted (after singing this duet, listen to measures 5–8 of the piece from which it was adapted. The upper voice descends immediately from E♭ to C; the lower voice descends more slowly from C to E♭).

f. Schubert, "Death and the Maiden" (after singing this duet, listen to the first eight measures of the piece from which they were adapted).

2. Dictation. The instructor will play the three brief duets in a random order within each group. Identify the duet and sing it back.

Group 1

Group 2

Group 3

3. Playing. Practice minor scales in thirds and fifths. These can be played with either hand alone or with both hands together. The example is given in d minor and also should be transposed to other minor keys.

4. Playing. You are given an interval that occurs in more than one minor key. Improvise a short progression of intervals that leads to the tonic note of one of the possible keys played in unison or an octave apart. Use only thirds, fifths, and sixths (in addition to the concluding unison or octave).

Example

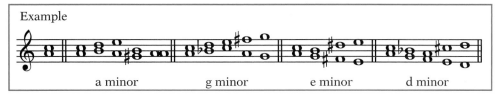

a minor   g minor   e minor   d minor

a.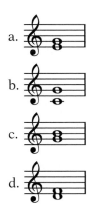

b.

c.

d.

Name: _____

Date: _____

Instructor's Name: _____

Lesson 26: Exercises

26-1. For the given keys, identify the requested intervals.

> a. e minor: its three major thirds <u>G–B, C–E, D–F♯</u>

b. e minor: its four minor thirds _____

c. d minor: its six perfect fourths _____

d. b minor: its three major thirds _____

e. g minor: its one augmented fourth _____

f. f♯ minor: its two minor seconds _____

g. c minor: its five major seconds _____

26-2. For any minor key, identify the interval between these scale-degrees, always calculating upward from the first note to the second.

a.	$\hat{1}$–$\hat{5}$	<u>P5</u>
b.	$\hat{1}$–$\hat{3}$	___
c.	$\hat{1}$–$\hat{6}$	___
d.	$\hat{1}$–$\hat{7}$	___
e.	$\hat{1}$–♯$\hat{7}$	___
f.	$\hat{4}$–$\hat{6}$	___
g.	$\hat{5}$–$\hat{7}$	___
h.	$\hat{5}$–♯$\hat{7}$	___
i.	♯$\hat{7}$–$\hat{4}$	___
j.	$\hat{2}$–$\hat{6}$	___
k.	♯$\hat{7}$–$\hat{6}$	___
l.	$\hat{6}$–♯$\hat{7}$	___
m.	$\hat{5}$–$\hat{1}$	___
n.	$\hat{5}$–$\hat{2}$	___
o.	$\hat{5}$–$\hat{3}$	___
p.	$\hat{6}$–$\hat{1}$	___

26-3. Name the minor scales that contain these intervals.

> a. G–B = $\hat{3}$–$\hat{5}$ in __e__ , $\hat{6}$–$\hat{8}$ in __b__ , $\hat{7}$–$\hat{2}$ in __a__

b. C–E = $\hat{3}$–$\hat{5}$ in _____ , $\hat{6}$–$\hat{8}$ in _____ , $\hat{7}$–$\hat{2}$ in _____

c. B–C = $\hat{2}$–$\hat{3}$ in _____ , $\hat{5}$–$\hat{6}$ in _____

d. G–D = $\hat{1}$–$\hat{5}$ in _____ , $\hat{3}$–$\hat{7}$ in _____ , $\hat{4}$–$\hat{8}$ in _____ , $\hat{5}$–$\hat{2}$ in _____ ,
$\hat{6}$–$\hat{3}$ in _____ , $\hat{7}$–$\hat{4}$ in _____

e. G–B♭ = $\hat{1}$–$\hat{3}$ in _____ , $\hat{2}$–$\hat{4}$ in _____ , $\hat{4}$–$\hat{6}$ in _____ , $\hat{5}$–$\hat{7}$ in _____

f. E–F♯ = $\hat{1}$–$\hat{2}$ in _____ , $\hat{3}$–$\hat{4}$ in _____ , $\hat{4}$–$\hat{5}$ in _____ , $\hat{6}$–$\hat{7}$ in _____ , $\hat{7}$–$\hat{8}$
in _____

g. E–B♭ = $\hat{2}$–$\hat{6}$ in _____

h. G♯–D = $\hat{2}$–$\hat{6}$ in _____

i. E♭–A = $\hat{6}$–$\hat{2}$ in _____

26-4. Name the minor scales that contain the following augmented seconds (or diminished sevenths), when scale-degree $\hat{7}$ is raised.

a. B♭–C♯   d minor

b. D♯–C   _____

c. D–E♯   _____

d. A♭–B   _____

e. A♯–G   _____

f. F♯–E♭   _____

26-5. Identify these intervals.

a minor: m3 ___ ___ ___ ___ ___ ___ ___

e minor: ___ ___ ___ ___ ___ ___ ___ ___

b minor: ___ ___ ___ ___ ___ ___ ___ ___

f♯ minor: ___ ___ ___ ___ ___ ___ ___ ___

d minor: ___ ___ ___ ___ ___ ___ ___ ___

g minor: ___ ___ ___ ___ ___ ___ ___ ___

c minor: ___ ___ ___ ___ ___ ___ ___ ___

Name: _____

Date: _____

Instructor's Name: _____

26-6. Identify these intervals.
    a. Bach, Chorale

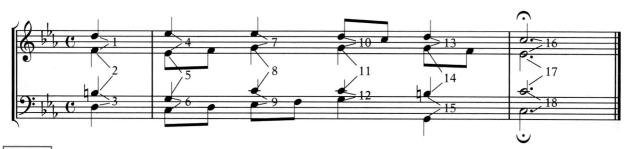

1. M6	4. ____	7. ____	10. ____	13. ____	16. ____
2. ____	5. ____	8. ____	11. ____	14. ____	17. ____
3. ____	6. ____	9. ____	12. ____	15. ____	18. ____

    b. Chopin, Prelude in c minor (adapted) (interval number twelve
       is an augmented sixth).

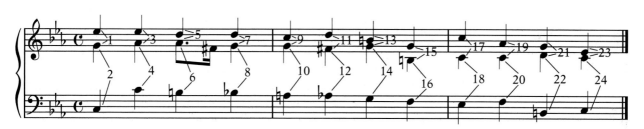

1. m6	4. ____	7. ____	10. ____	13. ____	16. ____	19. ____	22. ____
2. ____	5. ____	8. ____	11. ____	14. ____	17. ____	20. ____	23. ____
3. ____	6. ____	9. ____	12. A6	15. ____	18. ____	21. ____	24. ____

26-7. Compose duets by adding a melody above the given melody (some notes are already provided). Play your duet on the piano or other instrument before handing it in—be sure it sounds the way you want it to. Be prepared to sing in class both the melody you are given and the melody you have composed. Your melody should follow these guidelines:

1. Use only whole notes.

2. Create only the following intervals between the two melodies: thirds, fifths, sixths, octaves. Identify each interval by writing the appropriate number beneath the staff.

3. Don't write two consecutive fifths or octaves between the melodies.

4. Write a melody that moves mainly by step. Your melody should be as smooth, connected, and directed as the melodies you are given.

5. Don't use any accidentals—the leading-tone in the penultimate measure is provided.

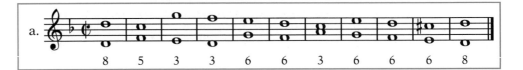

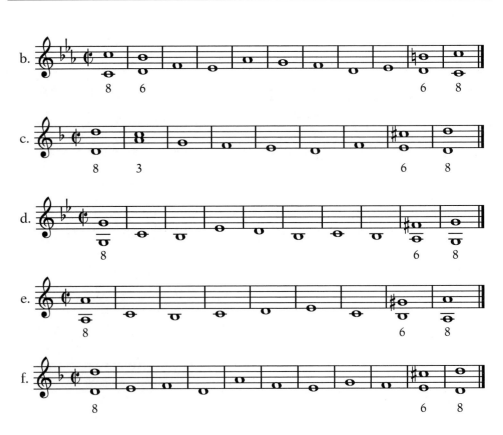

Chapter 4: Supplementary lesson

In this lesson you will learn about all intervals, doubly diminished and doubly augmented intervals, and intervals in harmonic and melodic minor.

In the preceding lessons of Chapter 4, we focused on those intervals that occur most commonly. The following charts offer a more comprehensive account, identifying each interval by its size, quality, and the number of semitones it contains.

Seconds	Diminished second 0 semitones (C♯–D♭)	Minor second 1 semitone (C♯–D)	Major second 2 semitones (C–D)	Augmented second 3 semitones (C–D♯)
Thirds	Diminished third 2 semitones (C♯–E♭)	Minor third 3 semitones (C–E♭)	Major third 4 semitones (C–E)	Augmented third 5 semitones (C–E♯)
Sixths	Diminished sixth 7 semitones (C♯–A♭)	Minor sixth 8 semitones (C–A♭)	Major sixth 9 semitones (C–A)	Augmented sixth 10 semitones (C–A♯)
Sevenths	Diminished seventh 9 semitones (C♯–B♭)	Minor seventh 10 semitones (C–B♭)	Major seventh 11 semitones (C–B)	Augmented seventh 12 semitones (C–B♯)

Unisons	Diminished unison (Does not exist—no interval can have fewer than 0 semitones)	Perfect unison 0 semitones (C–C)	Augmented unison 1 semitone (C–C♯)
Fourths	Diminished fourth 4 semitones (C♯–F)	Perfect fourth 5 semitones (C–F)	Augmented fourth 6 semitones (C–F♯)
Fifths	Diminished fifth 6 semitones (C–G♭)	Perfect fifth 7 semitones (C–G)	Augmented fifth 8 semitones (C–G♯)
Octaves	Diminished octave 11 semitones (C–C♭)	Perfect octave 12 semitones (C–C)	Augmented octave 13 semitones (C–C♯)

In fact, there are additional intervals not included on this chart. If you compress the size of a diminished interval it becomes *doubly diminished*. If you increase the size of an augmented interval, it becomes *doubly augmented*. Here are examples of doubly diminished or augmented thirds or fifths.

But doubly diminished and doubly augmented intervals are so rare in music—there are no scales and few musical contexts that produce them—as to make any further discussion unnecessary.

The common procedure of raising scale-degree $\hat{7}$ in minor keys (creating a scale called the harmonic minor) produces intervals that are not available in the natural minor scale.

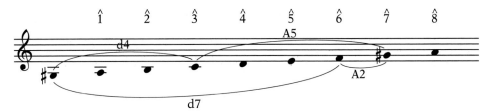

The intervals formed between scale-degrees $\hat{7}$ and $\hat{6}$ (diminished seventh/augmented second) and between scale-degrees $\hat{7}$ and $\hat{3}$ (diminished fourth/augmented fifth) cannot be found either in the major scale or in the unaltered minor scale.

5 Triads and Seventh Chords

Lesson 27: Triads

In this lesson you will learn about triads (root, third, and fifth), triad qualities (major, minor, diminished, augmented), natural triads, and chord symbols.

The *triad* is the basic harmony of tonal music. It consists of three notes: a fifth divided into two thirds.

Triads

The three notes of a triad can always be written on three consecutive lines or three consecutive spaces. When they are written like that, the lowest note is called the *root,* the middle note is called the *third,* and the highest note is called the *fifth.*

Root, third, fifth

There are four different qualities of triads—*major, minor, diminished,* and *augmented*—depending on the qualities of the thirds and fifths they contain. A *major triad* has a major third and a perfect fifth above the root (and thus a minor third between the two upper notes). A *minor triad* has a minor third and a perfect fifth above the root (and thus a major third between the two upper notes). A *diminished triad* consists of a minor third and a diminished fifth above a root (or two consecutive minor thirds). An *augmented triad* consists of a major third and an augmented fifth (or two consecutive major thirds).

Triad qualities

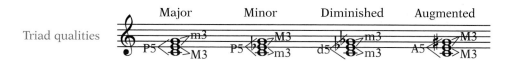

277

Any note can act as the root of a triad. A triad is named for its root so, for example, a C# major chord is a major chord with C# as its root and an f minor chord is a minor chord with F as its root. Here are some examples of major and minor triads:

Major and minor triads

        C# major   f minor   g minor   A major

There are seven *natural triads* (formed without any accidentals): C–E–G, D–F–A, E–G–B, F–A–C, G–B–D, A–C–E, and B–D–F. Of these, three are *major,* three *minor,* and one *diminished.*

Natural triads
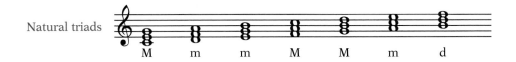

        M   m   m   M   M   m   d

By applying accidentals to these seven natural triads, it is possible to form any triad. For example, we can build the four different kinds of triads that share E as their root by applying accidentals to G and B, the other two notes of the natural triad on E: E–G–B.

Forming triads
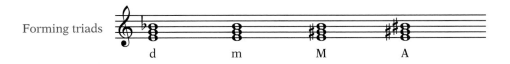

        d   m   M   A

Conversely, every possible triad uses the groups of three letter names defined by the seven natural triads: C–E–G, D–F–A, E–G–B, F–A–C, G–B–D, A–C–E, and B–D–F.

Composers and performers of jazz and popular music use a system of *alphabetical chord symbols* to name triads and other chords. Major triads are named with a capital letter that designates the root of the triad. Minor triads are named with a capital letter followed by a lowercase m (for minor). Diminished triads are named by a capital letter followed either by a small circle or the abbreviation "dim." An augmented triad is named by a capital letter followed by a plus sign (+). These symbols are illustrated here with triads built on the root D.

Chord symbols
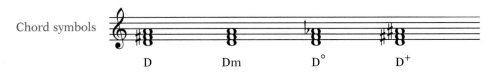

        D   Dm   D°   D+

The augmented triad is included here only for the sake of theoretical completeness. In musical practice, it is rare and occurs only under special conditions. As a result, the augmented triad is not discussed further in this book, or included among the In-class activities or Exercises.

So far, all of the triads discussed have been arranged in a tight little cluster, with the third and fifth found as close as possible above the root. But in actual music, many other arrangements are possible. One or more notes may be *doubled,* that is, represented by two or more different notes a unison or octave apart. As a result, a three-note triad often appears in music as a chord containing four or more notes. Furthermore, the notes of a triad, including the notes that are doubled, may be *arpeggiated,* that is, with the notes played consecutively rather than simultaneously. Rhythmic and melodic activity can serve to animate and activate a triad.

To figure out what triad is being played, eliminate all doublings and arrange the three notes in the smallest possible stack, on three adjacent lines or spaces. The lowest note in the stack is the root of the triad.

Identifying triads

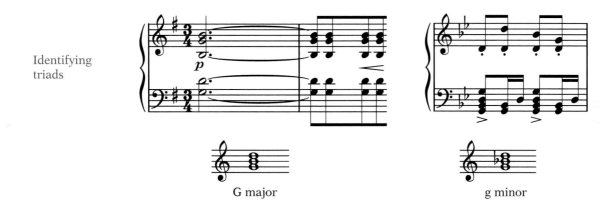

G major

g minor

Lesson 27: In-class activities

1. Singing. With the given notes as root, arpeggiate major and minor triads up and down. Sing the names of the notes.

a.

b.

c.

d.

e.

2. Singing. You are given a note and told if it is the root, third, or fifth. Arpeggiate down to the root, then arpeggiate the major or minor triad up and down. Sing the names of the notes.

a.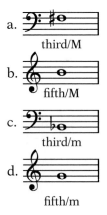

3. Singing (improvise). Choose a major or minor triad. Improvise a short melody that uses only the notes of that triad. Here are two samples:

4. Dictation. The instructor will play these three-note chords in a random order within each group. Identify them as a major triad, a minor triad, or not-a-triad.

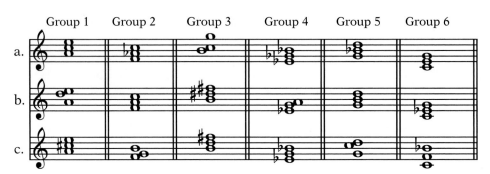

Group 7   Group 8   Group 9   Group 10   Group 11   Group 12

5. Playing. Play the requested triads with either hand (use the fingering 1–3–5). Remember that major triads are named with a capital letter, minor triads with a lowercase m, and diminished triads with °.

a. Cm play: C–E♭–G	k. A
b. G	l. D
c. Dm	m. Fm
d. Bm	n. G♯m
e. E♭	o. Gm
f. F	p. C♯m
g. A♭	q. Em
h. F♯°	r. Am
i. E	s. D°
j. B°	t. B♭

6. Playing. You are given a note, its identity as root, third, or fifth, and a triad quality. Play the triad.

a. B♭, third, minor   play: G–B♭–D

b. E♭, third, minor

c. B, fifth, minor

d. C, fifth major

e. B, third, diminished

f. A, fifth, minor

g. E, fifth, major

h. D, third, diminished

i. F♯, third, major

j. D, third, major

7. Playing. Play major and minor chords by changing the position of notes in the right hand while playing the root in the left hand.

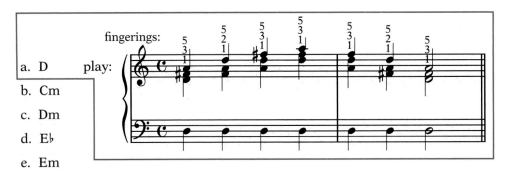

a. D

b. Cm

c. Dm

d. E♭

e. Em

f. F

g. G

h. Gm

i. A

j. B♭

Name: _____

Date: _____

Instructor's Name: _____

Lesson 27: Exercises

27-1. Identify the qualities of these natural triads (M = major, m = minor, d = diminished).

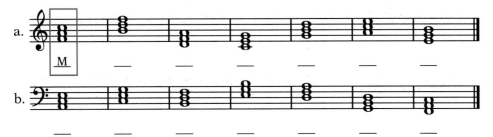

27-2. Create the requested quality of triad by adding accidentals if needed to the third and/or fifth of these natural triads (M = major, m = minor, d = diminished). Do not alter the root.

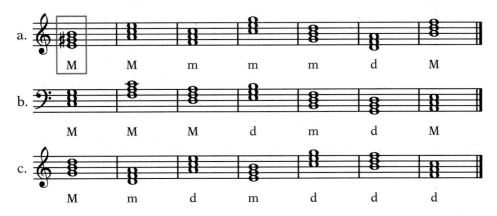

27-3. Write triads as indicated. Remember that a capital letter alone calls for a major triad; a lowercase m calls for a minor triad; and ° calls for a diminished triad.

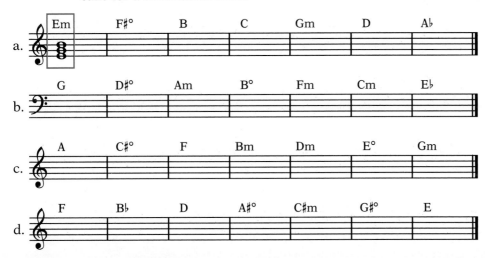

27-4. You are given a note as the root, third, or fifth of a certain quality
of triad (M = major, m = minor, d = diminished). Add two more
notes to complete the appropriate triad. Do not alter the note you
are given.

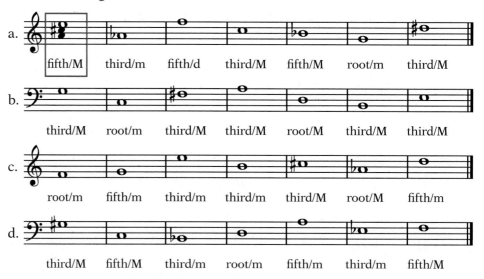

a.
fifth/M   third/m   fifth/d   third/M   fifth/M   root/m   third/M

b.
third/M   root/m   third/M   third/M   root/M   third/M   third/M

c.
root/m   fifth/m   third/m   third/m   third/M   root/M   fifth/m

d.
third/M   fifth/M   third/m   root/m   fifth/m   third/m   fifth/M

27-5. Rewrite these triads in the closest possible position. Identify them
with chord symbols (e.g., Em for e minor, G♯° for G♯ diminished,
B♭ for B♭ major).

a.

A   ___   ___   ___   ___   ___   ___

b.

___   ___   ___   ___   ___   ___   ___

Name: _____

Date: _____

Instructor's Name: _____

27-6. Identify the circled triads with chord symbols (e.g., Em for e minor, G#° for G# diminished, B♭ for B♭ major).

a. Chopin, Prelude in c minor (notice that the upper piano notes are written in bass clef until near the end of the passage. The chords marked with an asterisk (*) have an additional fourth note a seventh above the root—ignore that note. On the third beat of each measure, the melody has a dissonant note that is excluded from the chord).

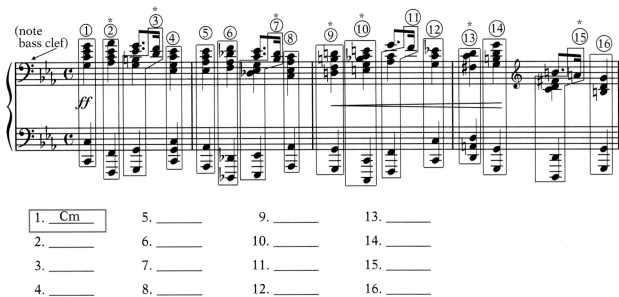

1. __Cm__	5. _____	9. _____	13. _____
2. _____	6. _____	10. _____	14. _____
3. _____	7. _____	11. _____	15. _____
4. _____	8. _____	12. _____	16. _____

b. Schumann, Song (the triads are formed by a combination of the voice and piano parts).

(continued)

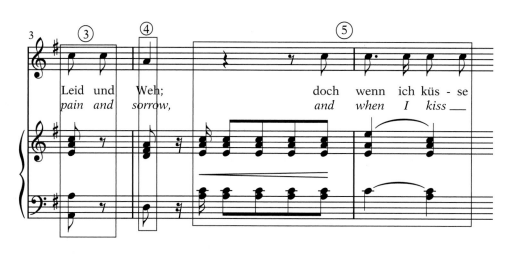

1. _____   2. _____   3. _____   4. _____   5. _____

c. Handy, "St. Louis Blues"

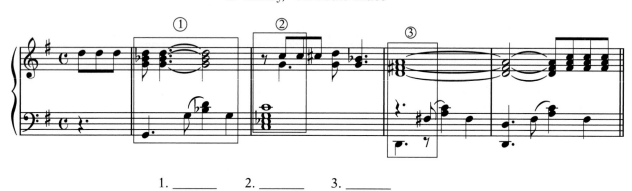

1. _____   2. _____   3. _____

d. Rodriguez, "La Cumparsita" (the notes in parentheses are embellishing or decorative—they do not belong to any triad. Do not include them in your identification of the triads).

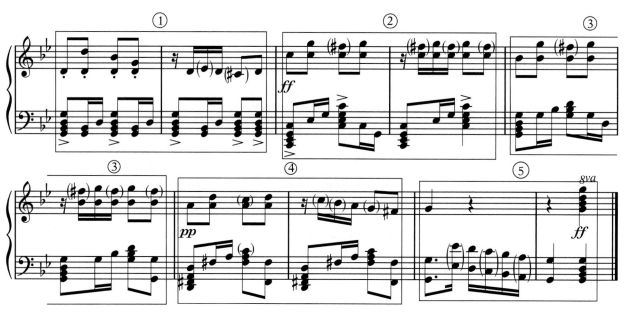

1. _____   2. _____   3. _____   4. _____   5. _____

Lesson 28: Triads in inversion

In this lesson you will learn about soprano and bass, inversion of triads (root position, first inversion, second inversion), and figured bass ($\frac{5}{3}$, $\frac{6}{3}$, $\frac{6}{4}$).

The highest note in a chord is called the *soprano;* the lowest note is called the *bass.* When the root of the triad is in the bass (i.e., when the root of the triad is the lowest sounding note), the triad is in *root position.* All the triads we have discussed thus far are in root position. But the third or fifth of the triad may also be in the bass. When that is the case, the triad has been *inverted.* When the third of the triad is in the bass, the triad is in *first inversion.* When the fifth of the triad is in the bass, it is in *second inversion.* Notice that the bass alone determines the position of the triad.

Triads in inversion

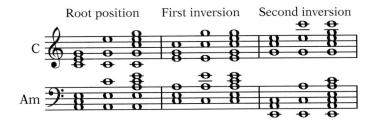

The first inversion of a triad is usually a weaker, less stable version of the root position. The second inversion, however, involves a significant difference. Recall that the interval of the perfect fourth is considered either consonant or dissonant, depending on the circumstances. In root position and first inversion, fourths occur among the upper voices and are thus consonant. In the second inversion, however, the fourth occurs between the bass and one of the upper voices—now there is nothing sounding below it and it is considered dissonant. As a result, a triad in second inversion is usually treated as a dissonant chord, and is used only under special circumstances, to be described later.

Fourths in triads

It is common to describe the position of triads, and other chords, using *figured bass* numbers. These numbers identify the intervals formed above a bass note (the lowest sounding note). When a triad is in root position, there are intervals a fifth and a third above the bass, so the triad is said to be in $\frac{5}{3}$ position.

Triads in $\frac{5}{3}$ position
(root position)

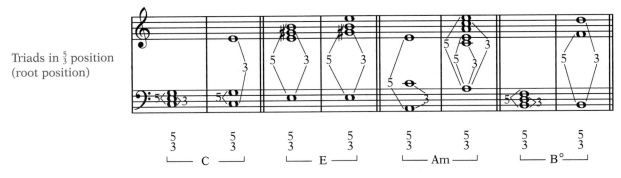

Notice that either or both the third and the fifth may be compound intervals and may be doubled. Notice also that the note creating a third with the bass may be either higher or lower than the note creating a fifth with the bass. The root may also appear doubled among the upper voices, an octave above the bass, but the number 8 is not normally included in the figured bass.

When a triad is in first inversion, there are intervals a sixth and a third above the bass, so the triad is said to be in $\frac{6}{3}$ position.

Triads in $\frac{6}{3}$ position (first inversion)

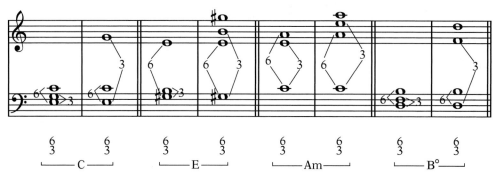

As with triads in $\frac{5}{3}$ position, the sixth and third may be doubled, may be compound, and may occur above or below each other.

A triad in second inversion is in $\frac{6}{4}$ position, with intervals a sixth and a fourth above the bass.

Triads in $\frac{6}{4}$ position (second inversion)

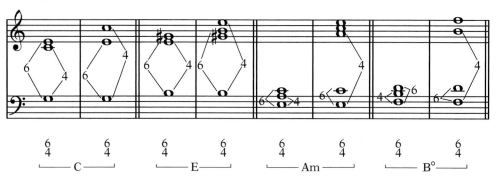

The sixth and the fourth may be compound and may occur above or below each other.

Alphabetical chord symbols do not usually distinguish between the root position and inversions of a triad. Sometimes, however, composers indicate the position of a triad by providing the bass note following the chord symbol.

Chord symbols

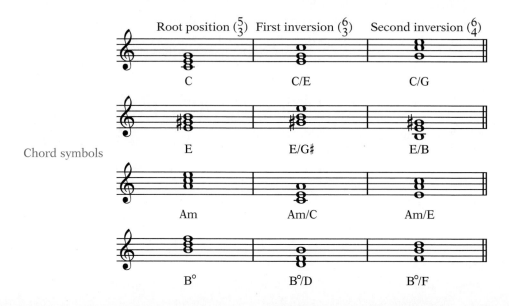

Lesson 28: In-class activities

1. Singing. You are given a note as the bass note of a triad in first or second inversion. Arpeggiate upward through the rest of the triad. End an octave above where you began.

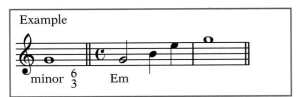

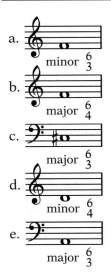

2. Dictation. The instructor will play these triads in a random order within each group. Identify them as root position ($\frac{5}{3}$), first inversion ($\frac{6}{3}$), or second inversion ($\frac{6}{4}$).

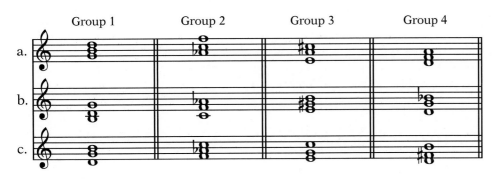

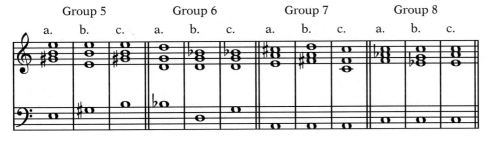

3. Playing. Play triads as indicated with either hand. (Remember that a capital letter stands for a major triad, a lowercase m for a minor triad, and ° for a diminished triad. In alphabetic chord symbols, the letter after the slash is the bass note.)

a. E_3^6 play: G♯–B–E	k C_3^6
b. D_3^6	l. $A\flat{}_3^5$
c. Fm_3^6	m. $D\sharp°_3^5$
d. Cm_4^6	n. Am_3^6
e. $E\flat{}_3^5$	o. Fm/A♭ play: A♭–C–F
f. A_3^6	p. G♯°/B
g. $B\flat{}_3^6$	q. Dm/A
h. F_4^6	r. Gm/B♭
i. $F\sharp°_3^6$	s. F♯°/A
j. $E°_3^6$	t. Cm/E♭

Name: _____

Date: _____

Instructor's Name: _____

Lesson 28: Exercises

28-1. You are given triads in root position (the figured bass is $^5_3$). Rewrite them in first inversion (figured bass: $^6_3$) and second inversion (figured bass: $^6_4$).

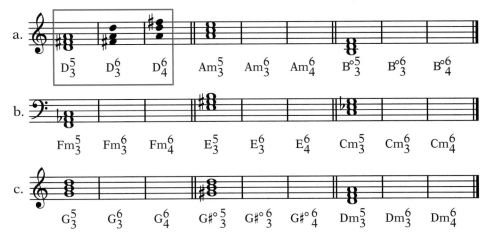

28-2. Write triads as indicated. Remember that $^5_3$ signifies root position, $^6_3$ signifies first inversion, and $^6_4$ signifies second inversion. In the alphabetic chord symbols, a capital letter stands for a major triad, a lowercase m for a minor triad, and ° for a diminished triad. If there is a letter after a slash, that is the bass note.

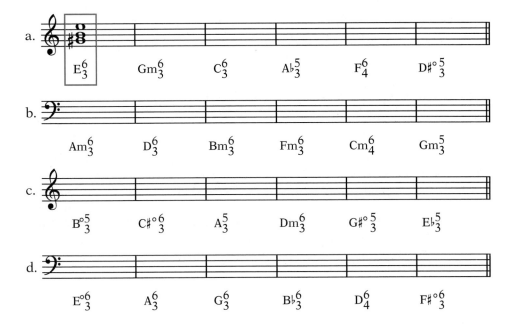

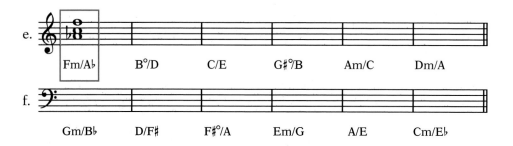

28-3. You are given triads in first or second inversion. Rewrite them in root position. Remember that you can always write a triad in root position on three adjacent lines or spaces of the staff.

28-4. Identify the circled triads by chord symbol (e.g., G for G major, Gm for g minor, and G° for g diminished) and figured bass numbers to indicate inversion ($\frac{5}{3}$ for root position, $\frac{6}{3}$ for first inversion, and $\frac{6}{4}$ for second inversion).

   a. Mozart, "Dove sono" (chords 7, 13, 20, 22, and 26 are seventh chords—they contain an additional note a seventh above the root. Disregard this note. Chords 5, 11, and 12 contain only two notes—they are incomplete. Assume that the fifth of the triad has been omitted. Ignore the notes in parentheses—they function as decorative embellishments, not as members of any triad).

Name: _____

Date: _____

Instructor's Name: _____

1. [B♭ $\frac{5}{3}$]   5. _____   9. _____   13. _____   17. _____   21. _____   25. _____

2. _____   6. _____   10. _____   14. _____   18. _____   22. _____   26. _____

3. _____   7. _____   11. _____   15. _____   19. _____   23. _____   27. _____

4. _____   8. _____   12. _____   16. _____   20. _____   24. _____

b. Bach, Chorale (ignore the decorative notes in parentheses. Chords 11 and 14 are incomplete—the fifth of the triad is omitted. Notice that in Chord 8, the soprano is still singing its E— that note is part of both Chords 7 and 8).

1._____	4._____	7._____	10._____	13._____	16._____	19._____
2._____	5._____	8._____	11._____	14._____	17._____	20._____
3._____	6._____	9._____	12._____	15._____	18._____	21._____

c. Haydn, Quartet (ignore the notes in parentheses).

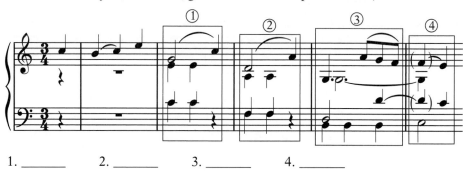

1._____   2._____   3._____   4._____

d. Schubert, "Death and the Maiden" (notice that the upper staff of the piano part is in bass clef throughout).

1._____   2._____   3._____   4._____

Lesson 29: Triads in major keys

In this lesson you will learn about triad names, Roman numerals, and triad qualities in major keys.

A triad can be built on each degree of a major scale. (We will use C major as our example, but all of the relationships can be transposed to any other major scale.) The name of the triad is the name of its root: tonic, supertonic, mediant, subdominant, dominant, submediant, and leading-tone.

Traid names
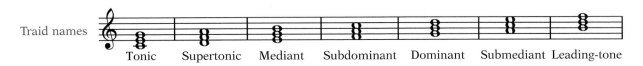

Triads also can be named using *Roman numerals,* with the numerals corresponding to the scale-degrees of the triad roots.

Roman numerals
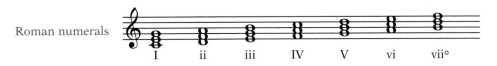

Of the seven triads in a major scale, three are major (I, IV, and V), three are minor (ii, iii, and vi), and one is diminished (vii°). Note that for major triads, the Roman numeral is uppercase, for minor triads it is lowercase, and for diminished triads it is lowercase with a °.

Triad qualities
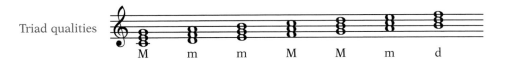

In identifying chords, Roman numerals are often combined with figured bass numbers: the Roman numeral identifies the root of the chord; the figured bass numbers tell the position of the chord.

Triads in major
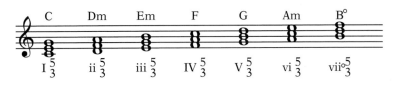

The figured bass $\frac{5}{3}$ is sometimes omitted—any Roman numeral without a figured bass after it will be assumed to be in root position ($\frac{5}{3}$ position). The figured bass $\frac{6}{3}$ is sometimes abbreviated 6 (the 3 is just assumed). In theory, it is also possible to construct $\frac{6}{4}$ chords on each degree of the scale. In musical practice, however, $\frac{6}{4}$ chords are used only under special conditions to be discussed in Chapter 6. Therefore, $\frac{6}{4}$ chords are omitted from the in-class activities and written exercises for this lesson. Another aspect of these harmonies, namely their functional relationships to each other and their combination into meaningful harmonic progressions, will also be deferred until Chapter 6.

Lesson 29: In-class activities

1. Singing. Sing the following arpeggiations of triads in a major key. Here are some ways to perform them: (1) sing on a neutral syllable like "la"; (2) sing with solfège syllables; (3) sing the qualities of the triads ("Ma-jor triad, mi-nor triad, mi-nor triad," etc.); (4) transpose to other major keys and sing the letter names of the notes.

2. Dictation. The instructor will play short progressions of triads in a random order within each group. Identify the progression you hear. Sing the bass.

Group 1

    a. I V^6 I   b. I V I   c. I vii°^{6} I

Group 2

    a. I vii°^{6} I^6 b. I IV I^6 c. I V I^6

Group 3

    a. I I^6 V   b. I IV^6 V   c. I IV V

3. Playing. Play triads in C major as shown. Transpose to other major keys. In the first progression, all of the chords are in root position (they are $\frac{5}{3}$ chords). In the second progression, all of the chords are in first inversion (they are $\frac{6}{3}$ chords).

4. Playing. You are given a triad that could occur in several different major keys (each minor triad could be ii, iii, or vi; each major triad could be I, IV, or V). Beginning with that triad, play triads down to each of the possible tonics, then up through an octave.

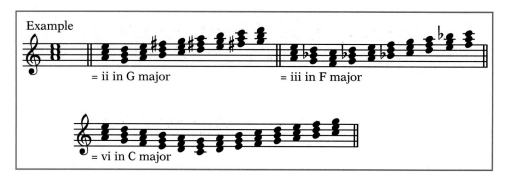

Example

= ii in G major   = iii in F major

= vi in C major

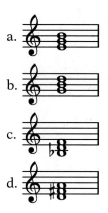

a.

b.

c.

d.

Name: _____

Date: _____

Instructor's Name: _____

Lesson 29: Exercises

29-1. Use Roman numerals and figured bass numbers to identify these triads in major keys.

29-2. You are given a major key and a Roman numeral with figured bass numbers. Write the appropriate triad.

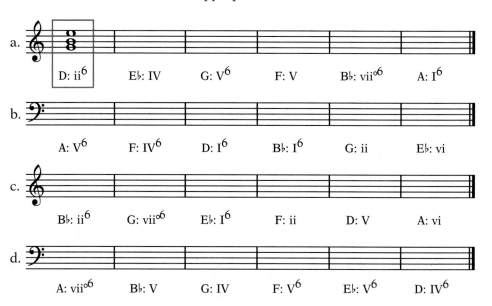

a.
D: ii^6 E♭: IV   G: V^6 F: V   B♭: vii^{o6} A: I^6

b.
A: V^6 F: IV^6 D: I^6 B♭: I^6 G: ii   E♭: vi

c.
B♭: ii^6 G: vii^{o6} E♭: I^6 F: ii   D: V   A: vi

d.
A: vii^{o6} B♭: V   G: IV   F: V^6 E♭: V^6 D: IV^6

29-3. Use Roman numerals and figured bass numbers to identify triads in these works.

a. Haydn, Quartet (disregard the notes in parentheses—they are embellishing notes and do not belong to any triad. In this passage, there is one triad per measure. The passage begins and ends on the tonic).

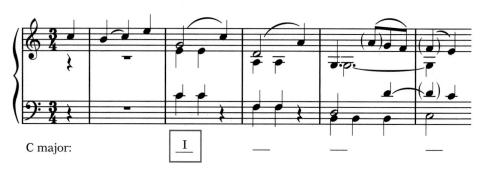

C major: I   ___   ___   ___

b. Bach, Chorale (disregard the notes in parentheses. This passage begins and ends on the tonic).

D major: ___   ___   ___   ___   ___   ___

Name: _____

Date: _____

Instructor's Name: _____

c. Schumann, Song (this passage moves from tonic to dominant).

G major: ___   ___ ___   ___ ___

d. Mozart, "Dove sono" (there is generally one harmony per beat,
    consisting of a bass note plus a chord, except at the ends of
    the two phrases—measure 8 and measures 17–18—where har-
    monies last for a full measure. Disregard notes in parentheses—
    they embellish the harmonies. In three places, there are chords
    we have not yet studied and the Roman numerals are provided—
    these are inversions of the dominant seventh chord, V^7).

C major: ___   ___   ___   ___   ___   ___   ___ V^4_3 V^6_5

(continued)

Lesson 30: Triads in minor keys

In this lesson you will learn about triad names, Roman numerals, triad qualities in minor keys, and the effect of raising the leading-tone.

As with the major, it is possible to build a triad on each degree of a minor scale. (We will use the key of a minor as our example, but all of the relationships can be transposed to other minor keys.) The name of each triad is the name of its root: tonic, supertonic, mediant, subdominant, dominant, submediant, and subtonic. Roman numerals also are used to name triads.

Triad names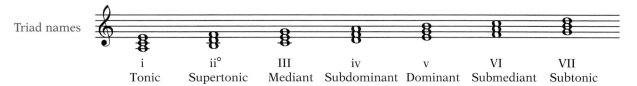

In using the dominant and subtonic triads, composers routinely raise the seventh degree of the minor scale to create a leading-tone (as discussed in Chapter 3). This gives these harmonies a greater impetus to move toward i (tonic). The common alteration in minor keys of scale-degrees $\hat{6}$ and $\hat{7}$ has the potential to affect other chords also, but use of a raised $\hat{7}$ to make V and vii° triads is by far the most common.

Alternative forms
of V and VII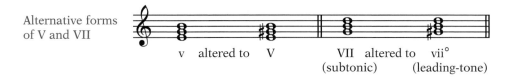

In the rest of this book, as in most music, we will assume that the dominant triad will be a major chord (V) and the leading-tone triad will be a diminished chord (vii°), both using the raised form of scale-degree $\hat{7}$. Of the seven triads in a minor scale, then, typically three are major (III, V, and VI), two are minor (i and iv), and two are diminished (ii° and vii°).

Triad qualities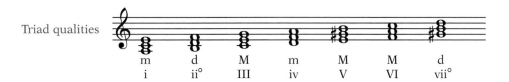

In identifying chords, Roman numerals are combined with figured bass numbers. As in major keys, the figured bass numbers are usually omitted when the triad is in $\frac{5}{3}$ position and abbreviated to 6 when the triad is in $\frac{6}{3}$ position. Also as in major, $\frac{6}{4}$ chords occur relatively rarely and under special conditions to be discussed later. They are thus omitted here.

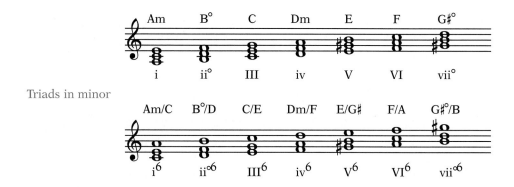

Triads in minor

Lesson 30: In-class activities

1. Singing. Sing the following arpeggiations of triads in a minor key. Here are some ways to perform them: (1) sing on a neutral syllable like "la"; (2) sing with solfège syllables; (3) sing the qualities of the triads ("Mi-nor triad, di-min-ished triad, ma-jor triad," etc.); (4) transpose to other minor keys and sing the letter names of the notes. Notice that scale-degree $\hat{7}$ is routinely raised in minor in making the V and vii° chords.

2. Dictation. The instructor will play short progressions of triads in a random order within each group. Identify the progression you hear. Sing the bass.

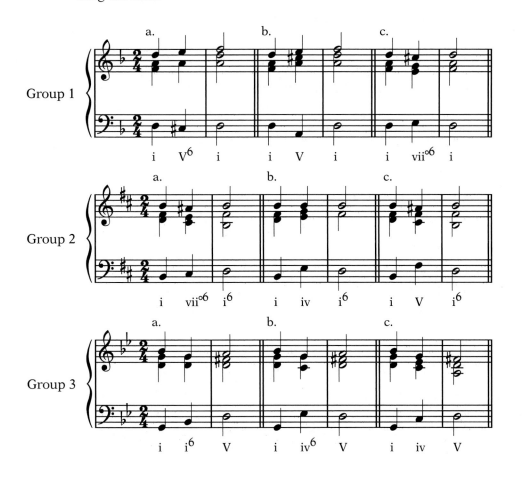

3. Playing. Play triads in the key of a minor as shown. Transpose to other major keys. Notice that scale-degree $\hat{7}$ is routinely raised for the V and vii° chords.

4. Playing. You are given a triad that could occur in several different minor keys (minor triads could be i or iv; major triads could be III, V, or VI). Beginning with that triad, play triads down to each of the possible tonics, then up through an octave. Be sure to raise the leading-tone in the V and vii° chords.

Example

= i in e minor   = iv in b minor

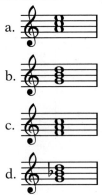

a.

b.

c.

d.

Name: _____

Date: _____

Instructor's Name: _____

Lesson 30: Exercises

30-1. Use Roman numerals and figured bass numbers to identify these triads in minor keys.

30-2. You are given a minor key and a Roman numeral with figured bass numbers. Write the appropriate triad. Remember that scale-degree $\hat{7}$ is always raised in making the V and vii° chords.

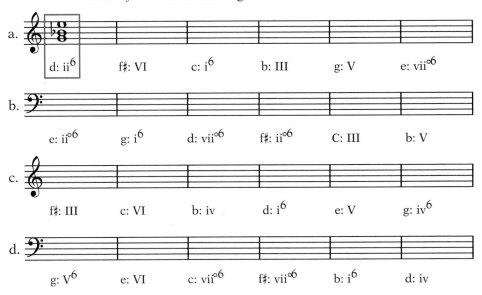

a.

d: ii⁶   f#: VI   c: i⁶   b: III   g: V   e: vii°⁶

b.

e: ii°⁶   g: i⁶   d: vii°⁶   f#: ii°⁶   C: III   b: V

c.

f#: III   c: VI   b: iv   d: i⁶   e: V   g: iv⁶

d.

g: V⁶   e: VI   c: vii°⁶   f#: vii°⁶   b: i⁶   d: iv

30-3. Use Roman numerals and figured bass numbers to identify triads in these works.

a. Schubert, "Death and the Maiden" (when you see a chord that contains only two notes, assume that it is an incomplete triad with the fifth of the triad omitted. In this passage, the young woman ceases begging for her life and Death begins his unforgiving answer. Notice that the upper staff of the piano part is in bass clef starting in the middle of the third measure and disregard the notes in parentheses).

b. Bach, Chorale (disregard the notes in parentheses).

c minor: ___   ___   ___   ___

Lesson 31: Seventh chords

In this lesson you will learn about seventh chords, major-minor (dominant) seventh chord, inversion of seventh chords, dominant seventh chords in major and minor keys, figured bass symbols, and chord names.

A *seventh chord* consists of a triad plus the interval of a seventh over a shared root. A seventh chord contains a *root, third, fifth,* and *seventh* and can be written on four successive lines or spaces on the staff.

Seventh chords

The quality of a seventh chord depends on the qualities of the triad and seventh that comprise it. The most important kind of seventh chord is called a *major-minor seventh chord,* because it consists of a *major triad* and a *minor seventh.*

Major-minor seventh chords

The major-minor seventh chord is also called a *dominant seventh chord,* because it is the quality you get when you build a seventh chord on the scale-degree $\hat{5}$ (the dominant) in a major key. As with triads, seventh chords can be named in two ways: (1) a Roman numeral that identifies the scale-degree of the root; or (2) an alphabetical chord symbol, with the root identified by a letter.

Dominant seventh chords in major

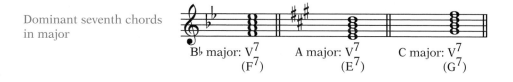

In minor keys, scale-degree $\hat{7}$ is raised when creating a dominant seventh chord. As a result, a minor key and its parallel major will have the same dominant seventh chord.

Dominant seventh chords in minor

As with triads, seventh chords whose root is also the lowest sounding note (bass) are said to be in *root position.* And, also as with triads, seventh chords can be *inverted* by placing notes other than the root in the bass: *First inversion* places the third of the seventh chord in the bass; *second inversion* places the fifth in the bass; *third inversion* places the seventh in the bass.

Inversions of seventh chords

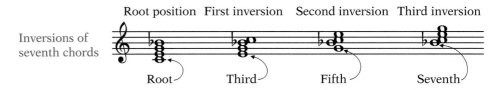

Figured bass numbers are often used in conjunction with Roman numerals to indicate inversion. Chord symbols are also useful for indicating inversion: the actual bass note is shown after a slash.

Figured bass and chord symbols

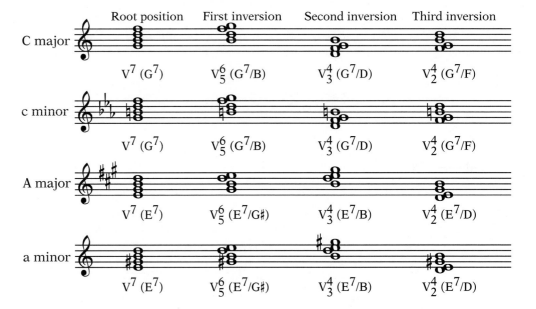

Lesson 31: In-class activities

1. Singing. With the given notes as root, arpeggiate major-minor seventh chords (dominant seventh chords) up and down. Sing on a neutral syllable such as "la" or with the names of the notes. Name the two keys (a major key and its parallel minor) of which this chord would function as V^7.

a.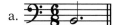

b.

c.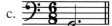

d.

e.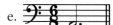

f.

2. Dictation. The instructor will play short progressions of chords in a random order within each group. Each progression contains a dominant-seventh chord or one of its inversions ($\frac{6}{5}$ = first inversion; $\frac{4}{3}$ = second inversion; $\frac{4}{2}$ = third inversion). Identify the progression you hear. Sing the bass.

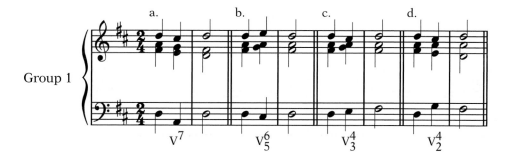

Group 1

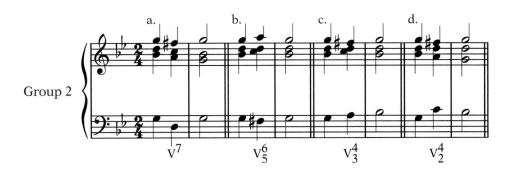

Group 2

3. Playing. Play the requested major-minor seventh chord with either hand. Remember that $\frac{6}{5}$ = first inversion; $\frac{4}{3}$ = second inversion; and $\frac{4}{2}$ = third inversion. In the alphabetic chord symbols, the letter after the slash is the bass note.

a. E^7 play: E–G♯–B–D		k. E^6_5	
b. A^7		l. D^4_3	
c. G^7		m. B^4_3	
d. B^7		n. F^4_3	
e. C^7		o. E^4_2	
f. D^7		p. A^4_2	
g. F^7		q. B♭^{7}/D	
h. B♭$^6_5$		r. D^7/F♯	
i. C^6_5		s. C^7/B♭	
j. A^6_5		t. B^7/F♯	

4. Playing. You are given eight V^7 chords. Resolve each to the root and third of its tonic triad (which may be either major or minor).

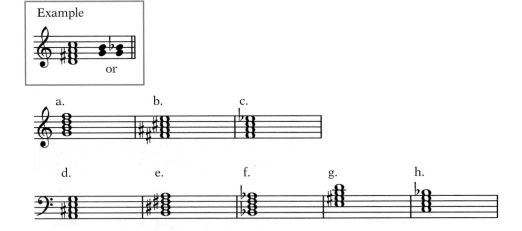

Name: _____

Date: _____

Instructor's Name: _____

Lesson 31: Exercises

31-1. Create major-minor (dominant) seventh chords by adding accidentals (if needed) to the upper three notes. Do not alter the lowest note. Remember that a major-minor seventh chord has a major triad and a minor seventh above its root.

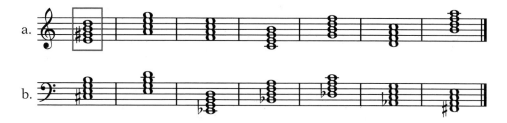

31-2. Write major-minor (dominant) seventh-chords as indicated (root position only). Remember that a major-minor seventh chord has a major triad and a minor seventh above its root.

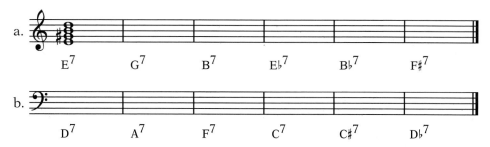

31-3. You are given a note as the root, third, fifth, or seventh of a major-minor (dominant) seventh chord. Write the rest of the chord in root position. Do not alter the note you are given.

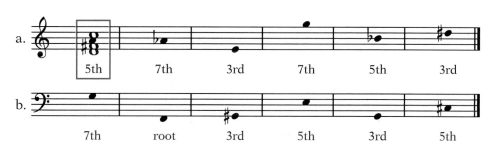

31-4. You are given major-minor (dominant) seventh-chords in root position. Rewrite them in first inversion (the third of the chord is in the bass), second inversion (the fifth of the chord is in the bass), and third inversion (the seventh of the chord is in the bass).

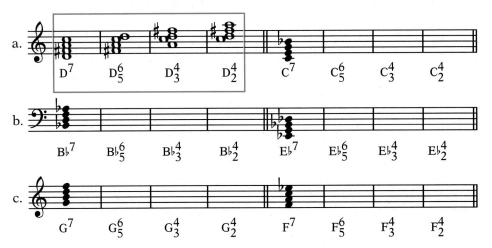

31-5. Write major-minor (dominant) seventh-chords as indicated (root position and all three inversions). Remember that 7 means root position, $^6_5$ means first inversion, $^4_3$ means second inversion, and $^4_2$ means third inversion.

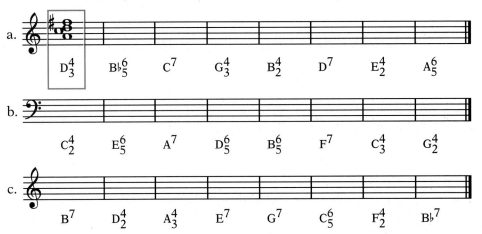

31-6. Use Roman numerals and figured bass numbers to identify these seventh chords in major and minor keys (V^7 and its inversions only). Remember that 7 means root position, $^6_5$ means first inversion, $^4_3$ means second inversion, and $^4_2$ means third inversion. And notice that, in minor keys, scale-degree $\hat{7}$ is raised when forming the dominant-seventh chord in all of its positions.

Name: _____

Date: _____

Instructor's Name: _____

c.

Bb major: ___   ___   ___   ___

d.

b minor: ___   ___   ___   ___

e.

g minor: ___   ___   ___   ___

f.

F major: ___   ___   ___   ___

31-7. You are given a major or minor key and a Roman numeral with figured bass numbers. Write the appropriate seventh chord (V^7 and its inversions only). In minor keys, the dominant seventh chord is always made with raised $\hat{7}$ (the leading-tone).

a.

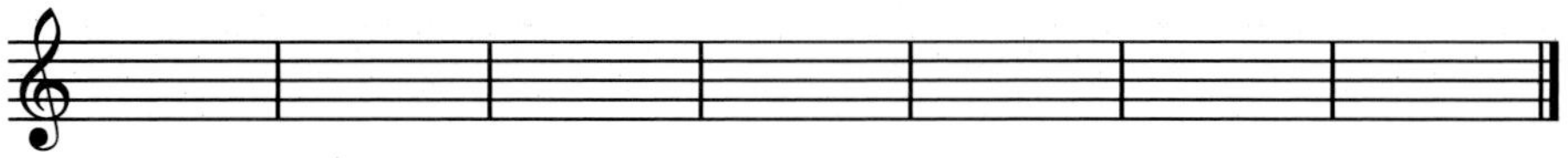

    F: V^6_5 d: V^7 C: V^4_2 e: V^6_5 Bb: V^6_5 G: V^7 a: V^4_3

b.

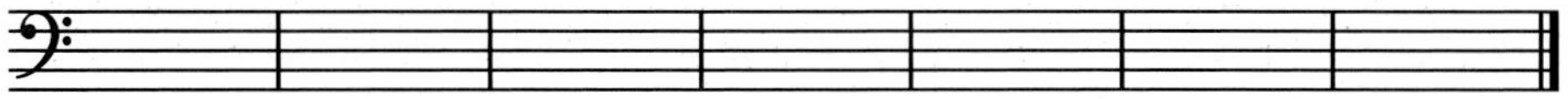

    d: V^6_5 Eb: V^6_5 f#: V^6_5 b: V^7 F: V^7 C: V^7 D: V^7

c.

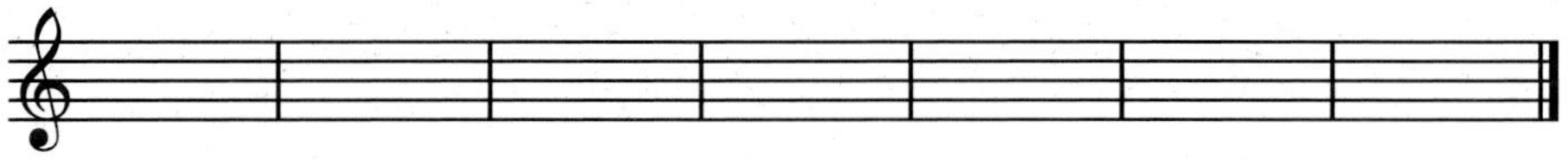

    D: V^6_5 d: V^4_2 f#: V^7 C: V^4_3 e: V^7 g: V^7 A: V^4_2

d.

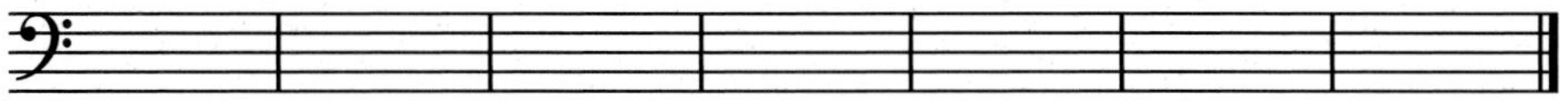

    a: V^7 A: V^7 g: V^4_3 Bb: V^7 b: V^6_5 G: V^4_3 Eb: V^4_2

31-8. You are given a V^7 chord (or one if its inversions). Name the tonic note of the key to which it belongs. (The key may be either major or minor).

31-9. Use Roman numerals and figured bass numbers to identify triads and seventh chords in these works.

a. Schubert, "Heidenröslein" (this piece begins in one key [G major], moves to another [D major], then returns to where it began. This process is called "modulation." In the second measure, the harmony is an inversion of a seventh chord built on scale-degree $\hat{2}$. Each harmony lasts for one full beat and includes both the bass note in the left hand and the chord in the right).

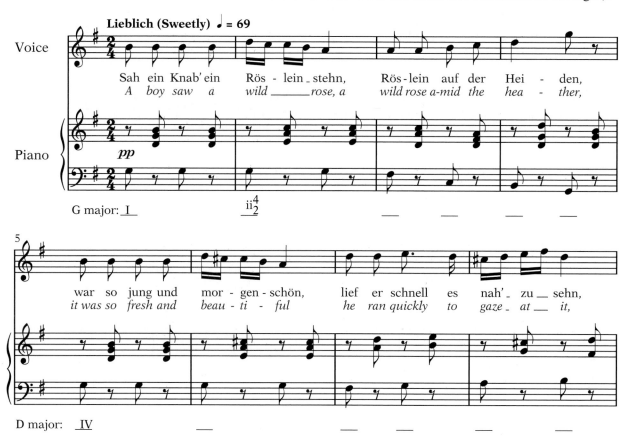

Name: _____

Date: _____

Instructor's Name: _____

b. Rodriguez, "La Cumparsita" (within both tonic and dominant harmonies, the D in the melody is embellished with notes above and below it. Disregard the notes in parentheses).

c. Lang, Song (one unfamiliar chord—the first inversion of ii⁷—is identified for you. Ignore the notes in parentheses—they embellish the harmonies you are asked to identify).

Langsam und Ausdrucksvoll (Slowly and expressively)

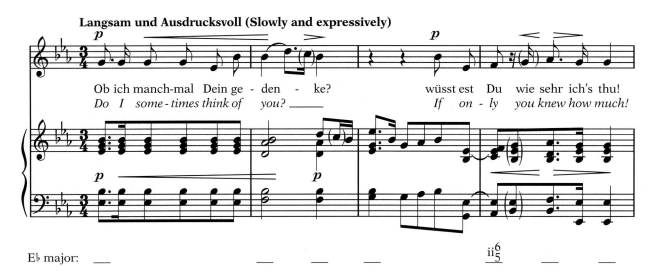

Ob ich manch-mal Dein ge - den - ke?   wüsst est Du   wie sehr ich's thu!
Do I some - times think of   you? _____   If   on - ly   you knew how much!

Eb major: ____   ____ ____ ____   ii$^6_5$ ____ ____

d. Mendelssohn, Piano Trio (ignore the notes in parentheses—they embellish the harmonies you are asked to identify).

Allegretto

D major: ____   ____ ____ ____ ____ ____ ____

e. Chopin, Prelude in A major (the notes in parentheses embellish the harmonies. That fact that these embellishing tones occur on the downbeat gives them particular expressive force).

A major: ____ ____

Chapter 5: Supplementary lesson

In this lesson you will learn about qualities of seventh chords, natural seventh chords, inversions of seventh chords, and seventh chords in major and minor keys.

The previous lesson focused on the major-minor (dominant) seventh chord. This supplementary lesson gives a full account of seventh chords.

There are five kinds of seventh chords in common use (illustrated here with D as their root).

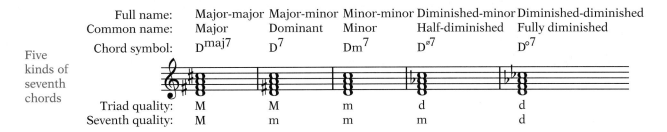

	Major-major	Major-minor	Minor-minor	Diminished-minor	Diminished-diminished
Full name:	Major-major	Major-minor	Minor-minor	Diminished-minor	Diminished-diminished
Common name:	Major	Dominant	Minor	Half-diminished	Fully diminished
Chord symbol:	D^{maj7}	D^7	Dm^7	D^{ø7}	D^{o7}
Triad quality:	M	M	m	d	d
Seventh quality:	M	m	m	m	d

(Five kinds of seventh chords)

It is possible to write seven different seventh chords without any accidentals—these are the *natural seventh chords*.

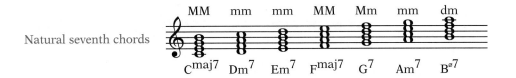

Natural seventh chords

MM	mm	mm	MM	Mm	mm	dm
C^{maj7}	Dm^7	Em^7	F^{maj7}	G^7	Am^7	B^{ø7}

All seventh chords involve these seven stacks of letter names: C–E–G–B, D–F–A–C, E–G–B–D, F–A–C–E, G–B–D–F, A–C–E–G, and B–D–F–A. Adding accidentals will change the quality of these natural seventh chords.

When talking about seventh chords within a key, Roman numerals with figured bass can be used either instead of or along with the system of alphabetic chord symbols. Just as with triads, the dominant and leading-tone seventh chords in minor are normally made by raising scale-degree $\hat{7}$.

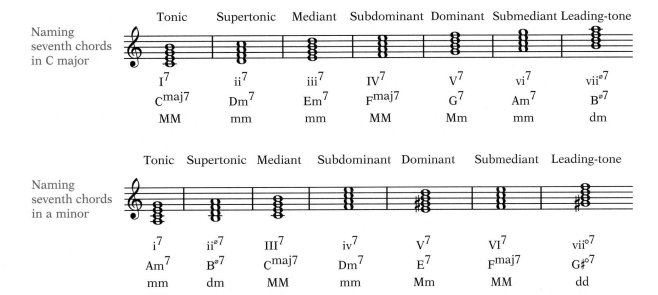

Naming seventh chords in C major

Tonic	Supertonic	Mediant	Subdominant	Dominant	Submediant	Leading-tone
I^7	ii^7	iii^7	IV^7	V^7	vi^7	vii^{ø7}
C^{maj7}	Dm^7	Em^7	F^{maj7}	G^7	Am^7	B^{ø7}
MM	mm	mm	MM	Mm	mm	dm

Naming seventh chords in a minor

Tonic	Supertonic	Mediant	Subdominant	Dominant	Submediant	Leading-tone
i^7	ii^{ø7}	III^7	iv^7	V^7	VI^7	vii^{o7}
Am^7	B^{ø7}	C^{maj7}	Dm^7	E^7	F^{maj7}	G$\sharp^{o7}$
mm	dm	MM	mm	Mm	MM	dd

Any seventh chord can appear in inversion as well as root position. The figured bass works as follows: 7 for root position, $\frac{6}{5}$ for first inversion, $\frac{4}{3}$ for second inversion, and $\frac{4}{3}$ for third inversion. Here are the five kinds of seventh chords in all four positions with D as the root.

Figured bass

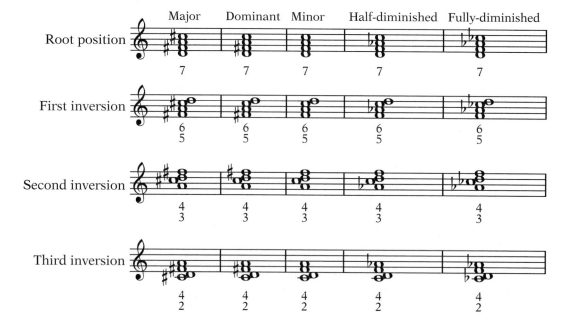

Chord symbols are also useful for indicating inversion: the actual bass note is shown after a slash.

Chord symbols

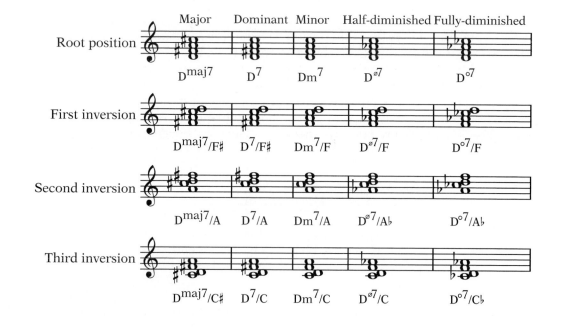

6 Fundamentals of Harmony

Lesson 32: Tonic and dominant

In this lesson you will learn about harmonic progression, tonic harmony, dominant and dominant seventh harmonies, and harmonizing a melody.

A *harmonic progression* is a succession of harmonies in which each leads purposefully to the next. Each harmony has its own distinctive character and its own role to play. The *tonic* harmony generally conveys a feeling of stability and repose. Progressions often start on the tonic and very often end on it. Normally, tonal motion is directed toward the tonic as a goal.

The main function of the *dominant* harmony is to lead to the tonic. Indeed, the most basic harmonic progression involves three chords: I–V–I. It begins on the tonic (in a state of poised repose), moves to the dominant (which has a strong tendency to move to the tonic), and concludes on the tonic (conveying a sense of arrival and completion).

I–V–I

The progression is often written in this standard, conventional way. Each triad is written in four *voices:* a soprano (the highest sounding note in each chord, written on the treble staff with an upward stem); an alto and a tenor (the next highest notes, written on the treble staff with a shared downward stem); and a bass (the lowest note, written by itself on the bass staff). Because triads contain three notes but are conventionally written in four voices, one note in each triad is *doubled* (i.e., occurs two times).

The progression I–V–I can be intensified by adding the interval of a seventh above the root of the dominant triad—that turns the dominant triad into a dominant seventh chord. The tendency of the dominant to resolve to the tonic is strengthened by the presence of the dissonant seventh.

I–V⁷–I
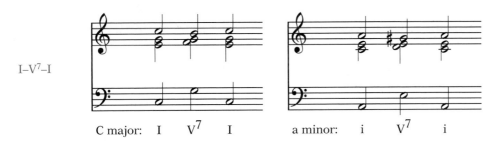

The presence of the seventh makes the V^7 chord dissonant and tense, more eager to resolve to the tonic. The seventh of the V^7 chord (scale-degree $\hat{4}$) usually resolves down by step to the third of the tonic triad (scale-degree $\hat{3}$). (In writing this progression, it is sometimes more convenient to leave the V^7 incomplete by omitting the fifth of the chord and doubling the root.)

Lots of melodies can be *harmonized* using the tonic and dominant harmonies (I and V or V^7). To harmonize a melody, follow these steps (illustrated with four different melodic fragments in the key of D major).

1. Identify the scale-degree of each melody note and figure out if it belongs to the tonic triad (scale-degrees $\hat{1}$–$\hat{3}$–$\hat{5}$), the dominant triad (scale-degrees $\hat{5}$–$\hat{7}$–$\hat{2}$), the dominant seventh chord (scale-degrees $\hat{5}$–$\hat{7}$–$\hat{2}$–$\hat{4}$), or more than one of these. (Notice that scale-degree $\hat{5}$ is the only one shared by tonic and dominant harmonies.)

2. Choose a good, strong progression of harmonies and write the bass line.

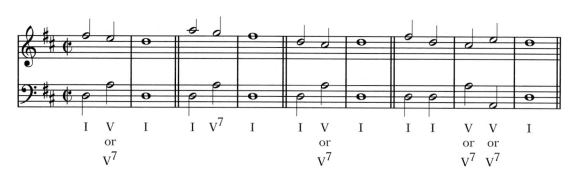

3. Add inner voices (alto and tenor) to fill out the chords.

Here is a simple way of realizing the progression I–V^7–I that makes it particularly easy to play at the keyboard.

Keyboard realization

These left-hand chords can be used to harmonize melodies played by the right hand or sung.

Harmonizing at the keyboard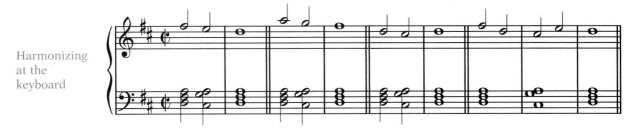

Lesson 32: In-class activities

1. Singing. Sing these melodies, using a neutral syllable like "la," solfège syllables, or scale-degree numbers. Think about the harmonies and the harmonic progression that each melody outlines. Transpose to other keys. Melodies e and f below work well as a four-part round.

2. Singing (improvise). Improvise melodies that arpeggiate tonic and dominant, beginning and ending on the tonic. Here are two samples:

3. Singing. Sing these short four-voice chorales. Students should have the opportunity to sing each of the parts.

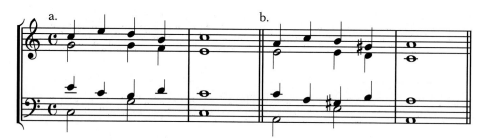

4. Dictation. The instructor will play a major or minor scale to establish a context, followed by I, V, or V^7. Identify the chord you hear.

5. Dictation. The instructor will play these three-chord progressions in a random order within each group. All of the progressions include only I and V or V^7, all in root position. Identify the progression and the chords it contains.

6. Playing. Play the following progressions. Transpose to other keys.

7. Playing. Harmonize these short melodies by adding three lower voices.

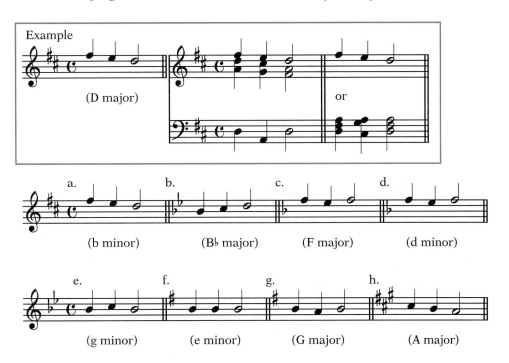

Name: _____

Date: _____

Instructor's Name: _____

Lesson 32: Exercises

32-1. Using only I and V or V⁷, harmonize these short melodic fragments (derived from works in the anthology). Supply one chord for each note in the melody, and identify each chord with a Roman numeral (some chords and Roman numerals are provided for you). The melody note you are given should be the highest note in each chord. Try to move the voices as smoothly as possible (avoid large leaps). When you have harmonized a melody, transpose what you have written to a different key, as indicated. Play what you have written at the piano before handing it in—be sure it sounds the way you want it to. After you have finished, compare your work with the actual music from which the melody is adapted.

Remember the three-step procedure for harmonizing a melody:

1. Identify the scale-degree of each melody note and figure out if it belongs to the tonic triad (scale-degrees $\hat{1}$–$\hat{3}$–$\hat{5}$), the dominant triad (scale-degrees $\hat{5}$–$\hat{7}$–$\hat{2}$), the dominant seventh chord (scale-degrees $\hat{5}$–$\hat{7}$–$\hat{2}$–$\hat{4}$), or more than one of these.

2. Choose a good, strong progression of harmonies and write the bass line.

3. Add inner voices (alto and tenor) to fill out the chords.

a. Chopin, Prelude in A Major, mm. 1–8

A major: V   B♭ major:

b. Arlen, "Over the Rainbow," mm. 9–11

E♭ major: D major:

c. Ellington, "It Don't Mean a Thing," mm. 27–30

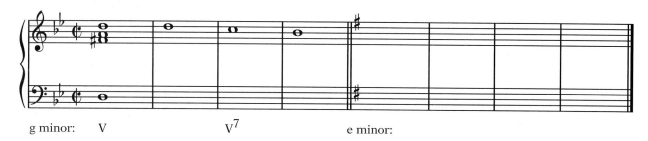

g minor: V   V⁷   e minor:

d. Chopin, Prelude in c minor, m. 1

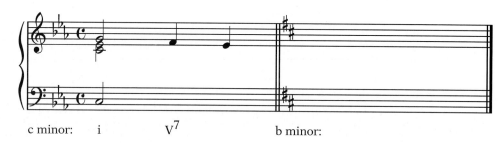

c minor: i   V⁷   b minor:

e. Joplin, "The Entertainer," mm. 5–8

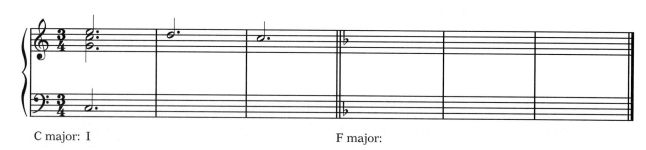

C major: I   F major:

f. Schubert, "Death and the Maiden," mm. 1–4

d minor: i   e minor:

Name: _____

Date: _____

Instructor's Name: _____

g. Handy, "St. Louis Blues," mm. 33–40

G major: I

A major:

h. Mozart, "Dove sono," mm. 1–8

C major: I   I   I   V^7

B♭ major:

32-2. Using only I and V or V^7, add three upper voices for the following bass lines (derived from works in the anthology). Supply one chord for each bass note and identify each chord with a Roman numeral (some chords and Roman numerals are provided for you). Try to move the voices as smoothly as possible (avoid large leaps). Play what you have written at the piano before handing it in—be sure it sounds the way you want it to. After you have finished, compare your work with the actual music from which the melody is adapted.

a. Chopin, Prelude in A Major, mm. 1–8

A major: V

b. Arlen, "Over the Rainbow," mm. 9–11

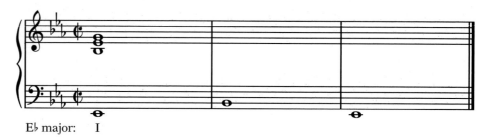

E♭ major: I

c. Ellington, "It Don't Mean a Thing," mm. 27–30

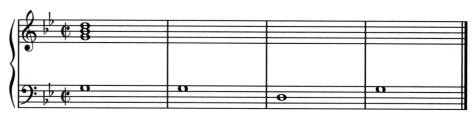

g minor: i

d. Chopin, Prelude in c minor, m. 1

c minor: i

Name: _____

Date: _____

Instructor's Name: _____

e. Schubert, "Death and the Maiden," mm. 1–4

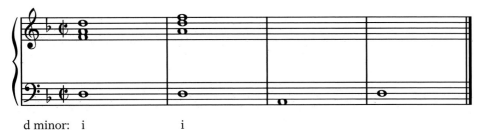

d minor: i   i

f. Haydn, Quartet, mm. 48–56

C major: I

g. Mozart, "Dove sono," mm. 1–8

C major: I   I   I

32-3. Identify the circled chords as I, V, or V^7. All nine passages end with the same two chords—a dominant followed by a tonic. Think about why that should be so.

a. Schubert, "Death and the Maiden" (the third and eighth chords are incomplete, but you should be able to figure them out even with one note omitted).

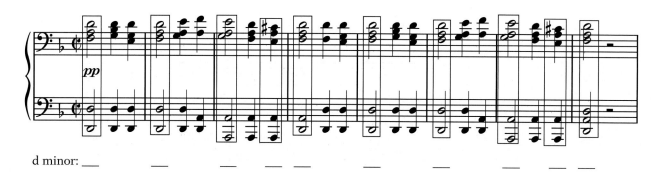

d minor: ___   ___   ___   ___   ___   ___   ___   ___   ___

b. Joplin, "The Entertainer"

C major: ___   ___   ___

c. Bach, Chorale (this is the concluding phrase of the chorale).

E♭ major: ___   ___   ___

Name: _____

Date: _____

Instructor's Name: _____

d. Ellington, "It Don't Mean a Thing"

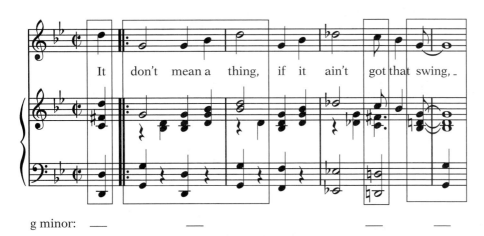

It   don't   mean a   thing,   if   it   ain't   got that   swing, __

g minor: ___   ___   ___   ___

e. Lang, Song

Ob ich manch-mal dein Ge - den - ke?   wüsst est Du   wie sehr ich's thu!
Do I some - times think of   you? _____   *If   on - ly   you knew how much!*

E♭ major: ___   ___   ___

f. Chopin, Prelude in c minor

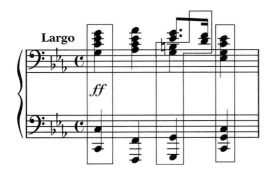

c minor: ___   ___   ___

g. Chopin, Prelude in A Major (the entire piece, like this passage, consists of an alternation of tonic and dominant harmonies).

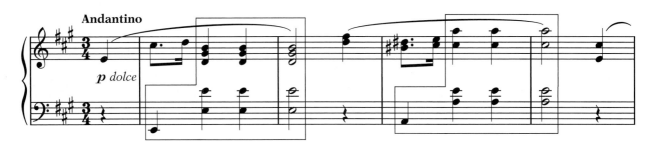

A major:

h. Handy, "St. Louis Blues" (despite the key signature, this passage is in g minor, and the piece as a whole moves back and forth constantly between G major and g minor).

g minor:

Name: _____

Date: _____

Instructor's Name: _____

man roun' _____   by her a-pron   strings _____

i. Rodriguez, "La Cumparsita" (like many popular dances, this tango consists largely of tonic and dominant harmonies).

Violin

Piano

g minor:

(continued)

Lesson 33: Expanding I and V

In this lesson you will learn about embellishment and prolongation (nonharmonic notes), passing notes, neighboring notes, passing chords (V^4_3 and $vii°^6$), neighboring chords (V^6, V^6_5, V^4_2, and IV), and the cadential $^6_4$.

The tonic and dominant harmonies, and any other harmonies, may be *embellished* with foreign notes. These decorative, *embellishing notes* are always just one step away from a note that does belong to a harmony, and they have the effect of *prolonging* or extending a harmony. They often are called *nonharmonic notes*.

There are two main types of embellishing notes: *passing notes* and *neighboring notes*. A passing note fills in the space between two harmonic notes. It may be ascending or descending, accented or unaccented.

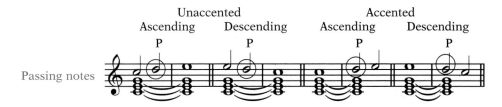

Unlike a passing note, which connects two different notes, a neighboring note moves away from and back to a single, stationary note. A neighbor may occur above (upper neighbor) or below (lower neighbor) and it may be accented or unaccented.

These neighboring notes are *complete:* they depart from and return to a harmonic tone. Neighboring notes also can be *incomplete,* attached to a harmonic note before or after, but not both.

Just as individual notes may have a passing or neighboring function with respect to other notes, entire harmonies may have a passing or neighboring function with respect to other harmonies. The second inversion of the V^7 chord (V_3^4), for example, is often used as a passing chord to connect I with I^6. Its bass note, scale-degree $\hat{2}$, acts as a passing note: it comes by step from I and continues by step to I^6. In addition, $vii^{\circ 6}$ has the same bass note and often has the same passing function.

Passing chords
(V_3^4 and VII^6)

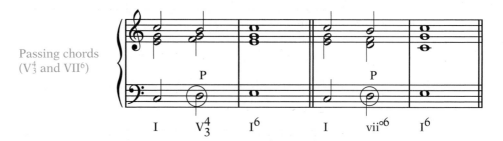

The first inversion of the dominant or dominant seventh chords (V^6 and V_5^6) is often used as a *neighboring chord* to connect two statements of I. The leading-tone in the bass acts as a *neighboring note:* the bass of the I chord moves down a step to the bass of V^6 or V_5^6, then right back to its starting point.

Neighboring chords
(V^6 and V_5^6)

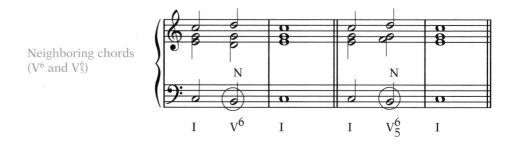

In a somewhat different sense, the subdominant triad (IV) can also function as a neighboring chord to I. The common progression I–IV–I prolongs the tonic harmony and the IV chord frequently supports a melodic neighboring note, either $\hat{3}$–$\hat{4}$–$\hat{3}$ or $\hat{5}$–$\hat{6}$–$\hat{5}$.

Neighboring
chord (IV)

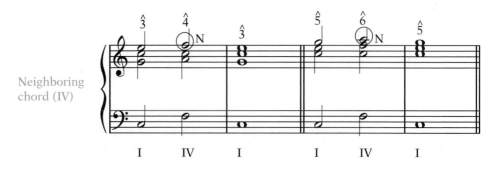

So far all of the passing and neighboring chords we have discussed are used to embellish or prolong tonic harmony. But the dominant can also be embellished. One particularly common kind of embellishment involves preceding the third and fifth of the dominant triad with their upper neighbors. This produces a chord that looks like the second inversion of a tonic triad (I_4^6) but functions as an embellishment of the dominant. This is called the *cadential $_4^6$* because it frequently occurs at cadences.

Cadential $_4^6$

Lesson 33: In-class activities

1. Singing. Sing these melodies, which elaborate a tonic triad with passing and neighboring notes. Identify all nonharmonic tones as either passing or neighboring. Transpose to other keys.

2. Singing. Sing these melodies, which elaborate tonic and dominant harmonies. Identify all nonharmonic tones (circled on the music) as passing or neighboring.

a. Joplin, "The Entertainer" (some of the embellishing notes are *diatonic*—they use notes within the scale—and some are *chromatic*—they use notes with sharps or flats that lie outside the scale).

b. Mozart, "Dove sono" (the first, second, and fourth dominant chords are embellished with an accented passing note. The third dominant chord includes a seventh [F]).

c. Rodriguez, "La Cumparsita" (a melodic figure that contains both upper and lower neighbors is called a *double neighbor*).

d. Haydn, Quartet (here is another double neighbor, but the second one is incomplete).

e. Schubert, "Death and the Maiden" (the first two measures span the interval of a third, D–F, within the tonic harmony. The third measure also spans a third, but within the dominant harmony, E–C♯).

f. Chopin, Prelude in A Major (the D in parentheses in the first measure is a neighbor to C♯, which is itself a neighbor to B).

3. Singing. Sing these melodies, which arpeggiate progressions that contain passing or neighboring chords.

4. Singing. Sing these duets with one student or group of students on a part. Then switch parts. Identify the circled notes as passing or neighboring. Notice that dissonant intervals occur only on the second beat of the measure and only as passing or neighboring notes; the note on the first beat is always consonant.

a.

b.

c.

5. Singing. Sing these duets. They involve neighboring and passing harmonies—try to identify them. After you have sung, compare the duets
to the music from which they are adapted.

a. Lang, Song, mm. 1–4 (adapted)

b. Mendelssohn, Piano Trio, mm. 1–3 (adapted)

6. Singing. Sing these two passages as a vocal quartet. Only tonic and
dominant harmonies are used; identify all nonharmonic notes as
either passing or neighboring.

a. Schubert, "Death and the Maiden," mm. 1–8 (this passage is the
piano introduction to the song. It sounds like a dirge in d minor
and it represents the character of Death).

b. Schubert, "Death and the Maiden," mm. 37–43 (this passage is the piano postlude to the song. It takes the music from the beginning and shifts it from d minor to D major. Death has triumphed).

7. Dictation. The instructor will play these short progressions in a random order within each group. Identify the progression. The progressions in Group 1 involve passing and neighboring notes; the progressions in Group 2 involve passing and neighboring harmonies.

Group 1

Group 2

8. Playing. Play these progressions that elaborate tonic and dominant harmonies with passing or neighboring notes. Transpose to other keys.

9. Playing. Play these progressions, which involve passing or neighboring harmonies. Transpose to other keys.

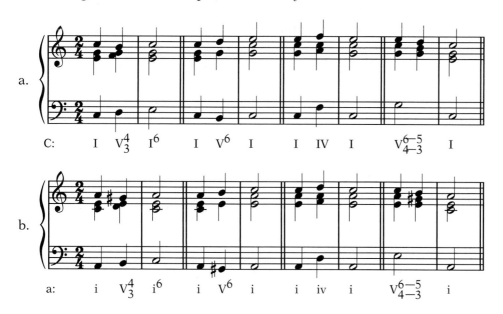

10. Playing. Improvise short melodies with your right hand while playing these chords with your left. Try to play steadily with a definite rhythm. The melodies you play will use the tones of the chords, and embellish those tones with passing and neighboring notes. If you wish, you may sing rather than play your melody.

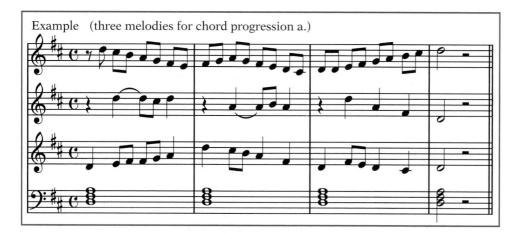

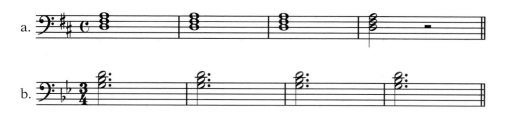

Name: _____

Date: _____

Instructor's Name: _____

Lesson 33: Exercises

33-1. Compose duets by completing a melody above the given melody. On the second half of each measure, add a half-note that is passing note or a neighboring note. Play each duet at the piano before handing it in—be sure it sounds the way you want it to. Be prepared to sing both the melody you are given and the melody you have written in class.

33-2. Identify the circled notes as passing or neighboring by writing P or
N directly above each note (some are done for you). Remember
that a passing note connects two harmonic tones that lie a third
apart (it involves two steps in the same direction) while a neighbor
tone departs from and/or returns to a single note.

a. Mozart, Sonata (for most of the passage, the bass and soprano
move together in parallel motion).

b. Haydn, Quartet (accented, incomplete lower neighbor notes are
featured first as part of the descending line in the highest voice
and then in the ascending line in the lowest voice).

c. Arlen, "Over the Rainbow" (the prevailing harmony is E♭ major—
only one note does not belong).

Where troub-les melt like lem-on drops, a-

Name: _____

Date: _____

Instructor's Name: _____

d. Schubert, "Death and the Maiden" (there is only one harmony in each measure—the notes that don't belong to the harmony are neighboring or passing notes. The double-neighbor figure is used in measures 1 and 5).

e. Mozart, Sonata (the bass line arpeggiates the harmony—either tonic or dominant. The melody embellishes those harmonies with passing and neighboring notes, including the double-neighbor figure).

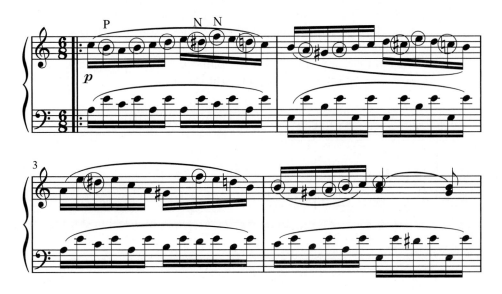

f. Handy, "St. Louis Blues" (in measure 2, the passing note C♯ connects the harmony tone C with its upper neighbor D. The key signature tells us this piece as a whole is in G major, but this passage is in g minor).

33-3. Compose a melody for each of these chord progressions (involving tonic and dominant only). The melodies you write will use the tones of the chords, and embellish those tones with passing and neighboring notes. See In-class activity 33-10 for some examples. Play your compositions on the piano before handing them in—be sure they sound the way you want them to.

Name: _____

Date: _____

Instructor's Name: _____

33-4. Harmonize these melodies by adding three-note chords in the bass
clef (tonic and dominant only). Some chords are provided for you.
Begin by singing the melody several times to get familiar with it.
Try to figure out what harmonies it suggests and which of its notes
are nonharmonic tones.

a. Arlen, "Over the Rainbow"

If hap-py lit-tle blue-birds fly be - yond the rain-bow, why oh why can't I?

b. Chopin, Prelude in A Major

c. Haydn, Quartet (adapted)

d. Joplin, "The Entertainer"

e. Mendelssohn, Piano Trio

f. Rodriguez, "La Cumparsita"

Name: _____

Date: _____

Instructor's Name: _____

g. Schubert, "Death and the Maiden"

33-5. Use Roman numerals and figured-bass numbers to identify har-
        monies. They are either passing harmonies (like V^4_3 and vii°⁶) or
        neighboring harmonies (like V⁶, V^6_5, or IV).

a. Handy, "St. Louis Blues" (both the tonic harmony and the
    neighboring harmony that prolongs it are heavily embellished
    with passing and neighboring notes).

I hate to see _   de ev'-nin' sun go   down _____

b. Haydn, Quartet (the tonic is elaborated by a neighboring harmony. Despite the key signature, this passage is in A major).

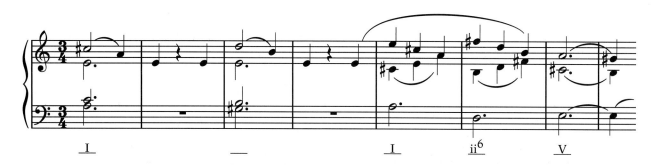

c. Mendelssohn, Piano Trio (the tonic harmony at the beginning and end of the passage is prolonged by neighboring harmonies that involve both an upper neighbor [E] and a lower neighbor [C♯] in the bass).

d. Lang, Song (a passing chord connects I with I⁶).

Name: _____

Date: _____

Instructor's Name: _____

e. Schubert, "Death and the Maiden" (the passing chord that connects I with I⁶ is actually a seventh chord, not a triad. Its root is C♯—ignore the seventh [B♭] in labeling it).

33-6. Harmonize these melodies by adding three lower voices. The notes of the melody you are given should be the highest in each chord. Roman numerals and some bass notes are provided. Play your compositions before handing them in—be sure they sound the way you want them to. When you have finished, compare your work to the passages from which these melodies are adapted.

a. Schubert, "Death and the Maiden," mm. 18–19

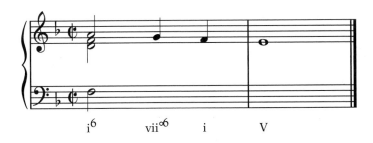

b. Mozart, Sonata, mm. 1–4

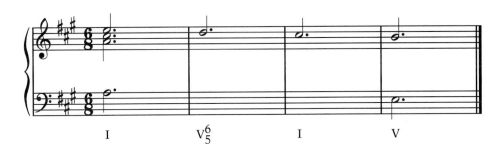

c. Lang, Song, mm. 1–3

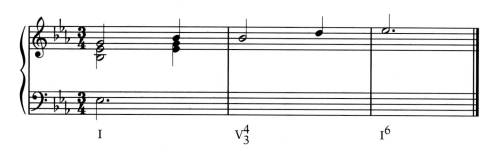

d. Handy, "St. Louis Blues"

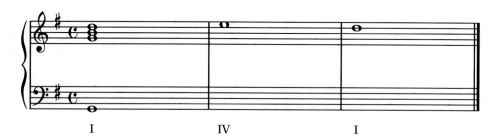

e. Mendelssohn, Piano Trio, mm. 1–5

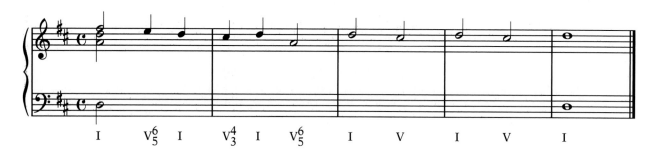

Lesson 34: Approaching V

In this lesson you will learn about dominant preparation chords (ii and IV).

Just as the dominant leads to the tonic, there are harmonies that lead to the dominant. Chords like these are called *dominant preparation* or *predominant* chords, and the most important are ii and IV.

In the progression from ii to V, the bass moves up by fourth or down by fifth. That is a very strong kind of harmonic motion, imitating the motion from V to I. (Note that ii in root position rarely occurs in minor keys because composers generally avoid writing diminished triads in root position.)

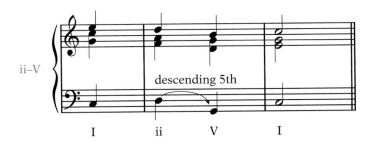

In first inversion, ii⁶ works well in major and minor. Its bass note is scale-degree $\hat{4}$, which moves smoothly by step as ii⁶ progresses to V.

IV has the same bass note as ii⁶, and when it moves to V, its bass also moves smoothly by step. Like ii⁶, IV acts as a neighboring chord to V, approaching it from a step below.

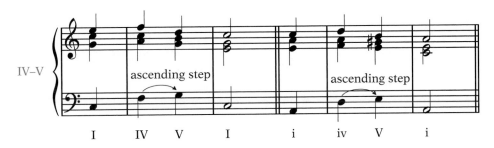

IV thus has two different roles: sometimes it leads to I (discussed in Lesson 33) and sometimes it leads to V (as a dominant preparation chord). Dominant preparation chords (ii, ii^6, and IV) can also lead to V^6 or to the dominant seventh chord in any of its positions.

Here is a simple way of realizing the progression I–IV–V^7–I that makes it particularly easy to play at the keyboard.

Keyboard realization

I   IV   V^7 I   i   iv   V^7 i

In this arrangement, the progression can be played with the left hand alone, and used to harmonize melodies played by the right hand or sung.

Lesson 34: In-class activities

1. Singing. Sing these melodies, which arpeggiate progressions involving dominant preparation chords. Identify the harmonies. Transpose to other keys.

2. Singing. Sing these four-part chorales, with one student or group of students to a part. Identify the harmonies.

a. Bach, Chorale (here are two different harmonizations of the same melody—it is the last phrase of the chorale).

a.

b.

b. Mozart, "Dove sono," mm. 1–8 (after you have sung this vocal quartet, compare it to the passage from which it is adapted).

c. Haydn, Quartet, mm. 77–92 (after you have sung this vocal quartet, compare it to the passage from which it is adapted).

3. Dictation. The instructor will play four-chord progressions in a random order within each group. Some involve dominant preparation chords and some do not. Identify the progression.

4. Playing. Play these progressions. Transpose to other keys.

5. Playing. Harmonize these short melodies by adding three lower voices.

6. Playing. Improvise melodies with your right hand while playing these chords with your left. Try to play steadily with a definite rhythm. The melodies you play will use the tones of the chords, and embellish those tones with passing and neighboring notes. See In-class activity 33-10 for examples. You may wish to sing rather than play your melody.

Name: _____

Date: _____

Instructor's Name: _____

Lesson 34: Exercises

34-1. Harmonize these melodies by adding three lower voices. The notes of the melody you are given should be the highest in each chord. Roman numerals and some bass notes are provided. Play your compositions before handing them in—be sure they sound the way you want them to. When you have finished, compare your work to the passages from which these melodies are adapted.

a. Handy, "St. Louis Blues," mm. 1–7 (many other passages use a similar melodic and harmonic framework).

b. Mozart, Sonata, mm. 17–18

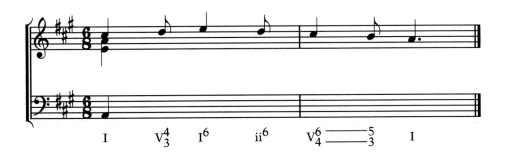

c. Chopin, Prelude in A Major (adapted).

d. Chopin, Prelude in c minor, m. 1 (the F after the third beat is a passing note).

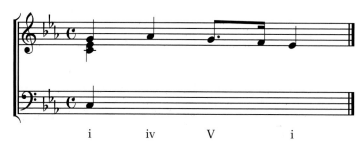

i   iv   V   i

e. Haydn, Quartet, mm. 2–5 (adapted. The F in measure 3 is a passing note).

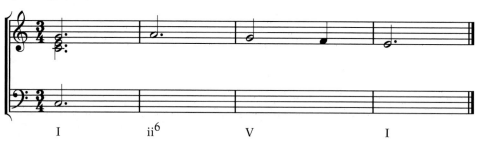

I   ii⁶   V   I

34-2. Use Roman numerals to identify the harmonies in these works.

a. Schumann, Song (this phrase moves from an initial tonic to a concluding dominant, which is preceded by a dominant preparation chord).

Wenn ich in dei - ne Au - gen seh',   so   schwin-det all' mein Leid und   Weh;
When I in - to your eyes ___ look,   then   fades ___ all my pain and sorrow;

b. Bach, Chorale (in the sixth and seventh chords, the alto voice has an accented dissonance—ignore those notes in your identification of the chords).

Name: _____

Date: _____

Instructor's Name: _____

c. Haydn, Quartet (the fourth chord represents an arrival on the tonic, but it is embellished by accented neighbor notes in both soprano [first violin] and tenor [viola]).

d. Schubert, "Heidenröslein" (on the first beat of the fourth and sixth measures, the dominant is embellished by the cadential $^6_4$).

e. Mozart, "Dove sono" (this passage has a noble simplicity—it uses the simplest harmonies and only the seven notes of the C major scale).

(continued)

di _ pia - cer, ___ do - ve an-da - ro i giu - ra - men _ ti,
end _ could _ know; ___ I re - mem - ber fond vows and fer - vent–

di quel _ lab-bro men-zo - gner, di quel lab - bro _ men - zo - gner.
All were _ bro-ken _ long a - go, _ all were bro - ken _ long a - go.

f. Mendelssohn, Piano Trio (the last four measures of the piece are
all tonic—but the tonic is extensively embellished with neighbor
and passing notes, and with one neighboring chord).

Name: _____

Date: _____

Instructor's Name: _____

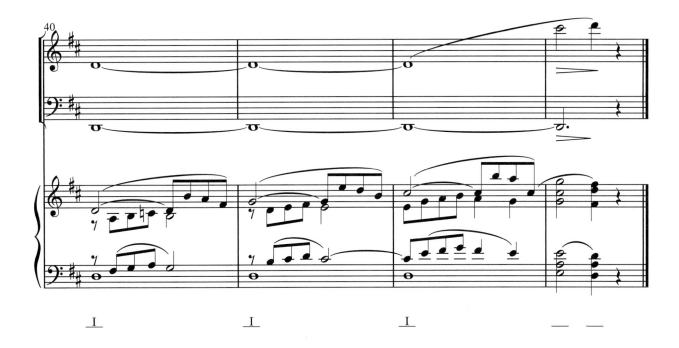

g. Handy, "St. Louis Blues" (in this piece, the subdominant is often used as a neighboring chord to prolong tonic, but in the second measure of this passage, it is a dominant preparation chord).

St. Lou-is wo-man ___ Wid her dia - mon' rings _____ Pulls _ dat

(continued)

man roun'_____   by her a-pron   strings_____

h. Mozart, "Dove sono" (V usually resolves to I, but in this passage
   it is often diverted to vi instead as a way of building tension and
   anticipation for the final blazing tonic arrival).

Name: _____

Date: _____

Instructor's Name: _____

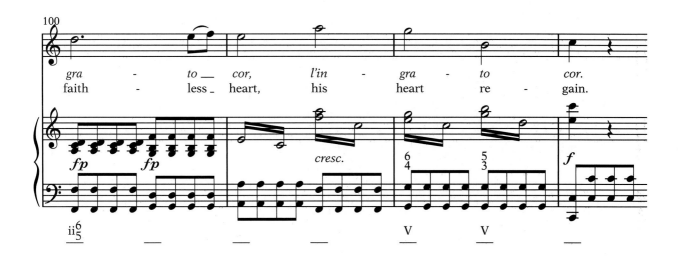

i. Joplin, "The Entertainer" (there are only three harmonies in this passage, with the second acting as a neighbor to the third).

34-3. Compose a melody for each of these chord progressions (involving I, IV, and V^7 only). The melodies you write will use the tones of the chords, and embellish those tones with passing and neighboring notes. Play your compositions on the piano before handing them in—be sure they sound the way you want them to. See In-class activity 33-10 for examples.

a.

Lesson 35: Phrase and cadence

In this lesson you will learn about phrase, authentic cadence, half cadence, period (antecedent and consequent), and plagal cadence.

A *phrase* in music is like a sentence in language: a self-contained utterance with a beginning, middle, and end. Phrases in music are groups of measures, often groups of two, four, or eight measures. Like sentences, musical phrases end with a form of punctuation—in language the punctuation is a period; in music it is called a cadence.

There are two principal types of cadences: *authentic cadences* and *half cadences*. An authentic cadence involves a progression from dominant to tonic (V–I), providing a strong sense of arrival on the tonic at the end of a phrase. The V–I progression can occur anywhere in a phrase; only when it occurs at the end of a phrase is it called an authentic cadence. Musical phrases vary considerably in length and content, but a particularly common arrangement is a four-measure phrase that begins on the tonic and ends with an authentic cadence.

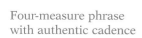

Four-measure phrase with authentic cadence

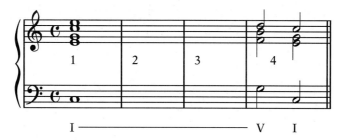

Here are five different realizations of that prototype:

a. Joplin, "The Entertainer"

b. Lang, Song

Ob ich manch-mal dein Ge - den - ke?   wüsst est Du   wie sehr ich's thu!
Do I some - times think of   you? _____   *If   on - ly   you knew how much!*

c. Ellington, "It Don't Mean a Thing"

d. Haydn, Quartet

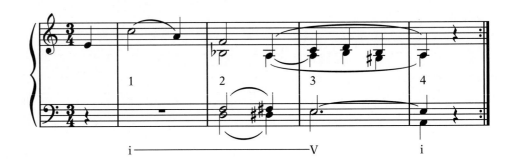

e. Chopin, Prelude in c minor

The second principal type of cadence is the *half cadence,* which involves an arrival on the dominant (V). Because the dominant has a more tense, unresolved quality than the tonic, a half-cadence does not sound like a definitive ending, more like a temporary pause in the musical flow (more like a comma or even a question mark than a period). A common arrangement is a four-measure phrase that begins on the tonic and ends on the dominant.

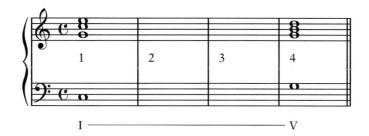

Four-measure phrase
with half cadence

Here are three realizations of that prototype.

a. Schumann, Song

Wenn ich in dei - ne Au - gen seh',   so   schwin-det all' mein Leid und   Weh;
When I in - to your eyes ___ look,   then   fades ___ all my pain and   sorrow;

b. Mozart, Sonata

c. Ellington, "It Don't Mean a Thing"

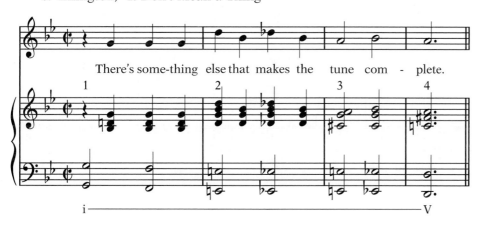

There's some-thing else that makes the tune com - plete.

Longer phrases are created by combining shorter ones. An eight-measure phrase, for example, might result from a combination of two four-measure phrases, and might combine with another eight-measure phrase to create a sixteen-measure phrase—these larger combinations are called *periods*. A particularly common arrangement involves one phrase that ends with a half cadence followed by another that ends on the tonic. When these two balanced phrases begin in the same way, the first is called an *antecedent* and the second is called a *consequent,* while their combination is called a *parallel period.* Here are two parallel periods:

a. Mozart, Sonata

b. Haydn, Quartet

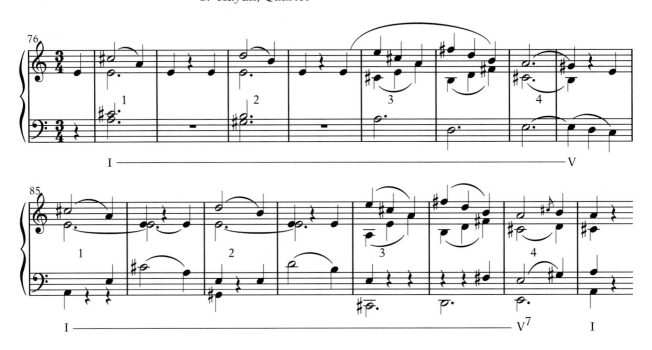

There is one additional type of cadence that occurs from time to time, although not nearly as often as the authentic and half cadences. The *plagal* cadence involves a progression from subdominant to tonic (IV–I). The sub-dominant has none of the strong pull toward the tonic that the dominant has. As a result, the plagal cadence is weaker than the authentic cadence and, in fact, usually occurs after an authentic cadence as a kind of extra confirmation. Here is one example:

Schumann, Song

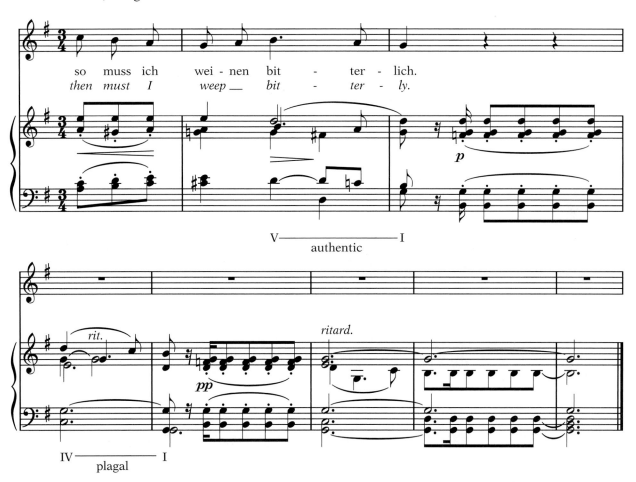

Lesson 35: In-class activities

1. Singing. Sing the following melodies and identify the type of cadence, marked with an arrow (authentic or half). Authentic cadences usual-ly end with scale-degree $\hat{1}$ in the melody, or occasionally with scale-degree $\hat{3}$ (over the tonic harmony). Half cadences usually have scale-degree $\hat{2}$ in the melody, or occasionally scale-degree $\hat{5}$ or $\hat{7}$ (over the dominant harmony).

a. Arlen, "Over the Rainbow"

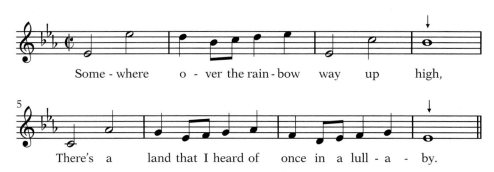

Some - where   o - ver the rain - bow   way   up   high,

There's   a   land that I heard of   once in a lull - a   -   by.

b. Ellington, "It Don't Mean a Thing"

There's some-thing else that makes the   tune com - plete.

c. Ellington, "It Don't Mean a Thing"

It   don't mean a   thing, if   it   ain't got that swing. _

d. Haydn, Quartet (this is a parallel period).

e. Haydn, Quartet

f. Joplin, "The Entertainer"

g. Mozart, Sonata (this is a parallel period).

h. Mozart, "Dove sono" (this is a parallel period, with the second phrase stretched out to ten measures compared to the eight measures of the first phrase).

i. Schubert, "Death and the Maiden"

2. Dictation. The instructor will play four-chord progressions in a random order within each group. Identify the progression you hear and describe the type of cadence with which it ends (authentic, half, or plagal).

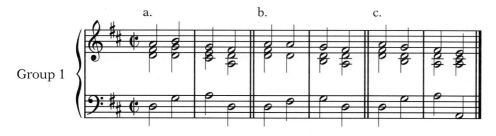

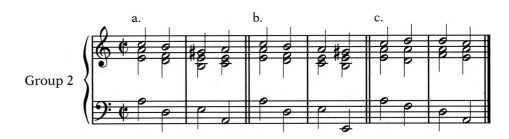

Group 2

3. Playing. Improvise melodies with your right hand while playing these chords with your left. Try to play steadily with a definite rhythm. The melodies you play will use the tones of the chords, and embellish those tones with passing and neighboring notes. See In-class activity 33-10 for examples. You may wish to sing rather than play your melody.

a. Four-measure phrase ending with an authentic cadence.

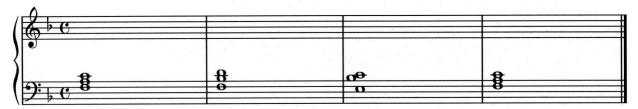

b. Four-measure phrase ending with a half cadence.

c. Parallel period (your melody for measures 1–2 should be the same as for measures 5–6).

Name: _____

Date: _____

Instructor's Name: _____

Lesson 35: Exercises

35-1. In the following passages, cadences are marked with an arrow. Identify them as authentic or half cadences.

a. Arlen, "Over the Rainbow"

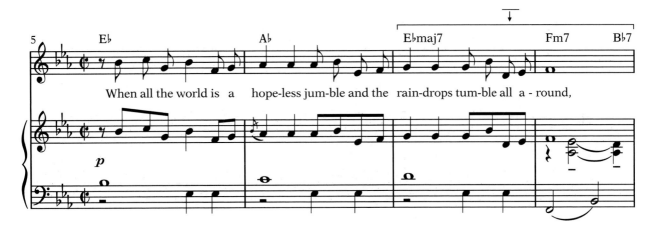

b. Handy, "St. Louis Blues"

(continued)

De — man I love — would not gone no - where. _____

c. Mozart, Sonata (the piece is divided into four-measure phrases, each punctuated with a cadence, and with two extra measures tacked on at the end).

Name: _____

Date: _____

Instructor's Name: _____

d. Rodriguez, "La Cumparsita"

e. Joplin, "The Entertainer"

f. Schubert, "Death and the Maiden"

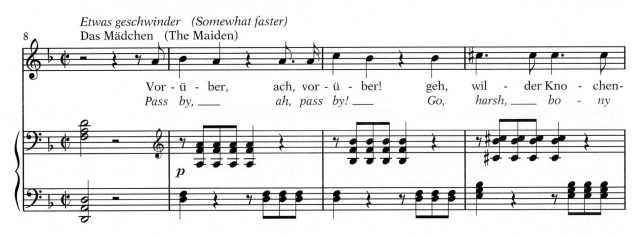

Etwas geschwinder   (Somewhat faster)
Das Mädchen   (The Maiden)

Vor - ü - ber,   ach, vor - ü - ber!   geh,   wil - der Kno - chen-
Pass by, ___   ah, pass by! ___   Go,   harsh, ___ bo - ny

(continued)

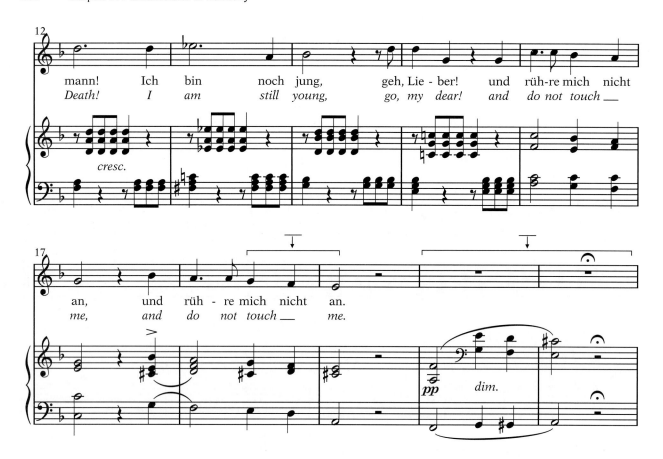

35-2. Compose a melody for each of these chord progressions (involving authentic and half-cadences). The melodies you write will use the tones of the chords in the left hand, and embellish those tones with passing and neighboring notes. Play your compositions on the piano before handing them in—be sure they sound the way you want them to. See In-class activity 33-10 for examples.

a. Four-measure phrase ending with an authentic cadence.

b. Four-measure phrase ending with a half-cadence.

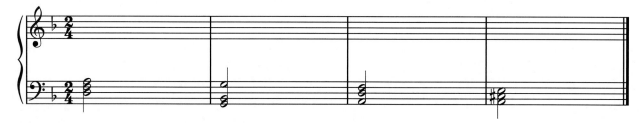

Name: _____

Date: _____

Instructor's Name: _____

c. Parallel period (your melody for measures 1–2 should be the
same as for measures 5–6).

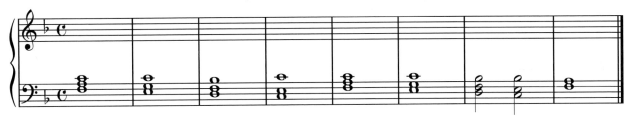

Chapter 6: Supplementary lesson

In this lesson you will learn about doubling, voice leading, smoothness, tendency tones, resolution of the seventh, and parallel fifths and octaves.

Triads have only three different notes, but composers often write chords that have four or more notes. As a result, one or more notes of the triad must be *doubled* (i.e., played more than once in the chord). Any note may be doubled with one important exception: Tones that have a strong tendency to resolve in a particular way (*tendency tones*) are not doubled. The *leading-tone*, which occurs as the third of the dominant chord, is such a tendency tone and should not be doubled.

Bass
doubled
(good)

Leading-tone
doubled
(problematic)

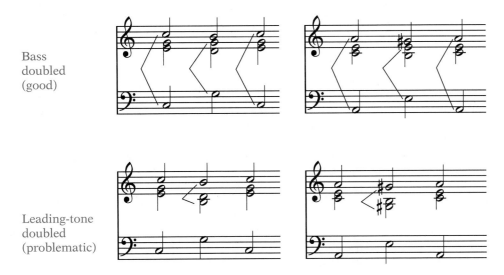

The notes of a chord are sometimes called voices: the highest note is the soprano, the second highest is the alto, the third highest is the tenor, and the lowest is the bass. The movement of the voices from chord to chord is called *voice-leading*. The bass voice often leaps, but the voice leading for the upper three voices is generally *smooth*, with each voice moving by small intervals (usually unisons, seconds, or thirds) to the nearest available position in the next chord.

Smooth
voice leading
(good)

Unsmooth
voice-leading
(problematic)

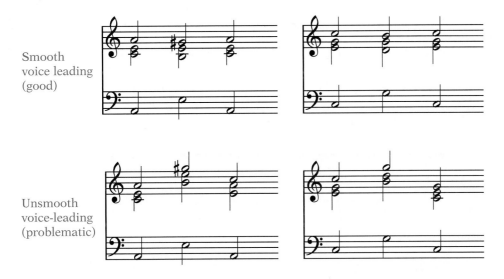

If two voices are an octave apart in one chord, they should not be an octave apart in the next chord. That is called *parallel octaves*, because the two voices are moving in *parallel motion* (in the same direction by the same interval). *Parallel fifths* are similarly avoided. This preference for avoiding parallel perfect consonances is deeply characteristic of classical music, much less so of popular styles.

Parallel fifths and octaves (avoided by classical composers)

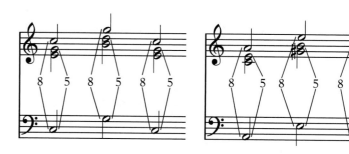

There are two important conventions governing the treatment of the seventh in seventh chords such as V⁷. First, the seventh is a dissonance and thus has a strong tendency to resolve to a consonance. Normally, dissonances resolve downward by step. In this case, the seventh of the V⁷ chord is scale-degree $\hat{4}$—when the V⁷ chord moves to I, scale-degree $\hat{4}$ moves down to scale-degree $\hat{3}$ within the tonic chord.

Resolving the seventh (down by step)

Second, because the seventh has such a strong tendency to resolve, it should not be doubled. In this way, it is just like another tendency tone, the leading-tone.

Anthology

Harold Arlen, "Over the Rainbow" (lyrics by E. Y. Harburg)

Harold Arlen (1905–86) was one of a generation of composers (including Jerome Kern, Irving Berlin, Richard Rodgers, and Cole Porter) responsible for a "Golden Age" in American popular song during the second quarter of the twentieth century. He wrote songs for Broadway musicals and Hollywood films, and many have become standards. "Over the Rainbow" was written for the film *The Wizard of Oz*. In it, the character Dorothy (played by Judy Garland in the film), sings of her longing to escape drought-parched Kansas during the Great Depression to a land where "dreams really do come true." The music is performed in many different ways, but it is presented here as Arlen wrote it, for voice and piano with chord symbols.

Over the Rainbow

Lyrics by
E. Y. Harburg

Music by
Harold Arlen

(continued)

(continued)

57
Eb
2.

I?   If

rall.

62
Eb   Fm7   Bb7   Eb6

hap-py lit-tle blue-birds fly be-yond the rain-bow, why oh why can't I?

rit.   pp   l.h.   ten.

Johann Sebastian Bach, Two Fugues from *The Well-Tempered Clavier*, Volume 1 (No. 15 in G Major and No. 16 in g minor)

J. S. Bach (1685–1750) is a dominant figure in the history of Western classical music. He wrote hundreds of works for voices and instruments in countless combinations. His *Well-Tempered Clavier*, Volume 1, was written in 1722 and consists of twenty-four Preludes and Fugues in all the major and minor keys (Volume 2, written later, follows the same plan). It was written for the harpsichord, but sounds good on any keyboard instrument. The Fugue in G Major is written for three voices—that is, three distinct musical lines—while the Fugue in g minor is written for four voices.

Fugue No. 15 in G Major

Johann Sebastian Bach

(continued)

(continued)

Fugue No. 16 in g minor

Johann Sebastian Bach

(continued)

Johann Sebastian Bach, Two chorales from the *St. Matthew Passion*

Amid the dramatic action of Bach's *St. Matthew Passion* (completed in 1729), the chorus pauses from time to time to sing contemplative chorales—these are hymns for four voices: soprano, alto, tenor, and bass. Five chorales in the *St. Matthew Passion* use a melody composed many years earlier by a composer named Hans Leo Hassler. Each of Bach's harmonizations of this melody is different in interesting ways. Two of the chorales are given here, each in two formats. Version A presents the chorale much as it appears in Bach's original score, with each vocal part on a separate staff. Instruments accompany each part. Beneath the score, there is a figured bass—this is the bass line of the chorale with numbered instructions to a keyboard player for producing appropriate chords. Version B gives the chorale in a compact format with soprano and alto sharing the treble clef and tenor and bass sharing the bass clef, and with an English translation suitable for singing.

Chorale No. 1 from the *St. Matthew Passion*

Johann Sebastain Bach

(continued)

blas - sen im letz-ten To - des - stoß, als - denn will ich dich fas - sen in mei - nen Arm und Schoß.

blas - sen im letz-ten To - des - stoß, als - denn will ich dich fas - sen in mei - nen Arm und Schoß.

blas - sen im letz-ten To - des - stoß, als - denn will ich dich fas - sen in mei - nen Arm und Schoß.

blas - sen im letz-ten To - des - stoß, als - denn will ich dich fas - sen in mei - nen Arm und Schoß.

B)

Be - side Thee, Lord, I've tak - en My place for - bid me not! If pain's last pale-ness
Hence will I ne'er be shak - en Though Thou to death be brought.

hold Thee, In ag-o - ny op - pressed, Then, then will I en - fold Thee With - in this arm and breast.

Chorale No. 2 from the *St. Matthew Passion*

Johann Sebastian Bach

(continued)

B)

Com-mit thy ways, O   pil - grim On   time's dark, storm-y   seas,   Who   mea-sures out their
To   Him who or - ders   all   things Through sweet e - ter - ni - ties,

cours - es To clouds, winds, waves be - low; He   too will find   a   path - way Where-in   thy feet   may go.

Frederic Chopin, Two Preludes from Opus 28 (No. 7 in A Major and No. 20 in c minor)

Frederic Chopin (1810–49) wrote extensively for the piano. His Preludes (completed in 1839) are a set of twenty-four short piano pieces, one in each of the twelve major and twelve minor keys. In its systematic exploration of all the keys, it recalls *The Well-Tempered Clavier* of J. S. Bach. The composer and pianist Franz Liszt commented on these Preludes: "They are compositions of an order entirely apart: they are not merely, as the title would indicate, introductions to other pieces. Rather, they are themselves poetry. Everything in them seems fresh, elastic, created at the impulse of the moment, abounding with that freedom of expression which is characteristic of works of genius." Each of the Preludes has a distinctive character. The Prelude in A Major sounds like a gentle waltz, while the Prelude in c minor sounds like a funeral march.

Prelude No. 7 in A Major

Frederic Chopin

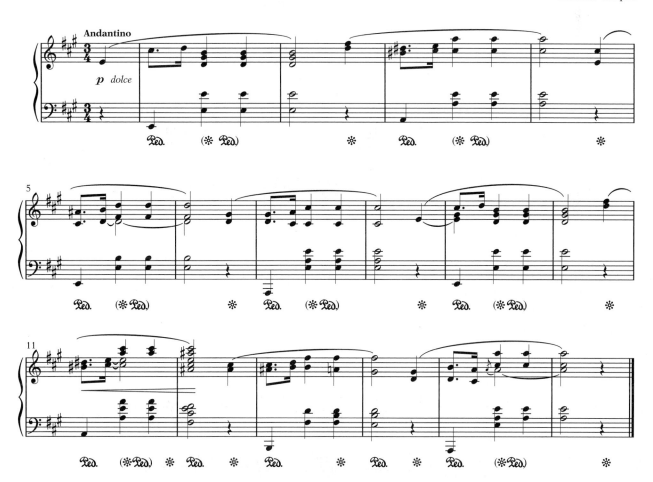

Prelude No. 20 in c minor

Frederic Chopin

Edward Kennedy ("Duke") Ellington, "It Don't Mean a Thing (If It Ain't Got That Swing)" (lyrics by Irving Mills)

Duke Ellington (1899–1974) is perhaps the most important composer in jazz history. He wrote roughly two thousand works, including hundreds of short instrumental pieces and popular songs. "It Don't Mean a Thing" dates from 1932, toward the beginning of Ellington's most fertile creative period. It was written for and first performed and recorded by Ellington's own big band. This is the original sheet music for voice and piano (with chord symbols).

It Don't Mean a Thing (If It Ain't Got That Swing)

Lyrics by
Irving Mills

Music by
Edward Kennedy ("Duke") Ellington

(continued)

William Christopher (W. C.) Handy, "St. Louis Blues"

W. C. Handy (1873–1958) is sometimes called the "Father of the Blues." He played a major role in the early popularization and wide dissemination of the blues throughout America and abroad. His early involvement with African-American folk music, especially the newly emerging blues in the Mississippi Delta and Memphis, strongly shaped his own later career as a composer, arranger, and performer. He wrote the "St. Louis Blues," probably his best-known piece, in 1914.

St. Louis Blues

William Christopher (W. C.) Handy

17

(continued)

(continued)

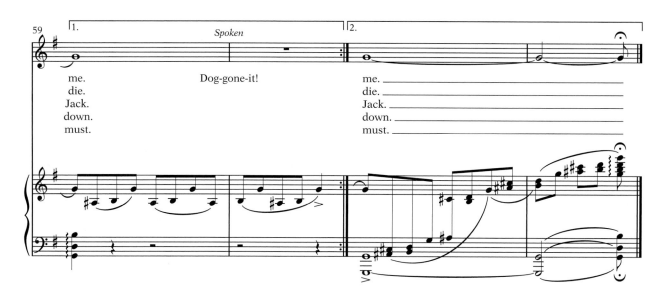

Franz Joseph Haydn, String Quartet, Op. 76, No. 3, third movement (Minuet)

Franz Joseph Haydn (1732–1809) was an amazingly prolific and influential composer, a mentor of Mozart, and a teacher of Beethoven. He is known as the "Father of the String Quartet" because he was the first to write a large number of works for a small ensemble of two violins, viola, and cello. His Opus 76 is a set of six quartets, and the third movement of the third quartet is a Minuet (a stately dance in ¾ time). In the published score, each instrument has its own staff (with the viola playing in alto clef), but it is presented here in an arrangement on a single great staff: the violins share the top line and the viola and cello share the bottom.

String Quartet, Opus 76, No.3, third movement (Minuet)

Franz Joseph Haydn

(continued)

Scott Joplin, "The Entertainer"

Scott Joplin (1867 or 1868–1917) is the preeminent composer of piano rag-time. Joplin tried to effect a fusion of popular ragtime with classical harmony and form. The result was what he called "classic rags." He wrote "The Entertainer" in 1902.

The Entertainer

Scott Joplin

(continued)

Josephine Lang, "Ob ich manchmal dein Gedenke (Do I Sometimes Think of You)" (text by Christian Reinhold Koestlin)

Josephine Lang (1815–80) was an important composer of German art songs (*Lieder*). Felix Mendelssohn praised her "divine genius" and commented: "She has the gift of composing songs and singing them as I have never heard before; it is the most complete musical joy I have ever experienced." She wrote about 150 songs, mostly during the 1830s and 1840s. The song included here was written in 1841 and its poetic text is an ecstatic outpouring of romantic love.

Ob ich manchmal dein Gedenke
(Do I Sometimes Think of You)

Text by
Christian Reinhold Koestlin

Music by
Josephine Lang

nicht ___ Du ___ seit dem wir uns ge-fun - den bist's al-lein was aus mir

spricht ___ Al - les An - dre seh ich schwan - ken um mich

her wie Traum und Schein! Dein _ ge - den - ken ist ___ mein Le - ben!

Dich zu lie - ben ist mein sein! ___ Dich zu lie - ben

(continued)

ist _____ mein sein!

Ob ich manchmal dein Gedenke?
wüsst est Du wie sehr ich's thu!
Dir auch noch die Schatten lenken träumender Gedanken zu.
Tag und Nacht, und alle Stunden,
o, dies Alles sagt es nicht
Du seit dem wir uns gefunden
  bist's allein was aus mir spricht
Alles Andre seh ich schwanken um
  mich her wie Traum und Schein!
Dein gedenken ist mein Leben!
Dich zu lieben ist mein sein!
Dich zu lieben ist mein sein!

Do I sometimes think of you?
If only you knew how much!
Directed to you are the shadows of dreaming thoughts.
Day and night, and at all hours,
oh, I can't express it.
You, since we found each other
  are the only one of whom I speak
All else I see swaying around
  me like dream and illusion!
To think of you is my life!
To love you is my existence!
To love you is my existence!

Fanny Mendelssohn, Trio for Piano, Violin, and Cello, Op. 11, second movement

Fanny Mendelssohn (1805–47) wrote a large body of works, mostly songs and short piano pieces, but including cantatas and orchestral works. Many remain unpublished even today, but the increasing availability of her music has begun to suggest its quality and range. Her Trio for Piano, Violin, and Cello, written in 1846, is one of her finest works.

Lied
(Song)

Fanny Mendelssohn

(continued)

(continued)

Wolfgang Amadeus Mozart, Piano Sonata in A Major, K. 331, first movement (Theme and Variations 1, 3, and 6)

Wolfgang Amadeus Mozart (1756–91) managed in his extremely short life to write an astonishing number of masterpieces of every kind, including symphonies, operas, concertos, string quartets, and sonatas. The Piano Sonata in A Major, the eleventh of eighteen piano sonatas, dates from 1778. Its first movement is a theme with six variations, three of which are included here.

**Piano Sonata in A Major, K. 331, first movement
(Theme and Variations 1, 3, and 6)**

Wolfgang Amadeus Mozart

(continued)

(continued)

VAR. VI
Allegro

Wolfgang Amadeus Mozart, "Dove sono (I Remember)" from *The Marriage of Figaro* (libretto by Lorenzo da Ponte)

Mozart's opera *The Marriage of Figaro* was first performed in 1786. Classical opera consists of arias (songs for a solo voice) and ensembles (vocal duets, trios, quartets, etc.) connected by a kind of singing speech called recitative. In the aria reprinted here, the Countess first sings regretfully of her husband's loss of affection for her, then hopefully that she might regain his "faithless heart." The music is presented in *piano-vocal score,* with the orchestral parts arranged for piano.

**Dove sono
(I Remember)
from *The Marriage of Figaro***

Wolfgang Amadeus Mozart

(continued)

la __ me - mo - ria di quel ben   non tra - pas - sò.
those __ hap-py mo - ments in my hour   of __ pain __   re - call.

Do - ve so - no i bei   mo - men __ ti   di   dol -
I   re - mem - ber days long   de - part - ed, Days   when

cez - za   e   di __ pia - cer; _____   Do - ve an-da - ro   i
love __   no end __ could __ know; _____   I   re - mem - ber fond

giu - ra - mèn - ti   di   quel lab - bro __ men - zo - gner! _
vows   and fer - vent All   were __ bro - ken __ long a - go. __

sf

(continued)

(continued)

gra - to   cor.
heart   re - gain.

Matos Rodriguez, "La Cumparsita (The Little Carnival Parade)"

The tango has its roots in the poor slum areas of nineteenth-century Buenos Aires in Argentina and has since become the most popular Argentine dance of the twentieth century. Matos Rodriguez (1897–1948) wrote "La Cumparsita (The Little Carnival Parade)" in 1916 as a marching song for the Federation of Students in Uruguay, of which he was a member. The song was later arranged as a tango by the composer and bandleader Roberto Firpo, and is probably the most famous tango ever written. It has since been rearranged countless times, but is provided here in the form in which it was first published, for piano and violin.

**La Cumparsita
(The Little Carnival Parade)**

Matos Rodriguez

(continued)

Franz Schubert, Two Songs: "Der Tod und das Mädchen (Death and the Maiden)" (text by Claudius) and "Heidenröslein (Wild Rose)" (text by Goethe)

Franz Schubert (1797–1828) was a masterful composer of symphonies, sonatas, and string quartets, but is perhaps best known for his *Lieder* (songs), of which he wrote more than six hundred. "Death and the Maiden" is a dialogue between a young woman who pleads for her life and the figure of Death, who claims her, promising that she will sleep softly in his arms. "Heidenröslein" is a simple, seemingly artless depiction of a boy admiring a flower.

Der Tod und das Mädchen
(Death and the Maiden)

Text by
Claudius

Franz Schubert

Das erste Zeitmaß. (The first tempo.)
Der Tod. (Death)

Gib dei-ne Hand, du schön und zart Ge - bild! bin Freund und kom-me nicht zu _ stra -

fen. Sei gut-es Muts! ich, bin nicht wild, sollst sanft in mei-nen Ar-men schla - fen!

Vorüber, ach, vorüber!
geh, wilder Knochenmann!
Ich bin noch jung, geh, Lieber!
und rühre mich nicht an,
und rühre mich nicht an.
Gib deine Hand, du schön und zart Gebild!
bin Freund und komme nicht zu strafen.
Sei gutes Muts! ich, bin nicht wild,
sollst sanft in meinen Armen schlafen!

Pass by, ah, pass by!
Go, harsh, bony Death!
I am still young, go, my dear!
and do not touch me,
and do not touch me.
Give me your hand, you beautiful, sweet creature!
I am a friend and do not come to punish.
Have courage! I am not cruel.
Softly in my arms you will sleep!

Heidenröslein
(Wild Rose)

Text by
Goethe

Franz Schubert

Sah ein Knab' ein Röslein stehn, Röslein auf der Heiden,
war so jung und morgenschön,
lief er schnell es nah' zu sehn, sah's mit vielen Freuden.
Röslein, Röslein, Röslein roth, Röslein auf der Heiden.

A boy saw a wild rose, a wild rose amid the heather,
it was so fresh and beautiful
he ran quickly to gaze at it, gaze with great joy.
Little rose, little red rose, rose amid the heather.

Robert Schumann, "Wenn ich in deine Augen seh' (When I Look into Your Eyes)," from *Dichterliebe (A Poet's Love)* (text by Heinrich Heine)

Robert Schumann (1810–56) wrote several song cycles (collections of songs with interrelated texts). *Dichterliebe (A Poet's Love),* written in 1840 to poems by the famous German poet Heinrich Heine, is probably the best known of these. The fourth song, "Wenn ich in deine augen seh' (When I Look into Your Eyes)" sets a deceptively simple two-stanza poem that seems at first to be a gentle love lyric, but ends with a surprising ironic twist.

Wenn ich in deine Augen seh'
(When I Look into Your Eyes)

Text by
Heinrich Heine

Robert Schumann

(continued)

lust;   doch wenn du sprichst: "Ich   lie - be dich!" so muss ich   wei-nen bit   -   ter -

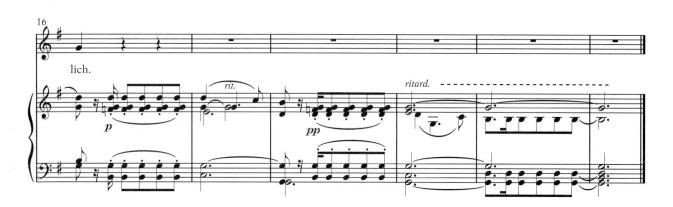

lich.

Wenn ich in deine Augen seh',	When I into your eyes look,
so schwindet all' mein Leid und Weh;	then fades all my pain and sorrow.
doch wenn ich küsse deinen Mund,	and when I kiss your lips,
so werd' ich ganz und gargesund.	then I become entirely well.
Wenn ich mich lehn' an deine Brust,	When I rest upon your breast,
kommt's über mich wie Himmels lust;	comes over me a heavenly bliss;
doch wenn du sprichst: "Ich liebe dich!"	but when you say: "I love you!"
so muss ich weinen bitterlich.	then must I weep bitterly.